CHANGING FACES

CHANGING
FACES

James J. Scott

Palmetto Publishing Group
Charleston, SC

Changing Faces

First Edition

Printed in the United States

ISBN-13: 978-1-64111-164-5
ISBN-10: 1-64111-164-X

DEDICATION

I would like to dedicate this book to my mother Rosa Scott-Johnson and all of the strong women in the world.

CONTENTS

PROLOGUE

After twenty-seven years of service in the United States Army, I decided the time had come to transition into civilian life. I began to schedule my retirement appointments as my months in uniform quickly drew to a close. Retirement appointments routinely begin with a mandatory pre-separation counseling packet and the Department of Labor's Transition Assistance Program (TAP) employment workshops, which feature information on job search strategies, resume writing, interviewing skills, job offers, and salary negotiation. The TAP as a whole is designed to focus on pre-separation examinations and the needs of service members. This transition process begins with the completion of the pre-separation counseling checklist, which allows service members to indicate the benefits and services they wish to receive, such as additional counseling for mental health. There are expected challenges upon leaving the army and, for many service members, they experience unexpected emotional side effects.

Transitioning from military life to civilian life isn't always easy, and many find it very difficult to say goodbye to the familial bonds they've made with friends in the service. The grieving period often catches people off guard, but unfortunately, far too many service members waive the pre-separation physical and psychological examinations in order to speed up the exit process. This is one of the biggest mistakes a service member can make, and I know that for me, these examinations most likely saved my life.

When I arrived for my physical, I had to fill out a standard prerequisite questionnaire that included a mental health assessment. When I flipped to that page on the clipboard, I immediately felt my old anxieties coming back, flooding my fingertips and making my heart beat faster. As my eyes scanned the questions, I wondered how honestly I really wanted to answer some of the questions about my unresolved issues. I had been hiding a secret about my well-being from my physician for a long time, waiting for the right moment to disclose it. But there never was a right time—there rarely is for this sort of thing—especially when I had never felt brave enough to admit I needed or wanted help. However, at that moment, as I held my pen poised above the questionnaire, I realized that this might be my last chance to get help before I left the military. If not now, when? The answer would likely be "never," and that felt like a much worse option than admitting my secret, so I wrote down the truth and waited for my name to be called. The minutes ticked by to the beat of the hanging clock's metronome, and I began to rehearse in my head how I would present my issue. It didn't feel like the sort of thing I could just blurt out, and yet there was no good way to present the information.

After a short while, a soldier came out into the waiting room.

"Lieutenant Colonel Scott?" he asked, surveying the room.

I stood up and he motioned for me to follow him through a door and down a hallway, the smell of antiseptic stinging my nose. I kept weighing my options in my head, wondering how to say what I needed to say, but nothing sounded quite right. The soldier led me to a room and asked me to take a seat, as someone would be with me shortly. I thanked him and sat down, still deep in thought. In trying to decide how to tell my story, the memories had started to come back, ones I'd avoided for so long. The burst of flames, the pain, the agonizing recovery, the way he'd just sat on the porch, grinning as he waited for us. When the door to the room opened, I jumped a little, too engrossed in my own mind.

"Hello," a middle-aged woman greeted me with a warm smile. Her friendliness helped to put me at ease, although I still wasn't sure how to broach the subject I needed to discuss. When she sat down across from me, the doctor studied my face for a moment, and luckily for me, unwittingly gave me the perfect opening I needed. I couldn't have planned it better if I'd tried.

"How did you get your burns and when?" she asked. I gathered my thoughts for a moment and decided to let the unfiltered truth out.

"I received these burns at the age of four in a house fire intentionally started by my father."

As soon as the words left my lips, I was surprised by the relief I felt. I'd guarded this secret for so long and it was the first time I'd ever shared the truth with a medical professional. In the past, I'd always said it was an accident, due to either faulty wiring or a gas leak in an old wooden house. This was partly due to my desire to get through the questions quickly, as well as not wanting to face the real, raw emotions associated with the truth. In some instances, I didn't want to cast a negative light on myself in front of military doctors. Doing so could lead them to believe I had mental issues, which could, in turn, negatively affect my position in the military in regards to possible promotions, maintaining my top-secret security clearance, or even remaining in the military at all—or so I believed. If the doctors pushed me when I told them about the "accidental" house fire, I would always say it was an accident, I survived, and I was having a pretty good life. When you feel like you have a secret to protect, you become very adept at saying your lines so others will see what you want them to see. Admitting that my own father had tried to murder my family and me had always felt like too much to handle, both for me and for others. But when I admitted this simple confession, that the fire had in fact *not* been an accident, I felt freer and lighter than I had in years.

The doctor gaped at me.

"Did you say *intentionally* started by your father?" she asked incredulously. It's not often one gets to surprise a doctor; they've seen and heard just about everything.

"Yes, ma'am," I replied. "As a matter of fact, I was hoping to talk with a counselor about some of the issues I have been dealing with as a result of this traumatic event that occurred so many years ago."

She nodded, and together we methodically went through the rest of my questionnaire, although I don't think anything quite topped my initial revelation. At the end, the doctor told me that she would, indeed, write me a referral for behavioral health services. As I left the office, I felt an immense sense of pride in myself. I had finally done it! At the age of forty-four, as a twenty-seven-year veteran of the US Army, I had finally worked up the courage to seek help for what my father had done. Forty years is a long time to be overdue, but I wasn't too late. I felt great, and as I walked outside, I felt like this was the first page of a new chapter of my life. However, sometimes going forward requires going backwards.

I decided to remain overseas as a government employee after I retired from the army in 2014. Living abroad in South Korea around a military base held a certain level of comfort and safety for my family and me. I was content in my life after my retirement and my days still held a certain level of routine for me. I woke up every morning at 0530 hours and turned on the coffee maker. As I waited for the machine to surrender the coffee to me, I usually spent a little time on social media to scroll through a few updates from my family back in the States. One morning, I noticed I had a message from my baby sister, Lynnette, the bright red notification drawing my eye immediately. I clicked on the message and all it said was, "Call me as soon as possible!"

My mind immediately began to spin with all the worst-case scenarios. What could have happened? What was so bad she couldn't tell me over the internet? Would I be able to get a flight back there in time? I clicked through each question in my brain as I immediately grabbed the phone and dialed my sister's number.

"It's me. I got your message. What's up? Is everything okay?" I asked as soon as Lynnette answered, as I tried to remain calm and stay focused.

"Our father passed," she announced.

A strange numbness overtook me when I heard the news. I wasn't quite sure how I felt about this new information, and it took a moment for me to realize I hadn't yet said anything.

"Oh." It wasn't much, but it was all I could think to say right then.

"He died three weeks ago," she said. "The prison officials could've told us sooner."

"Yeah, they could have," I agreed, latching onto annoyance at the slow pace of the US prison system as a tangible emotion I could handle at that moment. We later learned that my father's prison counselor, who had previously been great at contacting me over the years, had been unable to reach me because I hadn't yet updated my contact information when I left for South Korea. My brother hadn't spoken to our father since the fire, which left my sister as the only other contact. There had been a mix-up at the prison regarding the phone numbers she had given them, which had led to the long delay. Our father had died alone from heart failure due to a combination of complications from diabetes and high blood pressure. When the prison had finally gotten ahold of my sister, she'd made the decision to have our father cremated. In the space of a simple phone call, the man we had once called "Dad" was no more.

Our conversation lapsed into silence again. My sister and I tried in vain to find another talking point, but our father's death hung too heavy, too unavoidable, on the phone line.

"I should go," I finally said. "I have to finish getting ready for work."

"Yeah. Me too. I should get going, too," she agreed.

We said our goodbyes, and after I hung up I set the phone down on the table. I stared at it for a moment before I got up and walked back into the bedroom. I climbed into bed and stared at the ceiling, my coffee long forgotten. After being incarcerated for forty-one years, the man who had been my father had taken his last breath within the confines of a prison. My eyes remained dry, but I felt awful. In spite of the pain he'd caused us, I hadn't wanted my father to die alone. Everyone deserves that little bit of compassion, that little bit of human dignity, I suppose, to not have to endure death alone. Not if we don't want to.

As I lay there, staring at the ceiling of our bedroom as my wife slept softly beside me, I thought of my own mortality. It's not unusual to think of one's own inevitable death in the wake of the loss of a parent, but most of all I thought of how I didn't want to die alone like my father had. I thought of the scars on my face, daily reminders of what he had done, and of the visits I'd made to him in prison. Stress, diabetes, high blood pressure? No matter what he did, he was still my father and I had his genes. *How old was he?* I wondered. I didn't even know his real age. Was his behavior fueled by drugs or was it mental? Why did he do these things? How much time did I have to make a difference in my kids' lives? I wrestled with the compassion I felt for him and wondered why, at age forty-six, I was trying to rationalize my feelings as if I'd have to explain myself or accept some sort of responsibility. Why did I even care?

After a while, I got back out of bed. I had to go to work and wasn't about to call in to take the day off. I preferred to work; staying at home that day would've left me too isolated with my own thoughts, thoughts I didn't necessarily want to experience.

Later, I mentioned to my wife, Yolanda, that my father had died. I said it as an afterthought, as casually as if I'd told her that I remembered we needed to pick up some more milk from the grocery store.

"Are you okay?" Yolanda asked.

"Sure," I said. "I'm fine." But we all tell small lies to ourselves when we don't know what else to say.

The scars on my face serve as a daily reminder of the evil man I once called "Dad." There is no escaping either the scars or my father whenever I look at my own reflection in a mirror. On the day I learned of his death, I found myself thinking even more about him and our relationship, the visits I'd made to the prison, and the reason for his four decades of incarceration. Despite everything, in spite of the permanent markings I bore on my skin from what he had done, I still wrestled with the compassion I somehow still felt for the man who had tried to murder me. I didn't understand how, as a grown man with a family and children of my own, I couldn't feel completely done with this man, even after his death. Why did I care at all? Shouldn't I feel relieved, so to speak, to be rid of him? And yet, I did care. I didn't feel relieved. If anything, I just felt more conflicted than ever.

CHAPTER 1

Secrets in the South

During the fall of 1973, my mother made the decision to leave my father and move my siblings and me from Philadelphia to South Carolina. My mother had finally reached her breaking point after enduring years of physical and emotional abuse from my father, as well as from being subjected to his continual losses in his ongoing battle with drug use. My father had likely started with small potato drugs, but at that point he had escalated to regular use of LSD, often laced with heroin.

Heroin is known for its initial euphoric surge that users feel immediately after taking the drug, and once heroin enters the brain, it is converted back into morphine, which binds to molecules on the brain's opioid receptors. Following that initial euphoria, users lapse into a state often referred to as "on the nod," as they vacillate between wakefulness and drowsiness. Over time, this drug is highly addictive and deteriorates the brain's white matter, which can have a negative impact on a user's ability to regulate their behavior, their decision-making skills, and their responses to stressful situations.[1] Conversely, LSD isn't actually an addictive drug, unlike other hallucinogens, because it doesn't cause the uncontrollable drug-seeking behaviors found in other narcotics. However, users

---

1 "Heroin," DrugFacts: Heroin, National Institute on Drug Abuse, December 2016, <https://www.drugabuse.gov/publications/drugfacts/heroin>.

can build up a tolerance to LSD, which can be extremely dangerous due to the unpredictable nature of the drug.[2]

Such was the case with my father, whose behavior was, somewhat paradoxically, elevated to new lows by LSD. His paranoia increased over time, and during one such trip, my father got it into his head that my mother was having an affair. This was untrue, but there was no reasoning with my father. One day, my mother went to the bedroom to lie down while my father sat in the living room, his paranoia creating concrete accusations in his head as the minutes ticked by. Finally, he stood up, retrieved a butcher knife from the kitchen, and walked into the bedroom. My mother saw him as he entered, and just as he tried to bring the knife down and run it through her stomach, she rolled off the bed and landed hard on her hands and knees on the floor. Her quick reaction not only saved her life, but it gave my father's paranoia the moment it needed to dissipate, fading away like smoke.

One would think that an incident like this would be grounds enough for leaving, but the behavior was nothing new. Once, during their early courtship days before my parents married, my father and a friend jumped an off-duty police officer. My father and his best friend, Turk, were hanging out in south Philly outside of their usual territory. They were hungry and decided to go by McDonald's to grab a bite to eat. While standing in line, they got into a dispute with a guy, which quickly escalated into a full-fledged argument. My father's temper got the best of him again and the fight turned physical, with Turk lending a hand. However, little did they know, my father and Turk had picked the wrong fight with the wrong man. He turned out to be an off-duty police officer, and my father and his best friend were handcuffed and fingerprinted in the county jail. My mother borrowed bail

2 "Hallucinogens," DrugFacts: Hallucinogens, National Institute on Drug Abuse, January 2016, November 2016, <https://www.drugabuse.gov/publications/drugfacts/hallucinogens>.

money from her mother and got him out of jail. It wouldn't be the last time my mother would come to my father's rescue, and this encounter would later come back to haunt my father during the trials of his life a few years later.

Another time, my maternal grandfather attempted to stand up for my mother in light of the continual abuse she endured at the hands of her husband, and my grandfather threatened to shoot my father. My father's response was to physically attack my grandfather, beating him so badly that my grandfather had to spend a week in the hospital recovering from his injuries. The final straw for my mother came when my father broke into and robbed a pharmacy to support his drug use. After he was arrested, my mother pleaded for the courts to have mercy on my father and to commit him to a mental institution rather than prison. She told them that my father thought it was his house he was entering, not the pharmacy, and if they showed leniency and didn't send him to prison, my mother promised he would seek mental health treatment. I don't know if this is a decision that she later regretted, but had she just let him go to prison, perhaps the events of that summer night in Ridge Spring would have played out differently. Perhaps not, it's impossible to say, and any conjecture made at this point in time would be moot. But in any case, the courts agreed and my father was committed.

Shortly after my father entered the institution, my mother visited him. During this visit, the doctor took my mother aside into his office and gave her an important directive: to run as far away from my father as possible.

"It is going to be nearly impossible for him to break the hold of these drugs," the doctor told her. "Take whatever clothes and belongings you can gather and never look back."

My mother took his words to heart and after she left the hospital, she packed up our family, borrowed some money from family members, and fled from Philadelphia to South Carolina. She was only twenty- three years old and was attempting to start a new life with her three young children. My older brother, Kem, was nine, my sister was barely one, and I was nearing my fifth birthday.

Living in the South was a stark juxtaposition to the life we had known in Philadelphia. In the city, we had lived in a high rise before my father got his mother's townhouse after she passed. Mostly, I remember everything being loud. There were fights and music and sirens and blaring car horns locked in traffic. My father was in, if not good, then at least familiar company with the other drug addicts and gangs that ran rampant in our neighborhood. There is little doubt in my mind that my brother and I would've found ourselves in one of those gangs had our mother not moved us away.

To be fair to the City of Brotherly Love, it wasn't all bad. The food, especially as a kid, was wonderful, with butterscotch Tastykakes and greasy Philly cheesesteaks. The ice cream truck's simple tune would find its way through the cacophony of our street, and we'd savor those cones in the summer before turning on the fire hydrants and racing small sticks downstream. We'd play outside until the streetlamps came on because once they did, the neighborhood would start to transform. Those lights signaled a change in shift, and we'd go inside while the gangs and the drugs came out to play. There was always yelling and fighting and strangers coming to our door, and we'd have to wait inside, dealing with our own personal demon in the form of my father, until the sun came back and we could start our turn again outside. But the sun always went down and the streets always changed because, like Robert Frost said, "Nothing gold can stay."

We moved to Ridge Spring, about forty-five miles west of Columbia, South Carolina. It's a charming town with steadfast residents spanning ten generations. The land was originally curated by Native Americans before European settlers were given land grants in the 1700s. As the fields were plowed for farmland, evidence of the Native Americans' stewardship was found in the form of arrowheads and spearheads in the freshly tilled earth. The story has been passed down through the multitude of generations of Ridge Spring residents that it was actually the Native Americans that chipped away at the stone basin in the rock into which the spring water flowed, creating the town's namesake.

There were two prominent families in Ridge Spring, the Watsons and the Duboses. Between them, they owned the majority of the town and its land. In the name of progress, big businesses came to Ridge Spring looking to buy up land for factories. These families couldn't afford to lose their labor force from their farms and businesses to the factories, so they had no choice but to push back. These two families instead bought up more land around the town, resisting the change towards industrialization and thereby preserving Ridge Spring's status as a farming community. In the 1800s, cotton was the primary crop of the town and out of that necessity grew many beautiful plantation homes which still stand to this day. The rich soil proved to be desirable for many crops, most notably the peach. Although Georgia refers to itself as the Peach State, South Carolina actually leads in peach production in the United States, followed by Georgia and Virginia. The smell of peach blossoms is always thick in the spring air, but that sweetness doesn't compare to the taste of the peaches in summer.

The South had a certain tranquility to it. It wasn't as angry or violent as I'd known Philadelphia to be, but perhaps that's what led us to believe that things would be quieter, safer. We moved to an old house on the outskirts of Ridge Spring, about three miles or so from my grandmother. Even being as young as I was, I could really appreciate my new setting. Compared to the grumbling city we'd left behind, the South felt like paradise. I could play outside without fear, and everyone seemed friendlier, offering food and a smile without reservation. Families tended to settle in one spot for good, and it seemed like everyone was related, or at least claimed to be, which gave the whole town a welcoming, familiar vibe. Playing outside as the sun cast a fiery glow on the house, a warm breeze tickling my ears, life felt good, really good for the first time.

This isn't to say that everything was easy or without its difficulties in the South. The divide between ethnicities was still very evident, with white people living on one side of town and black people on the other. In the sixties, the five-and-dime store was like the Walmart of its day, serving everything from toys to soda pop and everything in between. During that time, Coca Cola was a rare treat, thickly sweet and drafted into glass drinking bottles. Ridge Spring's five-and-dime kept it in short supply, and the local black folks knew better than to order it for themselves. Today, it seems like such a small thing to be able to walk into any store and buy a Coke, buy a dozen if one feels like it. But for blacks in the South, it simply wasn't allowed. Technically it was possible—money exchanged for goods, a simple transaction. But, socially, such a purchase was another thing entirely. It's the same way in which older black men were expected to yield to all white folks on the sidewalk, stepping out of the way and tipping their hats so as not to appear "uppity." It was the rule of the day for blacks to remember their place and young black men had to learn this rule or face the consequences. The KKK ruled in the South, and when an uppity black person got out of line, they or their family would be warned.

Sometimes they would awaken to a burning cross on their front lawn, or maybe they would be evicted from their rented home, a property usually owned by a white man. Other times, a person could lose their job, or in extreme cases, their life. The

Civil Rights Movement continued to gain speed and power in the 1960s, particularly due to the work of Dr. Martin Luther King Jr., but in the face of progress, there is always pushback. The South and the KKK saw to that. During the 1950s and '60s, the KKK often formed alliances with southern police departments and governors' administrations. This practice was seen more in states like Mississippi and Alabama rather than South Carolina, but that didn't change the fact that as a black person in the South, you didn't always feel like you could trust the police to serve and protect all of the citizens.

When my mother returned to the South in 1974 with Kem, Lynnette, and myself in tow, my great-grandfather stressed to my mother that although she'd been gone for years, the racial customs of the South had largely remained the same. He wanted to ensure that Kem and I knew to use our manners when in the presence of the white man. We were to say "Yes, sir!" or "No, sir!" or "Yes, ma'am!" or "No, ma'am!" Kem and I were also told never to stare too long at anyone for our own safety. Although South Carolina was a peaceful respite from the angry, noisy city of Philadelphia, there was an underlying fear and threat of danger. For my family, however, our greatest danger lurked much closer to home.

When my mother moved my siblings and me down to South Carolina, she did so to be closer to her mother, my grandmother. My grandmother, Leona Mattie Burkett-Wigfall, had matriculated at Benedict College, pursuing a degree in elementary education, but life happened as it so often does, and she never completed her studies. At one time, she worked as a teacher's aid during a brief separation from my grandfather, particularly notable not only as a woman, but as a black woman in the South. She was young when she had my mother and their relationship was often more like that of sisters than that of mother and daughter. My grandmother carried a pistol, drank, smoked her share of cigarettes, and had a reputation for setting people straight when they crossed her. And yet for most of her life, she lived in domestic violence. Even the strongest women can become victims, heartbreaking as that reality is.

My grandfather was a World War II veteran and after he returned from the war, he married my grandmother; shortly after, they had my mother. My grandparents faced many of the same stresses as other young couples, especially with a young daughter, and the majority of their conflict arose out of finances. Despite my grandmother's degree, finances were difficult and my grandfather encountered a lack of opportunities in the South as a result of his skin color. In addition to their fights about money, my grandfather was also a lover of women who were not his wife, and this often resulted in epic physical fights, all witnessed by my mother.

At a young age, my mother yearned for the attention and love she felt she missed when her parents were warring, and she began to look for it in other places, resulting in the birth of my older brother when my mother was only fourteen. Her search for affection had led her to the house of an older boy, a boy of seventeen when she was not quite fourteen. She had been warned by her parents not to be "fast" like one of "those girls," the kind with the swollen bellies and the lost innocence of childhood. But she didn't listen, enamored by the promise of fulfilling what she felt she was lacking, and soon she became one of "those girls," her waistline thick with my brother, Kem. My grandparents threatened the boy's family to have him thrown in jail, what with my mother being so young while their son was practically a man, but my brother's grandmother begged my mother's parents to have mercy and they eventually relented. As a result, my brother's grandmother did everything she could to help support Kem until we fled Philadelphia to get away from my father and his drug addiction, including helping to care for Kem and buying him clothes.

My mother's parents kept the pregnancy a secret, and after he was born, they told family and friends that Kem was their son, not my mother's. Kem was given my mother's maiden name, Wigfall, and my grandparents cared for Kem, raising him and my mother as brother and sister, which enabled my mother to finish high school, an impressive feat for any teen mother but especially so in the '60s. Shortly after graduation and a few days before my birth, my mother married my father on June 28, 1969. At that point, she was able to take Kem back as her own to raise when he was four years old. Two years later, when Kem was six and entering the first grade, he realized that he didn't share a last name with the rest of us, as he still had our mother's maiden name. He begged our mother to change it to Scott so that we could all share the same family name. My mother complied, and Kem Wigfall became Kem Scott, and after we left Philadelphia, my mother didn't have any further contact with Kem's grandmother.

At the time of this writing, Kem is currently fifty-one, and it wasn't until a few years ago that he even had any idea that he didn't share a biological father with Lynnette and me. During the summer of 2014, my family was visiting Philadelphia from Korea. My godmother (my great-uncle's wife) had been gravely ill for a while, and shortly after we arrived in the United States, she passed away. My mother was already there, having made arrangements to visit my godmother in the hospital before she passed.

One day, while my mother was at the hospital, she ran into a relative of Kem's father. This relative mentioned to my mother that Kem's father and grandmother wanted to see Kem if he came to Philadelphia for the funeral. After the funeral and a little bit of deliberation, our mother finally revealed to Kem the truth about his biological father. Needless to say, this was quite the bombshell for my brother, who had spent nearly fifty years believing one truth about his life, only to discover that the man he'd always thought of as his father was in fact not his biological father. Our cousins, the ones who had grown up with our mother, encouraged Kem to see his father and grandmother. Having been raised alongside our mother, the cousins had known about Kem's parentage, but had kept it a secret for all those years. We were all gathered in the dining room of my great-uncle's house, and as my brother tried to absorb this new information, he was surrounded by a chorus that echoed ceaselessly that Kem should go see his father and grandmother.

I, however, was silent. Not because I didn't want him to go, but because I did. My brother can be very moody and become obstinate, especially when he feels pushed one way or another. Knowing that, I kept a strong poker face and told him that if he was willing to make the trip, I would go with him. He agreed, but I still tried to remain silent on the car ride over to his grandmother's house. I knew the smallest thing might trigger Kem into changing his mind and retreating, and I didn't want to set off his nerves and agitation. He could only push our mother so far, so I knew that if Kem's pressure cooker blew, I'd end up taking the brunt of his frustrations. Then again, what are younger brothers for?

As we drove through the streets of Philadelphia and through our old neighborhood, it felt both strange and comfortingly nostalgic. We arrived at his grandmother's home, and after Kem took a deep breath, my mother, Kem, and I went to the front door. Kem's grandmother had received a call from one of my mother's cousins that we might stop by, and as a result she had spent the entire morning waiting with hopeful anticipation. She was in her nineties and hadn't seen her first grandchild in nearly half a century, although she had yearned to see him for all those years. Today, finally, she was going to see Kem. When we knocked on the door, she was thrilled to see us and welcomed us into her home. Kem's father had not yet arrived, but that gave us a chance to get to know Kem's grandmother as she showed us family photos. I leaned over, looking for the resemblance between Kem and his father to verify that this was indeed true. And there it was in the photos: the family Kem had never known existed.

As we talked with Kem's grandmother, we were all taken in by her warmth. As the meeting progressed, Kem's nerves seemed to settle a bit. However, as our visit continued and Kem's father still hadn't arrived, Kem started to become visibly agitated. I suggested that we go for a walk, so Kem and I left our mother and his grandmother behind as we strolled along the pavement of our old neighborhood. Since he'd been older than I was when we'd lived there, Kem pointed to old places where he'd played and he reminisced about old childhood friends, most of whom had long since moved on from there. As we rounded one of the corners on the gray city sidewalk, we heard a familiar recorded tune. Sure enough, there was an ice cream truck parked at the curb. We stopped, and as I bought myself an ice cream cone, Kem lit up a cigarette. I rarely see him smoke, which only confirmed how nervous I suspected my brother really was.

As I ate my cone and Kem puffed on his cigarette, we began to circle back towards his grandmother's house. When we got close to the house, a car driven by what looked like an older version of Kem pulled up alongside us. As Kem's father climbed out of the car, I immediately grabbed my iPad and opened the camera app. Without a moment's hesitation, Kem and his father embraced, smiles stretching their cheeks as far as they would go. When they finally released one another from the hug, they each took a step back, still grinning as they held onto each other's arms. I watched my brother's face as I snapped photo after photo, and as Kem looked at his father for the first time, the years melted away and he looked all of seven, gazing at his dad with joy.

We all went into Kem's grandmother's house for a little while and talked some more as I continued to play photographer. Kem's father told us that he owned a popular disco club in the city and invited us to go check it out. We said goodbye to our mother and Kem's grandmother, and then we headed over to Kem's dad's club. We ordered beers, and I stayed fairly quiet as I observed Kem and his father talk about the family they shared. After about twenty minutes or so, the conversation began to slow, the sentences limping forward with increasingly longer pauses. It wasn't that everyone wasn't enjoying the time together, because we were; we'd just run out of things to talk about. One would think that nearly fifty years of separation would provide hours of talking points, but as time goes by, things tend to get whittled down to the bullet points. I don't want to compare my brother meeting his father for the first time to an obituary, but think about it: We live lives made up of hours and seconds and laughter and tears and struggles and triumphs and love, but in the end, everything is summarized in just a few sentences.

Before we left the club, everyone pulled out their smartphones and we linked to one another on Facebook. I promised to pass along all the photos I had taken, and then we swallowed the last of our beers and left. We returned to Kem's grandmother's house and stayed for maybe another thirty minutes or so, talking and taking even more photos before we finally said goodbye. Today, Kem maintains a relationship with his biological father, but it's a little strained. There are so many years lost between them that it can be difficult to play catch up, no matter how much all the involved parties might want to. We're all still Facebook friends and that internet circle has expanded to include two of Kem's half-sisters from his father's previous marriages, the links between us spidering out like leaves on a tree branch.

Parenthood can be a fairly malleable idea. Is a parent the person who contributes the biological component of a person? Or is a parent the person who is in the trenches of daily life, raising a child and teaching them what they need to know to become adults on their own? For most of Kem's life, he had spent it believing that my biological father was his as well. Of course, this was the same man who was in and out of jail and psychiatric institutions for drug-related crimes and then tried to kill us all in a house fire, so he wasn't there with the same consistency as our mother. My mother eventually remarried to my stepfather, Mack, who is a good man. They dated for nearly a decade before she finally agreed to marry him the summer after I graduated high school in 1988. We knew Mack as we grew up; he'd come around to help fix things around the house or work on the car when it started making telltale creaks and splutters. But he wasn't really a parental figure in our lives because throughout the rest of Kem's and my childhood, my mother held him at a little bit of a distance so she could raise us by herself. But sometimes all you really need is that one person, and I'm grateful that my mother was that for Kem and me.

My mother, at an age when many young women today are just finishing college and beginning their adult lives, shared her world with a violent, unpredictable man. Like the abusive relationship she had witnessed as a child, my father could be deeply kind and compassionate one minute, and then attempt to stab her the next. The cycle of abuse spiraled out from my grandparents to my mother and, just like she had witnessed her parents' unstable relationship, my brother and I watched hers as well.

Shortly after we moved to South Carolina, my father was released from the hospital and he and my mother reconciled. He joined us in Ridge Spring, and my parents seemed to want a fresh start. They chose to blame the past problems in their marriage on the stresses of the city, and whether or not they actually believed that, they wanted it to be true. And why not? The South was so different from Philly, and it was so much easier to put the blame on location rather than critically evaluate their own relationship or my father's addiction. Philadelphia was a convenient scapegoat and for a short while, that plan worked—until it didn't.

CHAPTER 2

Trial by Fire

The peach trees were ripe and the breeze was warm on a summer afternoon in Ridge Spring. My father was at our old house, the one we'd left with my mother, devising a plan with the help of a strong cocktail of marijuana and vodka. The house sat in the middle of a cornfield, about a quarter of a mile away from the main road, from which you could just see the top of the chimney peeking out. There was a screened porch around the back that led into the kitchen and the front porch stretched from end to end, the perfect spot to enjoy a night such as this one. The wooden planks squeaked under my father's feet as he surveyed the house with its faded paint. The windows were nailed shut, had been for some time. My grandfather had advised my mother to do this when we moved down from Philly to ward off an intruder before my father came down to South Carolina to join us. But, as it turned out, the most dangerous person to the family was willingly ushered in through the front door. My father circled the house, checking the windows, and was satisfied to find the nails were all still in place. He moved on to the next task and ripped the stove and clothes dryer away from the kitchen wall, severing the gas lines and allowing the fumes to seep into the house. And then, as he waited for the gas to fill what had once been a home, he began to destroy whatever was within his reach. Glass and china and porcelain littered the floor like broken stars, and once my father was satisfied with what he'd done, he picked up the phone.

My mother was done, really done with my father this time. She'd left him before, but this time she was going to make it stick. We'd left in such a hurry that we hadn't really taken much of anything with us, and at the time, the stuff hadn't mattered. Our bodies were out and safe—material belongings be damned. But now, safe at my great-grandfather's house, my mother realized we needed some of our things, Kem especially. He was in school and barely had more clothes than what he wore on his back, so when my father called, asking my mother to bring him cigarettes, she relented. My father knew it would be fruitless to beg her to come back, to plead with her as he had all those times before, but he knew she wouldn't refuse him something as simple as a pack of cigarettes. One last request before the end.

My mother hung up the phone and told my grandmother who had called. My grandmother's eyes narrowed; she despised my father and it pained her to watch her daughter go through this ebb and flow of abuse, time and time again. She volunteered—or more accurately, *insisted*—to come along to the house to get Kem's clothes with my mother. Kem, Lynnette, and I couldn't be left behind, so we were packed into the Buick at dusk, the honey light of the afternoon fading into the evening. After a quick stop at a convenience store for cigarettes, we drove the two miles to our old house. We drove down Main Street, the funeral parlor on our left and the nickel-and-dime that sold hot dogs on our right. We made a left at the train tracks, the Buick bumping over the rails into the white side of town. Plantation-style homes peppered each side of the road, and not a couple hundred feet past the tracks, we turned down the dirt road that led to the house. We were whole, in every sense of the word, in a way that we would never be again.

As we pulled up to the house, I craned my neck to look out the Buick's window and saw my dad sitting on the front porch with a glass of scotch and a devil's grin. Being only four years old, I didn't know what that meant yet. None of us did. Perhaps my mother was less cautious than she might have been otherwise, emboldened by the presence of my grandmother at her side. Maybe her attention was scattered between all three of us kids. Or perhaps she'd never considered that my father was capable of what happened next.

My mother opened the door, carrying baby Lynnette in her arms, and walked inside the house with my grandmother. My mother's eyes were met with the aftermath of my father's destruction, all the possessions she'd once loved broken and smashed like so many promises. She put Lynnette in a crib that sat in a small room just to the right of the front door and continued through the house. Kem and I followed her, confused by the sight of upturned furniture and broken glass. I was too young at the time to fully understand the complexities of a volatile marriage, but I knew what pain looked like I had seen it many times before on my mother's face, much like I did then as tears slipped from her eyes.

"Why?" she asked over and over. My grandmother yelled that he was crazy and evil for destroying the house, but still my father sat on the porch, unresponsive to anything but his glass of scotch.

Kem and I trailed our mother and grandmother into the kitchen. The air smelled funny; it wasn't right. I didn't know what it was, but my mother recognized the gas immediately.

"I'm going to cut it off from outside," she told my grandmother who stood near the door that led to the screen porch. "Please, please, don't light a cigarette."

Before my mother could go anywhere or turn of anything, my father came around to the house to the enclosed porch, visible only to my grandmother by his shadow. We had wandered right into his trap, like rabbits into a snare. He casually lit a long stem match and tossed it near the screen door to the kitchen that separated us from him.

The kitchen exploded with a boom. The fire blasted my face and arms and I watched in horror as my mother and grandmother were immediately engulfed in flames. Their skin began to peel and shred away like a roasting pig on a spit, but despite the pain, my mother flew into action. The only window was nailed shut, so she grabbed what was left of a kitchen chair and smashed it through the glass. She grabbed me and shoved me through the window first before climbing out after me, her skin ripping and falling away. My grandmother escaped through the screened porch and my brother, with his fire-kissed legs, ran out the front door. I scrambled towards the front of the house where I met Kem.

"I'm going to go get help," he told me, sounding far more mature than a boy of nine.

"Wait for me!" I begged, tears rolling from my eyes as I tried to stand on scorched feet.

Kem must have seen the extent of my burns, but he knew he'd have to be smart to keep me from following my big brother to the ends of the earth.

"I want you to come, but I need you to stay here with Mommy," he said. "Can you do that? Please?"

I agreed and watched as my brother took off running through the cornfield. By this time, my mother and grandmother had made it to the front of the house.

"Where's Kem?" my mother asked, her voice thick with pain.

"I don't know," my grandmother said, her skin falling away like autumn leaves.

My father just stared at us, dumbstruck that we had escaped and were standing before him as broken, melted versions of who we had once been. There was no contingency plan, no "in case of." The house had been intended to entomb us, and yet we'd fought. We'd survived.

"Where's Lynnette?" my mother suddenly asked, looking around frantically. All three adults looked back at the burning house. My mother knew she didn't have the strength to run inside and my grandmother had even less, so she turned on the one person who did. I had expected her voice to be angry or frantic, but it was neither.

"Please," she said evenly to my father, her tears running painful lines down her burned face. "Save my baby."

In a moment I'm not sure I'll ever understand, my father did as he was told. Perhaps it was the shock of seeing us all alive, or maybe it was a sudden moment of lucidity. Whatever it was, it carried my father into the house and he returned momentarily, the house exhaling black smoke behind him as he carried my baby sister, completely unharmed by the fire.

With the house engulfed in flames, there was no way to call 911, no reassuring wail of approaching sirens. Just the crackle of burning wood as we stood there with second- and third-degree burns, trying to decide what to do next. In the end, we eased our seared bodies into the Buick and drove to town. My grandmother stopped at a house in the white neighborhood while we waited in the car, too pained to move with the smell of charred flesh in our noses. I tried to think, tried to understand why my father had done such a thing, but there were no answers waiting for me. The rest of the night passed largely in a haze of dark pain, only momentarily lifted when I realized I was riding in my very first helicopter.

While other children my age were preparing to go to kindergarten for the first time and trying on new school clothes and worrying about whether or not they'd make friends, I was grasping at the shrunken, painful glimmer to which my life had been reduced. Instead of coloring with my classmates or learning the routine of school, my world was an endless cycle of doctors, surgeries, nurses, IV bags, dressing changes, and scrubbing.

When I regained consciousness in the hospital, all I could feel was the agonizing, unrelenting pain. It enveloped my whole body, coursing around me like an angry sea. In the midst of all this, a few questions managed to weakly break the surface: Where was I? Where was Mama? Where was Daddy? Where were Lynnette and Kem? The pain wouldn't let me wonder for too long before the riptide sucked me back under. After a while, I couldn't think of anything at all other than the constant ebb and flow of searing pain around my body. A combination of pain medication and sleep was my only respite, but even then, it never lasted for long. Waiting for me, pulling at me when I woke, was the fire on my skin. My only constant companion.

One of the earliest recorded burn treatments dates back to 1600 BC in Egypt when the use of resin and honey was recommended as a burn salve.[3] Hippocrates later used a combination of pork fat and vinegar in 400 AD, and cold water wasn't introduced as an acute remedy for burns until 900 AD,[4] although the later use of ice water had to be abandoned due to the propensity for burn shock that increased mortality rates in conjunction with the usage of ice water. The major flaw in earlier burn treatments, with the exception of the vinegar used by Hippocrates, was the lack of antibacterial care that led to a high mortality rate among burn victims. In fact, one ancient cure for burns was to pack the wound with feces—a method thankfully long out of practice by the time I arrived at the hospital.

---

3 Guido Majno, *The Healing Hand: Man and Wound in the Ancient World*, (Cambridge, MA: Harvard University Press, 1991) pg215.

4 A. Hirschwald, *E. G. Geschichte der Chirurgie und ihre Ausubung*, (Berlin: BD I; 1898)

I sustained second and third-degree burns that covered approximately 50 percent of my body on my face, ears, forearms, hands, thighs, feet, and portions of my scalp. Burns are ugly, they're scary, and they hurt. Above all, they hurt. Unless burns are treated right away, they will only get worse. They will continue to go deeper and deeper below the surface of the skin, because unless stopped, the heat will continue to cook the flesh. By compromising or destroying entirely the body's main barrier against infection, the skin, a burn victim's body becomes very vulnerable to infection. Unless immediate action is taken, a burn can seep into the skin and invade one's entire body. When caring for a burn, it is essential to remove the dead, necrotic tissue from the still living tissue in order to reduce the chances of infection. While there are now several methods of debridement, the one I experienced was called mechanical debridement. My wounds were dressed with wet-dry dressings, meaning my wounds were packed with wet gauze soaked in saline and then wrapped in a dry dressing. As the wet gauze dried, it adhered to the necrotic tissue.

Then it was time to change the dressing.

A nurse would come and remove the dressing, pulling away the dead skin from the soft, pink, living tissue inside. Then my body would be soaked in a saline solution before the nurse would scrub at my raw skin, removing as much of the dead tissue as she could, before my dressings were replaced and the cycle would begin once more. I'd scream, trying to get away from the pain, but there was nowhere for me to go. There was nothing outside the hospital walls for me for seven months. Seven months of dressing changes, of surgeries, of scrubbing. It never got easier. I never got over the pain.

Down the hall in another wing, my mother and grandmother lay side by side in their beds. 60 percent of my mother's body was covered in second- and third-degree burns, and as she lay in her own agony, my grandmother was forced to tell her what happened.

"Daughter," my grandmother said sadly. "I saw Scott throw a lighted match into the house. He did this to us."

The pain my mother experienced was no longer restricted to her physical injuries. She was forced to recognize that the man she had once loved, the father of her children, had laid a trap and tried to kill them. The charred flesh that now covered so much of her body and that of her mother's and two sons was courtesy of her husband. During her nine month stay in the hospital, she was left with a lot of time to think, time that was sometimes spent doling out blame to herself for what had happened. She blamed herself for going to the home of an older teenager and becoming pregnant with his child at only fourteen years old, still a child herself. She blamed herself for falling for another man a few years her senior, a man who was unpredictable and half-crazy. But she had paid for what she saw as her transgressions, paid a higher price than many do. She had once had smooth, soft skin, brown and pretty, but now her face was mottled with burns and scars so severe they altered her features.

After the long and arduous healing process, my mother caked her face with heavy makeup to cover the raised burns and she always wore long-sleeved shirts and pants, even in the middle of the summer. But she was and still is the most beautiful woman I have ever known, as strong as they come. The fire took away her drinking, smoking, and profanity, and in their place left a quiet spirituality, although her Philadelphia attitude never left her. She was one tough lady who cared about her children more than life itself, and it is because of her that we have life at all. When I was younger, I would watch my mother pray for what seemed like hours for our safety and our future, mine and Kem's and Lynnette's. I have carried the weight of those prayers with me throughout my life, and remembering my mother in those quiet moments of prayer has pushed me to do and be better. I felt it was my duty to lift her heavy heart and bring joy and pride to her sad eyes because of how hard she worked and prayed and fought for my siblings and me. She deserves more, a hundred times more, but I've given her what I can.

My grandmother's burns weren't as severe as my mother's, but there were several other factors at work against her. Death from smoke inhalation and burns is more common if the patient is older, female, or has a co-morbidity condition such as diabetes. All of these were attributes of my grandmother, and while at the hospital, she succumbed to her injuries. After the fire, she had managed to save everyone's life but her own, driving us to safety and banging on the door of that house in the white neighborhood, yelling for help. My grandmother had taken us out of the fiery wreckage of the house and delivered us to the painful purgatory of the hospital from which we eventually rose back into our lives, but she couldn't go with us. At least she didn't have to endure the pain anymore.

As my own body grew stronger, I underwent several surgeries. During my initial surgery, the doctors gave me multiple grafts using pig skin. Pig skin, although not a permanent solution, can provide some temporary cover for a healing burn. Some doctors have observed that perhaps some contribution to healing may occur from the deposition of growth factors, collagen, and perhaps other proteins from the raw undersurface of pig skin.[5] I later underwent additional surgeries, one for facial reconstruction and for my head sores, one to de-web my fingers that had joined due to my burns, and several follow-up procedures. It was months before I got the chance to see my mother again while we were both still in the hospital.

---

5 Chester N. Paul, MD, FACS, "Skin Substitutes in Burn Care," *Wounds* 20.7, 2008, Medscape, January 17, 2017, https://www.woundsresearch.com/article/9003

Because my mother was burned worse than me, my recovery went a little faster than hers, so when it came time for us to see one another, it was me who was taken to her. The nurses wheeled me down the hallway of the hospital, the sharp smell of antiseptic stinging my nose. I knew my mother was hurt like me, but I wasn't prepared for what she looked like. I'm not sure anyone can really be prepared to see their mother like that. She was bandaged from head to toe, save for her eyes, as she lay on her plain white hospital bed. She was not yet physically strong enough to sit up on the bed, so the nurses elevated her head slightly so she could see me.

When our eyes met, I saw her tears spill over, raindrops falling down on the bandages that held her together. I could see she was in so much pain; it was a pain with which I was all too familiar. I knew she wanted to hold me in her arms to console me, her small, scared, hurting child, but she couldn't lift her arms to me. I knew then how badly I wanted my mother, but it wasn't until I became a father myself that I truly understood how much that must have pulled at her heart to want to reach for me but be unable to do so. That parental love, what my father had been able to forego when he set his trap for us, it doubled in my mother as she looked at me. Although we weren't able to hold each other the way we wished we could, it was a relief to see her. To see that physical confirmation of each other, to experience each other's presence for ourselves instead of just through the words of the doctors and nurses helped to embolden us for our continued fight for recovery. We were the same, my mother and me, marked by our burns and bandages, but also through our desire to fight. We endured, and we weren't alone as long as we had each other.

As I reflect back on my mother during that time, only now as an adult can I imagine the physical and mental pain she must have been going through. I was all too aware of my own pain, but my mother's burns were worse. Her mother, as close to her as a sister, had died as a result of the fire. My siblings had been sent to stay with relatives; Lynnette was unharmed by the fire and Kem only sustained first- and second-degree burns on his legs, so he was discharged after only a couple weeks. My father, her husband, was in jail for what he'd done to us. Everything had happened so fast that day with the fire and maybe she blamed herself. I think parents in general carry around an extraordinary amount of guilt, wondering if they should've done this or that to optimize their children's chances to have a better life than they'd had. After all, isn't that what we all want for our kids, for them to have it better than we did? Even though it was my father's actions that had put us in our bandages in the hospital, I imagine she still took on the faults, or sins of the father, as it were. I don't blame her, but sometimes it's easier to forgive others than it is to forgive yourself.

Through all this physical and mental pain, my mother clung to her faith in God, one of the only things she felt she had left. There's a popular poem called "Footprints," or alternately, "Footprints in the Sand." The authorship is unconfirmed, as there are several people who claim to have penned the famous poem, but regardless of who wrote it, the words endure:

One night I dreamed a dream.
As I was walking along the beach with my Lord,
Across the dark sky flashed scenes from my life.
For each scene, I noticed two sets of footprints in the sand,
One belonging to me and one to my Lord.
After the last scene of my life flashed before me,
I looked back at the footprints in the sand.
I noticed that at many times along the path of my life,
Especially at the very lowest and saddest times,

There was only one set of footprints.
This really troubled me, so I asked the Lord about it.
"Lord, you said once I decided to follow you,
You'd walk with me all the way.
But I noticed that during the saddest and most troublesome times of my life,
There was only one set of footprints.
I don't understand why, when I needed You the most, You would leave me."
He whispered, "My precious child, I love you and will never leave you,
Never, ever, during your trials and testings.
When you saw only one set of footprints,
It was then that I carried you."[6]

I often think of my mother when I see that poem. My mother endured nine months in that hospital and at times, I'm sure she felt like giving up. But when she was lying in that hospital bed, unable to walk both physically and figuratively, God carried her until she was able to stand on her own.

Over the seven months that followed the fire, the hospital became my home. The marble floors, wheelchairs, operating rooms, IV bags, and needles were as familiar to me as couches and family photos are for others. There's a quote by Andy Warhol, "When a situation develops gradually, no matter how weird that situation is, you get used to it." While the event that landed me in the hospital was sudden, life in the hospital normalized over time. I never got used to the pain, but the comings and goings of nurses during shift changes, the checking of my vitals, visits from the doctors—all of these were part of my daily routine. Surgeries were a frequent

6 "Footprints in the Sand," January 26, 2017, https://www.onlythebible.com/Poems/Footprints-in-the-Sand-Poem.html.

occurrence for me as well. The surgical team grafted skin from the unharmed parts of my body to reconstruct the scarred and burned areas. Nearly every joint of my upper body required incisions and skin grafts to recover their mobility and flexibility. The burns had webbed my mouth closed to the size of a dime, which the doctors were able to fix along with my fingers, also webbed by the fire. After my fingers were cut apart, the doctors designed a plastic mold to fit on the back of my arms to help protect my healing skin. The total contact of this mold also reduced the buildup of collagen fibers to help them realign in more normal formations, rather than thicker, unyielding scar tissue. Hooks were placed on each of my fingernails and a rubber band was then attached between each hook to the base of the plastic mold on the backs of my arms. This allowed my fingers to remain spread apart to prevent them from webbing again. Although it was painful, the apparatus worked, although I was far from finishing my surgeries until my seventh grade year.

Finally, after several arduous months in the hospital, it was time for me to be discharged. The plan was to transfer me from the hospital to a rehab center in Florence, South Carolina. I don't remember a lot about that day, but I do remember the doctors and nurses bidding me farewell as a nurse wheeled me down the marbled hallways and out the front doors of the hospital. I don't even remember which relatives came to pick me up, but I remember being very sad. When you're stuck in a hospital for months on end, you form a community within those sterile walls. As people, we are social creatures and we want to connect with others, something that feels so necessary and important when you feel isolated from everyone else in the outside world. The doctors and nurses were the people with whom I'd spent the most time for more than half a year, and while I was sorry to leave them, it was time to go.

I had to leave my mother behind at the hospital, as she still needed round-the-clock care, but it was time for me to move forward in my own recovery.

After I left the hospital, I was taken to a rehab center so I could begin the arduous process of relearning how to use my limbs again after so many months of confinement in a hospital bed or wheelchair. With my siblings being cared for by relatives and my mother still in the hospital, I was on my own. Then again, even with the assistance of so many people, recovery is a lonely journey, often a struggle against yourself. The first task ahead of me was to learn how to use my hands again. After so many surgeries and de-webbings and time spent in the brace with the plastic mold and the hooks, my hands only somewhat resembled the hands I'd known before. They gave me a squishy foam ball and I had to learn how to close my fingers about its round surface and squeeze. It's a simple enough action that most people take for granted, but it was a struggle for me to do with my weakened, damaged fingers. I forced my fingers to tighten as they screamed in protest, every nerve begging me to stop. The pain was sharp and fiery and yet I persisted, pushing my hands past where they wanted to rest. Each day was a fight against my own limitations, but even at the tender age of five I knew that giving up was not an option. Eventually, I grew stronger and I began to regain a little bit of flexibility in my fingers and hands as the weeks passed. I graduated from the foam ball to a rubber one, and once my hands had regained a fair amount of strength, it was time for me to do something I hadn't done since the fire: walk.

I was put in a wheelchair and taken into a room where two sets of parallel bars, not unlike those used by gymnasts, stood waiting for me. Challenging me. There were taller bars and smaller ones, just my size. A nurse lifted me up out of my wheelchair and held me in front of the smaller set, instructing me to put my hands on the bars. I was fearful, but I did as she asked and placed my scarred hands on the cool metal. The doctors chanted encouraging words, telling me that I could do it, that it would be okay. I tried to believe them but the doubt bloomed within me anyway. Then, the nurse released me and I gripped the bars tightly in my hands. I was standing for the first time in months! My legs shook tremendously, like leaves in a windstorm, but I stayed on my feet. The nurse instructed me to take a step forward while I supported myself on the bars. Cheered on by the encouraging doctors, I pushed my left foot forward. The result was disastrous, and I crashed to the floor, pain knocking my hands and knees. I had wanted so badly to successfully take that step, but I was not yet strong enough to support my weight after so many months in a hospital bed. As an adult reflecting back on this time, I know that it was just the first day. But in that moment, I felt like I'd failed. It was my first real taste of feeling like I was unable to do what was expected of me.

I believe that I was born with a competitive spirit. I have failed many times in my life since that first day with the bars, but I have always been able to bounce back with more determination than ever before. Day after day in the rehab center, I tested myself on these bars, challenging myself. I began to dig deep within myself, finding strength I hadn't known I possessed, and I was not only able to stand, but I took steps. I soon mastered the bars and was able to walk the path without once giving into the safety net that the bars provided, my hands hovering above the bars—but never touching—or hanging at my sides. I felt safe walking this lane between the bars because I knew that I could grab for support if I had to. But then it was time for me to challenge myself further, to take away the security the bars offered. After weeks of aligning myself between those parallel bars, it was time for me to stand alone. No bars, no support system, just me and my own two feet. A nurse wheeled my chair to the middle of the hardwood floor, parked my wheelchair, and walked around to stand in front of me.

"Okay, James," she said. "Stand up and walk to me."

With a little help from another nurse, I was able to stand on my feet, but, for a moment, I was hesitant to step forward. My security was gone and all that was left for me to rely on was…me. I took a step towards the nurse. Then another. And another. My confidence grew with each step I took, and by the time I reached the nurse, I was ecstatic. I had done it! I had walked on my own. No bars, no helping hands. Just me.

I grew stronger every day, and after a couple of months in the rehab facility, I was running around the place like any other little boy. It was finally time for me to go, but go where? Mama was still in the hospital and Daddy was in jail, so I was sent to live with relatives. With each of my siblings staying with different people, our whole family was separated. It was strange that even though my brother and sister and I were staying only a few miles apart, it was months before we would see each other again. During the aftermath of the fire, my grandfather and other family members made the exodus from Philly to South Carolina. My grandfather and my grandmother's brother immediately arrived to ensure my father was captured and placed in jail. The next item on their list was to check on our welfare and safety. My sister hadn't received any physical injuries and my cousins, the Gibson family, didn't hesitate to take her in as their own. Kem received burns on his legs, but was released after a short stay in the hospital. He'd always been close with our grandfather, Boogie, because our mom had been so young when she'd had Kem, so Boogie was almost like his dad. My mother wasn't given very high survival odds, so Boogie decided to take Kem back up north to Philly for the summer to stay with him and his girlfriend, Momma Bennie Mae, as we called her. As was the case with nicknames, everybody seemed to be a Momma somebody. My survival odds were a little better than my mother's, but not by much. Still, I hung on as I lay in the hospital bed a few floors away from my mother as we fought the same fight.

We lost my grandmother thirty days after the fire on June 30, 1974, a date forever carved into my mother's memory, especially after sharing a hospital room with her. Was it our turn next? My mother and I fought for our lives as we remained separated from my siblings for what seemed like forever. I was too young to understand this journey. All I knew was that my pretty little baby sister who used to lay in that crib was gone, and my big brother who had run for help down that road away from me had vanished. I was all alone, and for the time being, our family was divided. I know this time had to be unbearable for my mom. She was all alone in the hospital, severely burned, her mother was dead, and all three of her children were living in different places. From her hospital bed, my mother could do little more than pray. But God answered her prayers, because after months of recovery, she came home to my great-grandpa's house. It was an unforgettable day for everyone.

Due to my mother's and my injuries, people often stared, and my brother grew to be very protective of us.

"Why are you staring at my brother?" Kem would demand when he caught someone staring. People would usually avert their eyes, embarrassed at having been caught.

My mother and I had to frequently return to the hospital for burn treatments and the occasional surgery. Although we had both been burned badly, her injuries were worse and she had to visit the hospital more often than I did. Whenever she had to have surgery, Kem, Lynnette, and I would stay with neighbors or relatives, sometimes for weeks at a time. We had to learn to rely on one another, supporting and encouraging each other.

One of the hardest parts of that time was that I couldn't understand. I didn't understand why this had happened to us, I didn't understand why my father had done what he'd done, and I didn't understand why I, and not my siblings, had to endure these physical pains. I would never wish it on either of my siblings, but I wanted to be like them—not like me, scarred and hurt and scared.

During this time, my mother earned her driver's license. She had always been a city girl and had never needed one before, but out in the country, where the buildings sometimes stretched far away from each other, a license was necessary. She drove us to Charleston for our burn treatments, about three hours away from Ridge Spring. During these trips, my mother and I would spend the whole drive talking. Many times, I spent a lot of those drives crying. I would wail and ask my mother all the questions to which there were no answers, like why God had allowed this to happen to me. She would try to explain, but each attempt only led to more tears falling down my marred cheeks. One day, I was feeling particularly sorry for myself when we were on our way home from the hospital. I was repeating my usual litany of complaints when my mother finally snapped.

"Stop feeling sorry for yourself!" she yelled, her voice emphatic and strong. "*Stop feeling sorry for yourself, because you could have been dead!*"

I sat there in the car, stunned. Without another word, my mother took the next exit off the highway and turned around, driving us back to the hospital.

What I saw that day at the hospital remains deeply embedded in my mind, even over four decades later. My mother took me back to the hospital and we saw some of the other children in the burn unit. While I had been crying over my own injuries, I hadn't stopped to think how lucky I actually was. Some of the other kids' limbs had been burned so badly that they'd needed amputations. I had complained about my scarred and once-webbed fingers, and yet I was incredibly lucky to have my hands at all. I had cried when I looked at my changed face in the mirror, but some of the other kids had faces that were horribly disfigured. While two-year-old Lynnette had cried at the sight of my face for the first time, some of the kids in the burn unit had faces that could make the average person sick, their faces distorted and raw. That day, my mother finally got through to me that I was fortunate to have lived. God had left me the ability to move around just like any other typical child my age. Sure, I'd had to fight against those parallel bars in rehab, but I could walk, run, jump, skip, dance—things some of these other kids would never again have the privilege of doing. It's unfortunate that it isn't until you're faced with the real possibility of losing something, like the ability to stand on two feet that you truly appreciate what a gift it is. That day, my mother reminded me that feeling sorry for yourself was not an option in our house. We were taught to be thankful for life and to recognize special blessings from God. I was lucky. I had lived.

CHAPTER 3

The Three Women Who Changed My Life

As my mother continued her recovery, she called upon friends and family to help care for Kem, Lynnette, and me. As no one was able to take all three of us in at once, my siblings and I ended up staying at different houses. When speaking with my mother about our family's journey after the fire, she told me of a piece of my history I didn't remember. For a short time, while she was still recovering in the hospital, I was sent to stay in a foster home for abandoned children without her knowledge. I don't personally have any memories of this time, so it was quite a shock for me to hear my mother speak of it. My mother and I were sitting together at Christmas, talking about our past, when tears began to gather and fall from her eyes as she told me of this missing puzzle piece.

My experience from the foster home was so traumatic that I completely blocked it from my memory. I don't have a single recollection from that place, only the stories from a report that my mother received from a family friend, Mr. Herrin. When I got out, my head was covered with bedsores, which nearly broke my mother's heart. I went to the foster home eating eggs and grits, but once I got out, I never touched grits or scrambled eggs ever again. To this day, the mere sight of grits makes me sick to my stomach. Something happened there that affected me to the core; at times,

I wish I could remember, but maybe it's best that I don't. Some things are better left uncovered.

After Mr. Herrin rescued me from the foster home, I continued to receive follow-up treatments at the hospital. He delivered me to the home of a cousin, whom I called "Momma Gladys," for a few months while my mother continued to recover in the hospital. Mrs. Gladys was my mother's third cousin and about twenty years her senior, and she worked in the cafeteria at the local middle school as a cook and a server. Momma Gladys and her husband were very nurturing people. They had kids of their own who were my mother's age who either lived in the home or nearby, functioning as the uncles I'd never had: Marion, Paul Jr., David, and John. Paul was the same age as my mom and Marion was about two years his senior. John was two years older than Kem and only a year younger than David. Their father was a quiet man and, in hindsight, there were a lot of quiet men in our neighborhood, those of the older generation. They were very stoic in their approach, and it appeared that the women ran things, at least at home.

Kem came by Momma Gladys's house from time to time, which always brightened my day, but he didn't live there with me. In retrospect, I suppose I understand because it was already a crowded field with all those boys in the house. Kem was the life of the party and I was the polar opposite, shy and reserved. It could've been my natural personality, but the burns had caused me to withdraw deeper into myself. Nevertheless, Momma Gladys's sons encouraged me and treated me like I belonged in their home, following the example set by their mother. Momma Gladys had passed middle age by then, and her speed of movement had slowed after years of working in the cafeteria at the middle school. She was short in stature and wore a pair of thick glasses attached to a string that hung around her neck. She stood barely over five feet and spoke in a very slow and southern tone, which reminded me of a black Aunt Bee from *The Andy Griffith Show*. I felt very safe at her house, but I often felt very alone because Momma Gladys would often stay in her room or sit in a rocking chair on the porch for what seemed like hours, watching people and cars pass by, fly-swatter in hand to shoo away the flies. Momma Gladys was on her feet all day, cooking meals for those antsy kids at the school, which had to be backbreaking work over time. It slowed her walk, but her smile and voice were just as warm as peach cobbler on a hot summer's day. She had a way of making me feel comfortable and I always enjoyed being around her.

Eating breakfast and dinner as a family was important back in those days, and that's when things could get a little testy. Everyone would be scattered to the four winds, either in their rooms, playing outside, or maybe just sitting on the porch. When dinner was ready and the lady of the house said it was ready and to come eat, she meant it! The announcement always started out with a loud but inviting, "Come eat!" but the hint of lag time and the idea of the food getting cold after Momma Gladys had spent her time cooking after a long day's work quickly turned the call from jovial to threatening.

"You better get in here and eat this food!" she'd exclaim. "And wash your hands!"

However, that was the extent of her anger, especially towards me.

"Foots, did you get enough to eat?" she'd ask me, her voice softer. "You know there's plenty!"

She often tried to convince me that I liked certain foods, much to my chagrin, and often teased me that I would either eat what was served or go to bed hungry. I could never tell if she was serious or not, but my belly was always full after every meal.

I would think about my mom in those moments and feel at ease with her stand-in. My mom instinctively broke that window in the kitchen and shoved me through it. She saved my life, and because of that unconditional love, I feel a closeness to women, especially older women. Momma Gladys provided that warmth like a blanket until I could see and touch my own mother again. Looking back, I know it had to have been a strain for Momma Gladys to take on another child, especially one like me who had burns and raw emotions. I could see the compassion in her eyes, almost a sorrow when she looked at me. I never forgot that look, and just like the tears in my mother's eyes, it inspired me to want to make her proud of me. There was no sticking point with Momma Gladys in the way I felt about her. She didn't take me outside to play or read me stories at night; instead, I believe it was just her presence. I didn't have my grandmother anymore, and maybe Momma Gladys filled that void for me. All I know is that she nurtured me after I left that foster home during a time when I needed a mother's touch, and I never forgot it. She cared for me until my mother came home, and when my mom finally did, that blanket of love was so familiar and a little warmer. No one could ever replace my mother.

When my mother was released from the hospital, we were all reunited, Kem, Lynnette and me. It was weird that my siblings and I had lived with separate families all within about a mile radius, but we hadn't seen each other often. There were people in the neighborhood whom I didn't see every day despite them living across the street, but they weren't my siblings. However, when my mom returned home from the hospital to live in my great-grandfather's house, we all came home. I know now that mothers have a special connection, a special type of love when it comes to their kids. I liken it to when I would arrive home before my wife when all of my kids were still at home. I would be in my bedroom and JJ, Josh, and Trinity would be in their separate rooms on the computer or doing some other activity, but as soon as my wife would come into the house and announce that she was home, all of the doors would pop open. The kids would gather in our bedroom and immediately start bombarding Yolanda with questions and conversation. They'd even have the nerve to ask for help with their homework, as if I hadn't been home for the past thirty minutes. Yolanda would shower them with hugs, even the boys, whom I would tease to no end about being so sickening around their mother, as if I had any room to poke fun. I must admit that I, too, got excited when Yolanda came home, but at least I played it off a little bit.

Now, take that level of excitement and multiply it by ten to imagine what it was like when my mother first came home from the hospital. It was like sleeping in hotels for a year before finally coming home to your own bed. My momma was home and walking and talking and full of energy, just like Kem and me. However, there was only one problem: Lynnette. She was so young and so pretty, especially during those days with her hair twisted in two plaits on either side of her head and adorned with bows. My daughter reminded me a lot of my sister when she was little. Lynnette's face was chubby and smooth and brown, the prettiest brown, with dimples to match (hence her nickname, "Dimples"). I saw Lynnette in that light, my beautiful sister, but she did not reciprocate. Lynnette saw me and cried, frightened sobs as she backed away from me.

"That's your brother!" our mom said, trying to reassure Lynnette that although I looked different from the burns, I was still the same old Foots. "Lynnette, that's your brother," she repeated in a calmer voice, quieting Lynnette's cries. I stood, frozen and awaiting directions, responses, and reactions. Kem was caught off guard as well, and for the first time in his life, became speechless.

It was almost as if we were sneaking up on a butterfly before it flew away.

"Do you remember your brother, Foots?" my mom asked Lynnette gently. Lynnette looked at my mom and then at me, possibly comparing our scars. A mother's love instinctively trumped her scars, but I was the foreign one. Lynnette studied me like a dog that had barked at her while walking down the street. I could see some of Lynnette's fear dissipate, but not all of it. I finally sat down on the couch in the living room and Lynnette's nerves began to ease enough so that she would consent to sit on the far end of the other side of the couch. It was a start!

Lynnette continued to survey me and I didn't force the issue. Over the course of several days, the ocean between us on the couch began to shrink. Then, finally, one day she touched my face and I smiled, and I guess she knew things were going to be all right. We became really tight after those days, fear turning into a mutual protection. I never forgot those moments as I periodically reflected in the mirror. I couldn't change my face; God wasn't answering that prayer, at least not in the way I would've loved for him to do. However, I learned that maybe it wasn't about the physical change, after all. It still hurt to see other people's reactions, but if I could win my sister over, I could win anybody over, because she didn't play with people back then. She still doesn't. The gang was back together and the calls to the dinner table were from my real mother's voice. How sweet it sounded!

Due to the severity of my mother's burns, she had periodic setbacks during her recovery. As a result, she would frequent the burn center, staying for a week or so at the hospital. During these times, Lynnette would always go to the Gibsons across the street, while Kem stayed with Momma Gladys or Mr. Herrin. As for me, I would stay with Patricia Denny and her husband, who adored me and had agreed to take me in while my mother was hospitalized. My mom had met Ms. Denny when the latter moved from Washington, DC to South Carolina. Ms. Denny was the most beautiful full-figured woman in all of the South, with light skin and an infectious personality. She could sing as well as any famous artist of the day and spoke with an elegance and confidence reserved for the fiercest of women, which immediately attracted my mother. They were both city girls operating in a southern town and felt a kinship with each another.

Ms. Denny's husband, Peewee, was a smooth operator in his own right, even though he was raised in the South instead of a big city. However, Peewee had served in Vietnam and returned home with some of the issues that came along with that war, fighting his own demons but never losing his kindness. When they met, Ms. Denny and my mother immediately hit it off, and when my dad followed us down South, they and their husbands made a regular foursome. The Dennys saw my father as a quiet and reserved man, which shocked them to no end when they found out he had intentionally burned down our house. She and Peewee had gone to the house after the fire had started and witnessed the blaze. Peewee once told me that the flames were so high and the heat was so intense that they'd had to stand at the road's edge to watch. He'd known my father briefly after my father moved down south, and Peewee couldn't believe such a quiet man like my father could have started the fire. My father had fooled us all.

Ms. Denny wanted to adopt me. She knew me before the burns and after the fire, and she wanted me with her after I was released from the hospital, but family won out. All the same, Ms. Denny wanted me to be a part of her family and treated me as such during my mom's frequent stays in the hospital. She'd always ask me if I liked it at her house and would I like to stay longer? I appreciated

Ms. Denny so much because she made me feel like a somebody. My nickname, Foots, was known by all, and to this day, everyone in Ridge Spring knows me as such. Ms. Denny called me "Footsie," and each time she said it, she sounded like she was calling her favorite person in the world. Her voice echoed in my mind like a beautiful song that always put a shy person like me at ease. Ms. Denny resembled Queen Latifah in many ways, her thickness and edge, but she didn't sing rap songs; instead, she really sang songs with a smooth and sultry voice. She could've been a star with that voice, like Jennifer Hudson, and it was calming to me. It was so soothing when I would hear her in the house, just humming or singing softly. I'm sure that's one of the qualities that mesmerized Peewee during their courtship days. He was country and she had that city accent and perfect diction, along with the fullness of her stature to go with that proper voice, and there was no doubt he was smitten.

I was so shy and emotionally scarred from the fire that I would drop my head around people and avoid looking them in the eyes. It was a protective defense mechanism. But during dinner, Ms. Denny wouldn't let me get away with that and she'd engage me in conversation.

"Footsie, did you have fun today?"

"Yes, ma'am," I'd reply, not making eye contact and keeping my head down.

"Hold that head up and let me see that pretty smile," she'd say. "I want you to look at me with those pretty eyes when you talk to me, okay?"

"Yes, ma'am," I'd say, risking a small smile. Ms. Denny began to build my confidence without me realizing it. All I knew at the time was that it made me feel good. Ms. Denny made me smile and she was a pretty beautiful person, inside and out, which made it all that much better. Peewee, in turn, would double back during our alone time and tell me that men should look each other in the eyes.

"You need to show confidence," he'd say. I understood what he meant, but it was difficult for me to trust any guys at this point, and Peewee's words didn't carry the same weight as Ms. Denny's. I can still hear her voice. It all makes sense now when I hear my wife sing. I can hear my cousin, Sandra, and I can hear Ms. Denny. The singing reminds me of a good place, a safe place. Ms. Denny nurtured me and gave me peace. She and Peewee treated me like their own son, and as I said, they wanted to adopt me.

Lynnette was in a similar situation with the Gibsons. The Dennys lived on the next street over from our house and the only thing separating the two blocks was a long chain-link fence dividing each neighbor's yard down a row of about eight houses. It was weird to be so close to my siblings, who were all within a half mile radius, but I rarely saw them unless we were home together with our mom between her visits to the hospital. Ms. Pat and Peewee had four other kids—Jamie, Brandy, Chris, and Kelcie—all of whom became my unofficial siblings, but it wasn't the same as having Kem and Lynnette with me. However, this was our norm until our mother was strong enough to come home for good, and during that time, I stayed with the Denny family on and off for the next two years.

When I entered the fourth grade, I became close with Greg Henman and his family. His mother, Ms. Henman, was a joyous personality and a beautiful, elegant woman with skin the color of tanned pecans. Her Indian black hair flowed over her shoulders and she looked like she'd walked straight out of the pages of *Ebony* magazine. She was a single woman raising four kids on her own after having recently relocated to the South from Connecticut, one of my mother's friends from before the fire. My mom had a connection with these women from the North who had also moved back home like she had. I enjoyed spending time with the Henmans because her kids were similar in ages to my siblings and me.

Greg and I were in the same class at school and he had older twin siblings, Debbie and Sheldon, who were both a year behind Kem. Kem and Sheldon hit it off immediately, with their similar personalities, and continued their friendship in later years. Debra was her mother's daughter in all respects, and just as beautiful. She reminded me of Denise Huxtable from *The Cosby Show* in both looks and style. Debra later attended SC State, as I did, and would've been the perfect fill-in for Denise's role on *A Different World*. Additionally, Greg had a younger sister, Ursula, who was the same age as Lynnette, and they were best buddies as well.

My friendship with Greg began at school. Greg had a talent for drawing, and one day I noticed one of his masterpieces in class.

"Can I take a look at that, Greg?" I asked.

"Sure," he said, handing it over.

"Wow!" I exclaimed. "Man, you are an artist!"

Greg just smiled.

After that, we began to hang out at recess and engage in foot races to show off and try to impress some girls. It was really more about the competition for me, and in those days, Greg was so fast he could fly. I was still a little chubby then, and Greg would light me up in a sixty-yard sprint. I was so competitive and it would eat me up inside to lose anything, but Greg was cool, and because of that, I could tolerate the loss. Greg also loved cars, but I knew absolutely nothing about them, so I guess opposites attract. Greg was just like my friend Junior in the way that he could hear a car coming down the road and before seeing it, he could tell you what kind of car it was, what type of engine it had, and if it was running correctly. Personally, I stuck to sports, but we enjoyed each other's company because of and in spite of our differences.

As a result, my mother allowed me to stay with the Henmans when she returned to the hospital from time to time. I was still very shy, but Greg and I had grown to be very good friends, and staying with the Henmans was a natural fit. Ms. Henman was a great cook and would call us into the house for dinner like we were the Waltons. We took turns blessing the food before each meal and it felt really warm and wonderful to be a part of a family unit…but it wasn't quite the same as being with my own family. The Henmans were wonderful, but I still yearned to be with my baby sister and my big brother.

Ms. Henman also ensured we got our clothes ready for school, and Greg and I would take turns on the ironing board, creasing our pants and starching our shirts. I'm not sure what it's like in other cultures, but starching your clothes before school was as serious as taking a bath before school. You had to look the part and be the part. I enjoyed staying there and Ms. Henman treated me like a part of the family. She didn't single me out or baby me, just allowed me to blend into the family like I was her third son. Ms. Henman had become the third woman in my life that I lived with for a little while from time to time, and I trusted and respected her. Women I trusted; men I did not. They fed me and nurtured me just like my mother. They taught me to look someone in the eye and iron my clothes, bless my food before consumption, and shower before bed. These women reinforced what my mother had taught me, that I was handsome and could do anything I set my mind to. They told me to stay well-mannered and to treat people kindly. To this day, I carry the spirit of these women, along with that of my mother, with me and I treat women differently. I hold them to the standards of all these women, right or wrong. The experience with the Henman family was great, but they were not my siblings. I still yearned to be with Kem and Lynnette every time I was sent away; I had a little hole in my heart where they should have been. Little did I know, all of this was preparing me for military life when I spent lots of time away from my loved ones.

These were the incredible women who left an indelible impression on me. I only stayed with each of them for a short time, but I never forgot them and I held them in the highest regard because they cared for me when I needed them. These three women were not alone in my life: My cousins, Dianne, Sandra, and Janice; their mother, Ms. Dorothy; my sister, Lynnette; and my own mother left each of their marks on me and made me want to protect and cherish women. As a result of all of these women in my life, I've always felt more comfortable and trusting around women than any man. Later in my life, after seeing my wife deliver each of our three children, and watching her bounce back from those births, confirmed my belief that women deserve all honor and respect. I have been fortunate to spend my life surrounded by strong and powerful women, and now I have been given the responsibility to raise my own daughter in that same tradition. Luckily, I've been surrounded by incredible examples.

CHAPTER 4

School Daze

A year had passed since my siblings and I had reunited with our mother, and everything seemed so normal. It's true, there had been many trips to the hospital, operations, and stay-overs with our cousins, but it was our new normal. But now, after having had to overcome so much and re-learn how to walk, I was faced with an even bigger challenge, probably one of the biggest challenges I'd ever faced: school. I was seven years old and it was time for me to start first grade. I got an early start in life in terms of experiencing hardships and learning tough lessons, but I got a late start in school due to those same factors. I was a year behind my peers, which meant that I was a little bigger than the other kids in my grade. As it turned out, that would serve as a plus for me.

The day had come for me to start my first day at Ridge Spring-Monetta Elementary School. I rode the bus to school, but I wasn't happy about it at all. I felt like I'd been set up to be mocked and to fail. Like any kid, I was nervous about starting school, but I was even more scared due to my burns and the fact that I had to wear a mask to aid the healing skin on my face. When I arrived at school, there were kids everywhere, an environment even more intimidating than I'd imagined. My teacher was there to greet me. I assume she had been briefed on me and my injuries beforehand, because she pampered me a little and went out of her way to extend her kindness and attention towards me to make sure I was okay. The amount of people staring at me was so stressful and I felt like I was on the verge of bursting into tears. I wanted to go back home to where I felt safe and no one stared at me for being different. However, things began to turn around once I got into the classroom. The other kids didn't understand about my mask yet, and because it was unfamiliar, they felt scared too. Half of the kids in my class were already in tears, and I was ready to join them, but it was then that things began to shift—we were all scared. This was all new, and we were in this together.

I believe timing is everything and fortunately for me, my arrival at school coincided with the popularity of wrestling on TV. Andre the Giant and Tony Atlas were some of the popular wrestling heroes at my school, especially the latter because he was the only African American wrestler that we knew of. There was one wrestler in particular who wore a mask similar to mine. He was actually born in Charleston, South Carolina, and his name was Johnny Walker, better known by his stage name, Mr. Wrestling II.

He was the favorite wrestler of Georgia governor and later president Jimmy Carter, and Mr. Wrestling II was even invited to the inauguration. However, the Secret Service demanded that were he to attend, he'd have to remove his mask for security purposes. Due to Mr. Wrestling II's popularity with his mask, he felt that appearing unmasked and exposing his identity would cause professional ramifications, so he ultimately declined Carter's inauguration invitation. However, Mr. Wrestling II did enjoy a private audience with Lillian Carter on several occasions. At the time, I really related to him because he was a star who thrived underneath the secrecy of a mask. He didn't have to unmask to be liked or popular. This gave me a little confidence in myself, because although my masks resembled stockings, my classmates immediately related the two of them, and by doing so, what made me different became a little less scary.

While in first grade, I became pretty good friends with a kid named Michael Gantt. We'd often have foot races, and because he was fast like me, we started to hang out during recess or playtime at school. He never probed about my mask or my injuries, which was really cool; I appreciated being treated just like any other kid. One day, we were playing close to the tree line at the edge of the recess yard. We had made paper airplanes and were throwing them over and over again until his drifted a little ways into the woods. We weren't supposed to go past the tree line and out of the teachers' sight, but we had to get his plane back. So when we saw that folded piece of white paper sail in between the trees, we both ran after it and began searching for it.

"Hey, can I see you without your mask on while nobody's watching?" he asked suddenly, completely out of the blue.

He caught me off guard and I paused for a moment, considering his unexpected words. But he was my buddy, so I told him I'd do it really quick. I reached back to the line of Velcro that held my mask in place at the back of my head and pulled. The Velcro made its crunchy, ripping sound, and then I reached for the bottom of my mask with both hands and pulled it up from under my chin to my forehead. I stood there for what felt like an eternity in a moment while I watched him without saying a word, waiting for his response.

"Cool!" he exclaimed before he turned to retrieve his paper airplane.

I was stunned. I wasn't sure what exactly I'd expected him to say, but "cool" definitely hadn't been it. As I watched him look for his plane, I didn't know if he was really preoccupied with finding it, or if he'd wanted to say a different word when he saw my face and "cool" just popped up in his brain first. I donned my mask quickly before he had a chance to change his response, pushing the Velcro strap secure once more. Then we ran back to the front of the tree line before the teachers noticed we'd ventured too far.

I had already liked Michael because he was my friend, but after that incident he became even cooler to me because he didn't react in a negative way when he saw my face. I had been so ready for him to recoil in fear or disgust, but everything had turned out okay. We were still friends—better, in fact, after that incident—and after that moment in the woods, we were able to get back to the serious business of flying paper airplanes. Looking back, I believe that that incident with Michael gave me the courage to go without the mask once the doctors eventually gave me the green light to ditch it. Michael moved away after first grade to a neighboring town, but it's funny to consider how small moments with people who pass through our lives so briefly can have such a huge impact on us and the way we view ourselves.

Unfortunately, not all the kids were like Michael. When I later revealed my face to some of my other classmates, they did not have the same positive reaction that Michael had. Some of their faces were filled with fear and despair at my different face. In later years, those expressions angered me because it felt like no matter how hard I tried to fit in and be a normal little boy, other people's initial reactions to my face were constant reminders of what I looked like. Much like after the first time I looked in a mirror when Lynnette cried in terror at my appearance at our reunion, I began to avoid mirrors and eventually grew to hate them. I wished there were no reflections so that I never had to look at myself. I did my best to avoid looking not only in mirrors, but also car and shop windows, anything that might accidentally show me my own face.

But even if I didn't look at myself, some of the other kids made sure I never forgot. Some kids were very blunt and directly asked me, "What happened to your face?" I was not usually bothered or offended by this sort of thing. By throwing my scars out in the open waters of the conversation, they were ultimately easier to move past. However, context is everything, and a change in tone and circumstance can make all the difference between honest curiosity and an excuse for humiliation and ridicule. Sometimes the question would be thrown out at me in a group setting and it would often be asked in a way that, in no uncertain terms, let me know they were disgusted by my presence. Oftentimes, I could hear kids whispering during lunch break or between classes. I did my best to ignore those whispers, unless someone told me that the whispers were about me.

Because I had started school later than the other kids in my grade, I was a little bigger than my peers, which, as I said, turned out to be in my favor. Physical altercations that resulted from their teasing would always end with me as the victor, but verbal altercations resulted in losses. What could I say when they teased me? It's not like I could argue that my face wasn't different, because it was. My father had irreparably changed my face and the damage from that night was far from just physical. In setting that fire, he had changed my life in more ways than one, and now I was enduring the other consequences of his actions. Oftentimes, I think it's easier to manage physical pain because it's something tangible, it's easier to understand. A fire burned my skin so my skin hurt, but there were defined avenues of treatment. When the other kids hurled insults at me, their words cut me in a deeper way that a surgeon's knife never could.

As a result of my physical appearance, I was very shy and had low self-confidence. Without someone like Michael to encourage me, I was at the mercy of the other children. I hated having to stand in front of the class and read; feeling everyone's undivided attention on me, feeling the way I did about my appearance—it was excruciating. Once a year, our school held a fire prevention week, during which, real firemen would come to our school and speak to all of the kids. I dreaded this event every year and tried to steel myself for what was to come, but it was always awkward and painful for me. During their annual speeches, the firemen always explained what to do in case of a fire at home. I would fold into myself, wanting to ball into the tightest knot that I could and disappear from the class, because each year, I would overhear kids whispering to one another, joking that I obviously hadn't followed the firemen's instructions.

Back in the classroom, teachers would reiterate the firemen's speeches and ask questions about what to do if there was a fire. All eyes would shift towards me, I suppose expecting me to say, "Stop, drop, and roll!" but I didn't want to participate. I didn't want to be the inadvertent center of attention during fire safety week. The other kids knew I'd been burned, but they didn't know the whole truth. They didn't know about my father, didn't know about my family's true history. They hadn't seen my father waiting on the porch, his satisfied grin when we pulled up in the car, knowing his horrible plan was about to come to fruition. They hadn't felt what I had, either during the fire or during the months and years that followed. They didn't know what it was like to hide from mirrors and reflections. Maybe if the other kids had known, then things would have been different. Maybe not. Bullying and cruelty are unfortunate truths of childhood.

In the next town over from Ridge Spring, there was a popular ice cream store called Tastee-Freeze. Getting to travel there and get a soft vanilla ice cream cone or a banana split during the hot summer months was an incredible treat. One summer afternoon, my friend's father decided to treat us to ice cream, so he loaded about six or seven of us kids into his pickup truck, and off we went. It was exciting to ride in the back of the truck, the wind swirling around us as we bounced and rumbled down the road, all of us excited and giddy with anticipation of the treats that waited for us at the Tastee-Freeze.

Everything went well at the ice cream shop, and all of us kids got our cones and climbed back into the bed of the pickup truck to return home. We were enjoying our ice cream and waiting to leave, when an older gentleman walked out of the Tastee-Freeze, his arms full of his own purchases. His eyes traveled over us in the truck and when his eyes found me, his face changed. He looked as if I'd scared him and he immediately dropped everything he was holding. The man stared at the ground for a brief moment at the wreckage of his purchases before he turned and went back inside. One of the other kids in the truck immediately jumped on the situation and proclaimed that because I was so ugly, I'd made the man drop his ice cream. In the moment, I laughed off the comment and tried to rationalize why the guy had really dropped his food—but I knew why he'd dropped it. Of course I did. Sometimes it seemed like anytime I felt close to being just a regular kid, there was always someone there to remind me that my face wasn't like everyone else's.

CHAPTER 5

Facing My Father, Part I

When I was about eight or nine, my family, with the exception of Kem, visited my father in prison for the first time since the fire. At the time, I really didn't understand what jail actually meant or how long my father's sentence was. All I had was this looping scene in my head of the house, the fire, the broken glass, the screams, and the scramble out of the house. It was as if someone was sitting on the remote and didn't know it, accidentally pressing rewind and play at random, over and over again.

Kem was still having problems dealing with the fire. My mother had tried everything she could think of to convince him to visit our father. She took him shopping for shoes and tried to talk about the good times with our father, but to no avail. Kem would not face the man he had once called "Dad" no matter what our mom said or did. Unlike my mother and me, Kem had only received burns on his lower legs, but he was so ashamed of those burns that he would wear long tube socks and tape them up to keep them from falling and revealing his scars. Other than Lynnette, Kem had physically suffered the least, but the psychological wounds ran far deeper than they appeared. Maybe it was because he was old enough to remember a calmer life before the scars, and couldn't really deal with the new normal.

However, this life of burns and scars was all I knew. I didn't have any pictures to look at to remind me of how I used to look before the fire, which was, at the time, probably for the best for me. I stared in that bathroom mirror for so many years at the same face, asking God why, but I never expected an answer. I figured that instead of hiding behind some mask or long sleeves or long pants, why not just deal with it? This is the only way I have known I look like, and God saw fit to make me look this way, so I dealt with it. Kem, however, saw things differently. He carried that weight and anger for us all. He couldn't understand how our mom could want to see a man that had caused so much pain to so many. What did she know that we didn't? Was our mother in denial or suffering from post-traumatic stress? Did she still love our father in spite of this travesty? Did she not see her own reflection in the mirror and understand how those scars got there? Did she think it was somehow an accident? Our mother showed us no anger towards our father and I went along with that, but Kem did not. He saw what a mess we were in, and he was not having it. On the day we went to the prison, my mom made one last-ditch effort to bring Kem along with us by going to his school to pick him up. However, Kem was not fooled. He saw us coming and took off running. He absolutely would not go with us, no way, no how!

The visit was not for me or my sister. It couldn't have been; we were way too young and didn't even sit at the table very much while our parents talked. My sister and I mostly played in the corner, but I often looked over at my mother and father, feeling fiercely protective of my mom and confused about why we were there at all. I couldn't understand why we were there with this man who had hurt us so badly, who had sent us to the hospital, whose actions had led to the splintering of our family. In retrospect, I believe my mom needed closure. It was weird at the time, because my mother never once looked angry while she spoke with my father. From my vantage point in the corner with Lynnette, I searched my mother's face for anger, but I never found it. Instead, I saw disappointment in a man she had once loved. I'm sure she was conflicted about this visit, about seeing a man responsible for taking the life of her mother and best friend. She surely had to question how a man could harm his own children, but my mother also knew of his mental issues. Did she carry the guilt with her while she searched for answers of why my father had done what he did? In a way, she seemed to feel sorry for him.

On the rare occasion I rejoined the table, I was quiet so as not to disturb my mother's conversation with my father. Nevertheless, my appearance drew my father's attention.

"Foots," he said, "how's school?"

"School's fine," I said.

"Are you taking care of your baby sister?"

"Yes."

I kept my answers short as I looked into his eyes, trying to figure out if this was the same man I'd seen on the porch with that glass of liquor. Was this some kind of illusion, some figment of my imagination? He was speaking to me as though nothing had happened, and my mother was talking to him as if he had only robbed the local store and would be home in a year. He wasn't acting like a man who had smashed all of our belongings before luring us into an inferno. I circled the table slowly, warily, like edging around an unpredictable bear. I studied my father's features and kept looking at my mom, trying to rationalize this moment in time. Kem wasn't there to keep me focused, but why was that? Was Kem still afraid of this man? Did he have a secret that he didn't share with me? Kem wouldn't have left Lynnette or me unprotected, or in a dangerous situation, so it had to be something else.

I pulled my eyes away from my parents and let my gaze wander around the room, over the other inmates and their family members. No one looked like a killer. In fact, they all looked normal, except for the few with what looked like a million tattoos, but I didn't stare at them for too long. Because of the man we were there to visit, I knew all too well what it felt like to be stared at, and I didn't want to do that to someone else.

All in all, our meeting lasted about two hours. Lynnette whined the whole time, but she was really too young and probably shouldn't have been there in the first place. However, Lynnette's whining ended up being the best thing for me because it kept me mostly distracted and prevented my mind from looping through its endless questions. Finally, my mom said her goodbyes and we got ready to leave. I was anxious to go home and I don't remember too much of what my father said to me before we left, except for one thing: "Make sure you take care of your mother and sister, and tell Kem hello for me."

I nodded when he said that and didn't think much of it at the moment, but my father's words stuck with me for a long time. I carried his goodbye with me for years, psychoanalyzing the audacity of his request. How dare he make such a request of me! Take care of my mom and sister? The way he was supposed to, or the way he actually did? *What a psycho,* I thought. Sometimes, I felt like I was balled up in a knot because I hadn't been brave enough to tell him he was a monster. *Why didn't I say that?* I'd ask myself. *I should've said that.* I held onto that lost moment for years until I finally got my chance while I was stationed at Fort Jackson. *I will say that.*

CHAPTER 6

Finding Myself in Sports

As I grew into adolescence, I began to look for ways to divert people's attention away from my face, and found I had two key skills: I was athletic and I could make people laugh. When I was younger, verbal altercations had always failed me, but as I got older, I found a way to gain the upper hand without having to resort to my fists. When I felt people were going to make fun of me, I would intercept the joke by saying something else to make them laugh or do something crazy to relieve some of the tension.

Despite my newfound comedic abilities, I still found myself getting into fights. Sometimes the jokes wouldn't be enough to divert the teasing, and I'd once again find myself in a fight. I always hated physical confrontations, but there was still a temporary gratification in momentarily silencing the almost daily abuse I received from my classmates. When a joke wouldn't suffice, my fist did nicely. Of course, that never really solved the problem, but I later found a different way to use my size and strength to my advantage. While being bigger than my classmates had formerly been an asset when it came to winning fights at recess, I channeled that power into something more positive as I got older. I could run faster, jump higher, and kick and throw farther than just about anyone in my class.

Recess, the one hour we received to play during school, was the highlight of each day for me. We would usually play some type of organized activity and early on, kickball became my sport. If you've never played, kickball is basically played like baseball but with a large rubber playground ball instead of a baseball and a bat that you would, of course, kick. When I was up at the plate, the pitcher never had an answer for any of my kicks. They could roll the ball fast or slow, spin it or bounce it, but the results were always the same. I would send the ball sailing a country mile over the defender's head, where it would bounce in the distant grass as I sprinted around the bases. When it was my turn to kick and I stepped up to the plate, the opposing team would always take several steps back in anticipation of my heavy hitter's kick. It was such an awesome feeling for me because it gave me a sense of something I felt so infrequently: pride.

There is a difference between demanding respect and commanding respect. When I fought with the other kids and the altercations turned physical, I was trying to demand respect. With my fists, I demanded they respect me as a person and not mock me for my scars, something that was completely out of my control. But as an athlete, I commanded respect on the field, and the other kids gave me that respect freely. It was odd to see people stand away from me due to my physical appearance, and yet crowd me because of my physical abilities. They were resistant to the way I looked and yet they were so impressed with what my body could do in sports. I realized that through my athleticism, I was giving them something else to see besides my injuries when they looked at me. Even if it was only for that moment when I walked up to the plate and all the outfielders backed up in anticipation for my kick, in that moment I wasn't the kid with the scars—I was the kid who was about to kick the ball over everyone's heads and score a run for my team.

In seventh grade, the end of my surgeries happened to coincide with the start of organized sports at school. Before I was old enough to play, I remember going to the games to watch the bigger kids play. If you've ever lived in a small country town, you know the importance of sports to the town's lifeblood, especially football. Everyone becomes very involved with local sports and the local school field is the only place to be on a Friday night. So, of course, I was there, too. I and the other younger kids would watch the games, which would inspire us to hone our own skills after school, just waiting for our own opportunity to become the next town star. In my eyes, the two best and most important positions on the football field were running back and quarterback. My favorite team was the Pittsburgh Steelers and my favorite player was none other than Franco Harris.

Franco Harris, a fullback from Penn State, was a first round draft pick in 1972 for the Pittsburgh Steelers. At the time, many people were surprised because they had expected Harris's teammate, the All-American running back Lydell Mitchell, to be selected first (he later went to the Baltimore Colts). But Harris proved to be a valuable pick because in his first season with the NFL, he rushed for a gain of 1,055 yards on 188 carries, which averaged out to 5.6 yards per carry. He also rushed for ten touchdown and caught four touchdown passes. During his rookie year, he also participated in a play that was later dubbed "The Immaculate Reception" during a playoff game against the Oakland Raiders. The Steelers were behind the Raiders with a score of six to seven and twenty-two seconds left in the fourth quarter. Terry Bradshaw's pass was deflected, and when defeat looked certain, Franco Harris snatched the ball just before it hit the ground and he ran it in for a touchdown, securing the win against the Raiders.

Although the Steelers didn't go on to win the Super Bowl that year, Harris ultimately won the championship with the Steelers four times and was the Super Bowl MVP two years later in Super

Bowl IX against the Minnesota Vikings. In that game, Harris rushed for 158 yards, more than the entire Vikings offense combined. That particular award as MVP was notable in the NFL's history as Harris was not only the first Italian American Super Bowl MVP, but also the first African American Super Bowl MVP. Franco Harris was consecutively nominated to the Pro Bowl nine times from 1972 to 1980 and, as of this writing, Franco Harris holds the Super Bowl records for most career rushing yards (354) and most career attempts (101). Although the Pittsburgh Steelers no longer "officially" retire the numbers of former players, it's generally understood that no one else will wear Harris's 32.

Because I was born in Philadelphia, most people would assume that I am a fan of the Eagles, but my allegiance is deeply rooted in the Pittsburgh Steelers. Between my first and second years in school, Kem and I spent the summer in Pittsburgh with our great-grandmother. It was an amazing summer and during that pleasant trip, the seeds of love for the Steelers were planted in my head. At the time, I equated the Steelers with the warmth and love of my great-grandmother's house, so I began to watch the Steelers' games. As I watched, I was drawn to Franco Harris because we had similar builds (mine was the smaller, child version, of course) and I liked to run the ball like he did when I played in neighborhood pickup games of football. A lot of the other kids really liked Lynn Swann, but Franco was my man.

Inspired by Franco Harris, I wanted to be a running back, but before seventh grade, I couldn't yet play for the team, so I had to get creative in my mission to get close to the school football team. I applied to be a team manager, which was really just a fancy, dressed-up way of saying "ball boy." Due to my athletic abilities, some of the older kids knew who I was and they respected the talent I had, so I was selected to become a manager. I was thrilled;

my selection to what was viewed as an elite club meant so much to me. As an added bonus, as a manager I got free access to the JV and varsity football games, so not only did I save a few dollars each game, I gained a little clout amongst my peers. It always gave me a thrill to be able to sail through the gate with a flash of my manager's pass, my own badge of honor.

As I said, small towns love their Friday night football, and there was really something about attending those games. The smell of popcorn and freshly mowed grass was a combination that meant football. As you walked through the entrance into the stadium, that smell would fill your nose and the school band's battle cry of the fight song filled your ears. All of the youngsters, us wannabes who desperately wanted to join the team when we were old enough, would watch the first quarter with a deep intensity. We studied the quarterback and running backs closely so that we could mimic their mercuric moves during the second quarter behind the stands. During the games, the cheerleaders would always throw miniature footballs into the stands, so some of the other kids and I would get one of balls and head behind the stands to start a little football action of our own. Every now and then, if we made good cuts like the big boys on the field, a grown up might look back at us and comment, saying, "Look at that little fellow run! He's going to be a baller." We'd always end our games before halftime to avoid the crowds, and then we'd turn our focus back to the actual football game out on the field. We'd watch with excitement and anticipation along with the rest of the crowd as each of us kids would fantasize about the day when we would be on the field wearing the blue and gold.

Football season would end and transition into basketball season, which I loved with an even greater passion. My favorite team was the Philadelphia 76ers, highlighting my connection to the

City of Brotherly Love, and my favorite player was Julius Erving, also known by the popular nickname "Dr. J." Over the course of his career, Dr. J scored over thirty thousand points and on a combined list of scoring for the NBA/ABA, as of this writing, he's still ranked the sixth highest scorer of all time, behind Magic Johnson, Kobe Bryant, Wilt Chamberlain, Karl Malone, and Michael Jordan, and the latter became my favorite player later in my life.

To this day, Dr. J is known for being one of the best dunkers to ever play the game. Although he wasn't the first to perform impressive dunks, Dr. J is credited with making the practice mainstream. Whereas players before used the dunk as a testosterone-fueled display of machismo and was regarded as somewhat unsportsmanlike, Dr. J utilized a lot more finesse as a way to avoid a blocked shot. Of course, slam dunks are still used as a display of power today, but Dr. J showed that they can be displays of skill as well, especially when launching one's self far away from the hoop to deliver a dunk. Dr. J displayed remarkable skill during his time playing professional basketball, but he performed a few particularly memorable feats.

In the 1976 ABA Slam Dunk Contest, Dr. J dunked the ball twice and brought a new style of dunking to the general consciousness of basketball fans by launching himself from the foul line to sink the ball. Dr. J wasn't the first player to dunk from the foul line, it had been done before by Jim Pollard and Wilt Chamberlain, but Dr. J was the first one to really bring it to a wide audience by performing it at this contest. Another notable feat occurred during the 1977 finals when Dr. J dunked over Bill Walton. This is still considered one of the strongest dunks ever attempted since it was preceded by Dr. J charging across the full length of the court while being chased by all five defenders. This coincided with a wider television audience for professional basketball, which, in turn, solidified Dr. J's status as an impressive dunker.

But perhaps his most impressive play was not actually a dunk, but a layup. During the 1980 NBA finals, Dr. J was heading for the hoop but was close to being closed out of a possible scoring position by both Mark Landsberger and Kareem Abdul-Jabbar. As Abdul-Jabbar was forcing him out of bounds, Dr. J, in mid-air, managed to reach over and score a right-handed layup, despite the fact that his whole body, left shoulder included, was already behind the backboard. This particular move is considered one of his signature moves and *Sports Illustrated* called it the "No Way, Even for Dr. J, Reverse Lay-up." Dr. J, on the other hand, referred to it as "just another move." While I felt that Franco Harris's playing style impacted my own moves on the football field, Dr. J didn't have that same influence on my basketball style. I was a small guard and didn't hit a growth spurt until ninth or tenth grade, finally reaching five eleven during my senior year of high school, so I wasn't much of a dunker the way Dr. J was. However, I was very quick on the court and my passion for the sport fueled that speed.

Aside from his impressive skills on the court, I felt another connection to Dr. J, because as it turned out, he had family in Ridge Spring, of all places! His cousins, who shared the last name Erving with the Doctor, were all tall and resembled their famous cousin. The younger cousins would all tell breathless, excited stories about meeting Dr. J and made outrageous claims that Dr. J would come play basketball with us in the summers in Ridge Spring. We all knew it would never happen, but we still loved to indulge ourselves in the fantasy of getting to play with our hero. Dr. J was a well-spoken, articulate superhero who said all the right things and was just so cool to us.

Motivated by this personal hero and my love of the game, I played basketball at every possible opportunity. Dirt courts, asphalt courts, old gyms, armories—anywhere. If there was a hoop,

I was throwing a ball through it. Off the court, there was so much I couldn't control. I couldn't control my injuries from the fire and my subsequent scars, I couldn't control the way the other kids teased me, I couldn't control the reactions of strangers when they saw me. But when I was on the court, I felt free and in charge of my life in a way I didn't anywhere else. I played football at a high level, but my love and passion lay in basketball. Basketball became my escape for many years until I wore my right knee down to four surgeries and finally a knee replacement at age forty-four.

As the school's basketball season approached, I began to campaign for a manager's spot on the team as I had with football. Due to my position with the football team, I was all but guaranteed the same job with the basketball team, but I had to make sure I stayed on the good side of the big boys who were on the team. The older guys had a little bit of influence as to who would end up as a manager. They could tell the coaches that they liked having this guy or that guy around, and I wanted every possible advantage I could get to secure my spot. As I mentioned before, the manager's card gave me free access to any of the home games, which usually cost around $1.50 to $2 for a ticket. That was big money for me in those days, since my mother didn't make much, so the manager's card was like a lottery ticket for me.

The card also allowed me to get some popcorn and a drink during halftime, which I thought was great. Fortunately, I'd played pickup games with a lot of the older kids and they knew my skills on the football field and basketball court, which worked to my advantage in getting the coveted manager's spot. I was a sixth grader, biding my time until I reached seventh grade and was able to join organized sports for the very first time. The manager's position allowed me to get as close to the action as I could without actually suiting up, which I loved. I would imagine myself running in touchdowns or shooting a basket, depending on the sports season, and I couldn't wait until I was old enough to showcase my talents.

In larger towns, there would be one group of kids playing football and another crew that played basketball, but in our small town, we played every sport. An athlete was an athlete and the football players would trade in their padding and helmets for the shorts and jerseys of the basketball team. For me, the feeling of anticipation I had at the start of the season was the same for me, no matter the sport. I loved them all and lived to play them. Sports consumed me and if I wasn't practicing, I was dreaming about playing. As I grew older and drew closer to seventh grade, and therefore able to try out for the team, I studied the best players and worked hard to improve my own moves, knowing that my time was near. I would find myself lost in daydreams, imagining myself on the basketball court, driving to the hole and throwing a Magic Johnson no-look pass. But before I could try out for the team, I had to do my time and wait until I was in seventh grade.

My sixth grade year drew to a close and as summertime approached, I knew the time to showcase my athletic skills was growing closer. It was time to close the gap between my older, eighth grade competition and myself. I had always played sports with the older crowd, but it was time for me to command respect on the field. I only stood at five six and really had to work hard to get my shot off on the basketball court. I had to get creative with scoop shots, reverse layups, and no-look passes. There were no breaks and the big kids always played hard against me, but that really paid off for me in the future. No one gets better by taking on the easiest challenges. I began to improve every week and my confidence grew, even though kids continued to ridicule me about my burns and about my father's incarceration. However, when I was on the court or on the field, I had a way to deal with all the teasing.

Sports were my outlet, my way to shut out all the hateful comments. I might have been the kid with scars, but I was also the kid who was charging past them on the basketball court and making incredible shots.

Before I reached that highly anticipated seventh year, I experienced something else significant. In fact, my experiences during my sixth grade year changed the course of my life. There was a system at our school, similar to other schools in the South, that placed students on certain academic levels based on grades, evaluations, and subjective inputs from teachers. Our school had four categories: 6-1 college track, 6-2 community college/business track, 6-3 auto mechanics/agricultural track, and 6-4 remedial/needs assistance track. I was placed in 6-2 due to the good grades I'd had up to that point. Good grades meant access to the sports teams; this was the rule my mother required and demanded of me, so I worked my hardest to follow that directive.

Aside from sports, I found myself drawn to one particular class: English. I can't distinctly recall whether or not it was the information that interested me or the teacher who instructed me, Ms. Peterson. That English class was my first encounter with a female African American teacher. In fact, I'd only had one other African American teacher, Mr. Davis in the fourth grade, so Ms. Peterson was the first female. She was very beautiful and elegant, and she spoke with great confidence while explaining things in a way that made some of the more abstract concepts of literature easier to grasp. I sat in the very front row and absolutely loved her class, excelling because she made everything so much fun. As a result of my good performance in her class, my teacher recommended that I advanced upward to the 7-1 track the following year and begin college preparatory classes. At the time, I did not fully understand the impact of that advancement; kids rarely understand the weight of those moments until much later. As a result of her recommendation, I moved up to the 7-1 track in seventh grade, and as a direct result of that, I attended college after high school.

This advancement from the 6-2 track to 7-1 the following year changed my circle of friends in school. There were less people that looked like me (African American), but it didn't matter, not to me. Most people in 6-2 lived in my neighborhood and we played together during school and after school. We knew each other's parents, dressed the same, and talked the same. Our parents all knew each other, or were at least friendly, and the 6-2 class's racial makeup was split fairly equally between white and African American. However, all of that changed when I moved up to 7-1, from the expectations of the teachers to our own conversations to the racial makeup of the class.

There were five black kids in 7-1: JB, Ronda, Patricia, Robbie, and me. Another boy named Kenny joined the group later, but he moved away after the ninth grade. Kenny was probably the smartest person I've ever met in my life and he was a straight-A student without even trying very hard, and I was sad to see him go. As a group of African American kids in 7-1, we were easy to spot amongst a predominantly white female class, and I was the newcomer. Those of us in 7-1 became the core group members that remained on the same track through high school.

Before joining 7-1, I hadn't really understood the importance of academics as they pertained to college. My focus had always been on sports first, academics second. In fact, maintaining strong academics was essential to getting to my primary goal of sports, as per my mother's rule. But once I joined 7-1, my feelings about academics shifted and I began to see them as being important in and of themselves, not just as a means to an end of getting to play sports. I had always been very competitive, so I didn't feel intimidated by the academics of 7-1, but from a social standpoint I felt a little out of place.

Once, some of my classmates were having a conversation about the upcoming Masters Tournament in Augusta. The Masters is a huge deal for golf fans, and since Augusta is only about forty-five minutes away by car from Ridge Spring, a lot of white parents would allow their kids to skip school to watch a few holes during the tournament. When my classmates talked about this, they didn't initially mention the word "golf," and I didn't have a clue as to what they were talking about. I listened to them discuss the tournament with excitement while I had a deeply puzzled look on my face, brow furrowed in confusion. When I finally found out the Masters was a golf tournament, I was completely shocked. I loved sports, but I thought golf had to be the most boring sport in the world, and I couldn't believe my classmates were excited to leave school to watch something as dull as golf. When I got older, I began to view golf differently and grew to play the game, spending a few dollars to learn how. I even joined a golf club before moving to Korea, something that my seventh grade self would have found astonishing.

The golf tournament made me feel separated from my classmates, not only because I didn't care for the sport, but also because the idea of going to Augusta was out of the question for me. My family didn't have the money to travel that far on a regular basis, so Augusta may as well have been on the moon as far as I was concerned. Incidentally, Alan Shepard played some golf on the moon on February 6, 1971, so really, Augusta and the moon had more of a connection to each other than I did to Augusta or my classmates when it came to that particular sport.

My classmates also discussed Clemson University and the University of South Carolina, and whether or not they would go to college there one day. Having just joined the 7-1 college track, I was way behind when it came to any sort of discussion of higher education, but I figured it out. While my classmates were talking about universities, my main goal was to figure out a way to take their attention away from my scars by focusing on something else, anything else to avoid those same questions about what had happened to my face. It was a new circle of friends, but they had the same old questions. I might've changed school tracks, but some things were, unfortunately, unwaveringly static.

My classmates' conversations were a little different than what I was used to in my neighborhood, and as a result, my diction began to change just by being around them. For example, "isn't" became "is not." The agreement between my subjects and verbs became a little more noticeable as well. The teachers expected it of me and my peers stared at me when something from my neighborhood, something that sounded a little foreign, came out of my mouth. I had to get it together quickly. As if I didn't have enough to work on in regards to my speech, compounding the issues was a very bad lisp. I received therapy during my third grade year from a speech therapist once a week for about thirty to forty-five minutes per session. I hated it because I would be pulled out of class and sent to her office to endlessly practice my *S* words. The only positive thing that came out of those sessions for me was the candy the speech therapist gave me at the end of each meeting.

Once she had cupcakes which was really cool, but even cupcakes weren't enough to balance out how much I hated those sessions. I found the whole situation extremely embarrassing. From the outside, one might think that a person with a lisp could make it stop, like a stutter. People seem to think that you can make a lisper just stop it in their mind, and they often seem like they just want to tell the person with the lisp to cut it out or go home and work on it, as if one night of deep soul searching will magically cure a speech impediment. At first, it was painful for me to say *S* words without my tongue coming out between my lips like a snake, but the speech therapist worked on exercises using all types of methods to get my tongue to behave properly. My lisp was just one more thing in my life that I had to fight past, one more thing that marked me as "other."

I had one friend in particular, whose name was Jerome Benjamin Davis, Jr, "JB" for short. I could tell from his initial appearance that he came from a well to do, God-fearing family. He spoke with clarity, his hair was curled, and his outfits looked like money. He wore corduroy pants and turtlenecks in the winter, something I'd never seen another kid wear until I met JB. He was the Billy Dee Williams of the seventh grade and all the girls wanted to sit by him at lunch. Because we didn't live in the same neighborhood, I had no idea if he liked sports or not until one day when we played together during recess. He had game, especially in basketball, and from that day on, our friendship just clicked into place. He became my best friend in school, along with Robbie, another guy in 7-1. JB didn't use any slang because his mother was an educator and he spoke very proper English, which was initially a little odd to me. As a result, I knew his upbringing was different from mine, even before I ever saw his house or met his parents. I admired him, and because we shared all of our classes together, I was in his social circle. We played during recess, chatted in class, and became close friends.

One day, I was invited to JB's home to play some hoops. Of course, I was always interested in any chance to play sports, so I asked my mother if she could drop me off and she agreed. JB only lived four miles away from me, but as my mother and I approached his home, it seemed like we lived worlds apart from one another. His family lived on the outskirts of town in a ranch-style home, a home that, up to that point, had only ever been occupied by white people. Outside the house, the landscape looked like something from a postcard, painted with sprawling macadamia nut trees. The lawn in front of JB's house was perfectly manicured and neatly dressed the curved driveway that formed a semicircle in front of their home.

As my mother parked, JB and his parents appeared out of the side door to greet us. JB's mother, a schoolteacher, was warm and friendly, speaking so clearly as if she herself had helped to develop the English language. His father was a kind but domineering figure who spoke with authority, as if he was in the boardroom as an executive of a major corporation. I had seen a family like JB's before, but it had been on *Leave it to Beaver*, and the family had been white. As I grew to know them better, JB's family became the standard in my eyes of what "right" looked like in regards to black success, family unity, and values. The house, the etiquette, the dress; they were a God-fearing, polite, and secure family. They became for me a tangible model from which I would someday draw the template of what right looked like for me early in life.

Later, in eighth grade, I had a classmate named Dianne Maddox. She was my buddy, a fellow 8-1er, and amazing at math, as well as a kind soul. I felt warm and comfortable around her, as if I could share anything with her and it would remain between us. Dianne was the kind of friend who would hand over her favorite pen or pencil to you without a moment's hesitation. She came from a large family with a bunch of sisters and one older brother, Richard, who as one year her senior and an amazing athlete. Richard and I played sports together and later we both joined the National Guard, and Dianne's older sister, Aileen, later attended SC State like I did and served as our chaperone during our visit to campus. However, during those days as kids, Dianne was my number one Maddox. During the summer between my eighth and ninth grade year, I saw Dianne in town at the local store. We chatted for a while, catching up on the time since school had let out for the summer, when out of the blue she invited me to a pool party at their home.

"Sure, I'll come," I said.

"Okay," she said, smiling. "It's next Saturday."

They lived maybe seven or eight miles from us and I'd never seen their home and didn't make the connection of having a real pool. I told my mom about the invite and she agreed to drop me off as the date of the party approached. Sure enough, when Saturday arrived, I made my preparations to head out to the Maddox's' home. Dianne had described the location to me and it was a familiar area, as we often passed the road leading to their home on our way to Aiken.

"Just make a right after you pass the store and you will see our house about a quarter of a mile on the left," Dianne had said.

As my mom drove up the road and made the right turn, I began to feel excited at the idea that I would get to see my friend and have the opportunity to hang out in a different area of town. We drove down the road and I saw a tennis court with a fence around it, and my first thought was that this was a strange place to have a country club. It really did look like a country club, with a beautiful white home near the tennis court and a pool in back. We passed the house and kept heading down the street.

"Do you know exactly where the house is, Foots?" my mom asked.

"She told me a quarter of a mile," I said.

We found a place to turn around after driving for about a mile and went back up the road. Sure enough, as we approached the white house, Dianne was standing in front, waving us down. I was excited to see her, but confused at the same time.

"You live here?" I asked Dianne, perplexed as my mother bid my goodbye and told me to call her when I was ready to be picked up.

"Yes," she said.

"Who does the tennis court belong to?" I asked.

"It's ours," Dianne replied.

"What?" I asked, astonished.

"We're going to go to the pool through the house, follow me."

As we entered the house, I saw a picture of a man in an army dress uniform. I later learned that the uniform rank insignia was for lieutenant colonel.

"Is that your father?" I asked.

"Yes," Dianne said. "He's retired now and works as a prison superintendent in Aiken."

"What does your mom do?"

"She teaches math at college," Dianne said. I studied the picture for a moment before Dianne motioned for me to continue through the home towards the back door, which led out to a deck. She opened the door, and as we stepped outside, I heard the sounds of laughter. I turned towards the direction of the voices and saw something I'd never seen before: an inground swimming pool at a residence. To my right on the deck stood a large, built man who looked like Jim Brown.

"Hello, young man," he said. "Your name is?"

"Foots," I said. "I mean, James."

"Well, James, are you going to swim today?"

"Yes, sir."

"Well, enjoy yourself and be careful."

"Yes, sir!" I said. I couldn't believe it. First JB and the Davis family, and now Dianne and the Maddox family with a tennis court and a pool to boot. I enjoyed my time at the pool party, but even more importantly, I filed that moment away in my mind. A soldier, a nice home, SC State, education and family—I saw what equated to black wealth for the second time in my life and it was a pleasant visual for me, a defining moment as I saw what could be possible for my own family and me someday.

JB's mother was one of the few people that called me James. In town, we all had nicknames given by family members shortly after birth, or by friends because of something you did or how you looked physically. Mine is Foots. Everyone in the neighborhood, including adults, used this name for me. In fact, to this day, you can travel to any town within a twenty-five-mile radius of Ridge Spring and if you say the name Foots, everyone will know it's me. You don't find a lot of people in the South using their real names unless you're classmates and the teacher is conducting roll call, or someone dies and you see their name printed in the obituary. I received the name Foots from my grandmother shortly after my birth. I was born two months premature and only weighed 2 lbs., so I was put in an incubator. My grandmother saw me in that incubator, with my feet propped up on the glass, and from that point on I had my nickname. Not Feet, but Foots! It's a strange nickname, but it wasn't even close to being the strangest name in the neighborhood. I was lucky, because there were other names like Pig, Black, Booger, Weasel, Dirty Nose (we just called him Dirty for short), Pookie, and so on. But JB's mom called me James. She made it sound so elegant, like I belonged in their neighborhood and it was okay for me to hang out with JB. She was so caring and always asked about my well-being, as well as told me to bundle up when the weather turned cold, so refined and classy like our very own Clair Huxtable.

Speaking of Clair Huxtable, there was one TV dad whom I saw as a man among men. I became invested in this particular show around the time I began basketball season in eighth grade. The boys' basketball game started immediately after the girls' game. We were expected to be present for at least part of the girls' game until the fourth quarter when we would head to the locker room to suit up for our own game. Most of the guys would be there from the start of the game, but I wouldn't arrive until the second quarter. Some of the kids assumed that I wanted to make an entrance by showing up after the game had already started, but that wasn't the case at all with me. I didn't care about making an entrance; instead, I was at home in my bedroom watching the TV show *Little House on the Prairie*. That's right, my TV dad role model was Charles Ingalls, played by Michael Landon. I was fascinated by him and he really was my first and favorite TV dad. I loved the way he took care of his family; he was a hard worker who sacrificed for those he loved. I was completely engrossed in each episode of the show and just had to watch them to the conclusion, no matter what else was going on—including a basketball game. Of course, I couldn't tell my friends about my admiration for Charles Ingalls or *Little House on the Prairie* because that would've just been one more thing for them to tease me about, and they already had plenty of ammunition. *Little House on the Prairie* made me feel warm inside when I watched it and it gave me another role model of what a man should be like. It didn't matter to me that the show was fictional; I admired him all the same. In fact, Charles Ingalls might have been cooler than Dr. J for me in those days, if you can believe it. I admired Charles Ingalls so much that when the show ended, I took my viewership and followed Michael Landon to *Highway to Heaven*. It wasn't the same, but some Charles Ingalls was better than no Charles Ingalls at all.

CHAPTER 7

Big Brother

To me, my big brother was the man. I wanted to dress like him, wear the same haircut as him, walk and talk like him. No one understood me like Kem did. He knew when I was in pain, or when I needed encouragement. He protected me like a father would a son; like our father should have protected me, protected both of us. With the exception of the minor burns on his legs, Kem was physically unscathed from the fire. However, the psychological scars were deep and painful and ever present, and at times, I could see the rage in his eyes. By virtue of being the eldest child, he had seen and remembered most of the bad parts of our father. The physical and mental abuse, the fights, and the incidents of destructive behavior our father had displayed. Kem always carried this burden with him and did his best to shield my sister and me from this particular type of pain whenever possible.

There was an incident when we were kids, when I was shooting hoops at a playground with Greg Henman on the other side of town. There was a family who lived near the playground with a reputation for being downright mean, the Morris family. Some of the siblings had been in jail or reform school and they carried knives and bats around with them to bully people they didn't like. There were feared by many, and I was no exception. As we began to play a couple of games, three of the kids from that fearsome

Morris family came to the court. Greg and I exchanged nervous glances, apprehension crawling up and down our limbs. We knew trouble was brewing. The three kids invited themselves into our game and challenged Greg and me to a contest of lopsided teams, the two of us against the older and more unhinged three of them.

The game began with a thunderous check, followed by one of them slamming the ball at my chest in an attempt to rattle me. This intimidation technique, however, was completely unnecessary because I was already terrified of this guy and very rattled just by his and his brothers' presence. I passed the ball to Greg and ran down the court for the give and go. Greg passed the ball back to me and as I caught it, one of the guys pushed me down to the ground.

"Get up," the guy growled.

I'd known it already, but now it was completely clear that this was never meant to be a friendly game of basketball. I climbed to my feet and threw the ball as hard as I could towards the trees edging the side of the playground.

"This game is over," I said.

The guy stepped closer to me, menacingly towering over me.

"If you don't go get that ball, I'm going to cut you," he said, his voice low and serious.

I told Greg to get his bike and head towards the street. Greg dashed for his bike, picked it up, and started to pedal. I ran after Greg and just as the bike began to accelerate, I hopped on the back seat. By then, the chase was in full pursuit as two of the siblings ran behind us. Greg could get tremendous speed on his bike, but the siblings were faster and started to close in on us.

"Go faster, please go faster," I begged Greg, panic flooding my voice. He did the best he could and pushed on. We were getting close to the middle school and I knew that if we reached the football field, we'd be home free. As we reached the field, I looked back over my shoulder and saw the scary siblings dropping back, increasing the distance between us. I breathed a huge sigh of relief.

As we approached the driveway of my house, I saw my brother in the yard. He could immediately see the lingering terror on our faces.

"What's wrong?" he asked, not bothering with a greeting.

Greg explained the confrontation in great detail and I chimed in immediately, adding to the drama of the moment. At first, Kem said nothing, but I saw the rage flare in his eyes. Without a word, he walked into the house. After a moment, he reappeared holding a bar that we used to curl free weights.

"Where are they?" Kem asked.

I turned towards the direction Greg and I had flown from on his bike and saw three figures walking across the field towards our house. Kem followed my gaze and immediately took off towards the three brothers, weight bar in hand. Greg and I stayed put, staring after Kem as he ran. The three brothers turned and ran when Kem started to gain some ground on them. I was told later by some onlookers that my brother chased those guys for a country mile through some woods behind the middle school and back towards the playground where they'd first come to us on the basketball court.

Because I didn't follow him, it seemed to take my brother a long time to return. I began to worry as I waited nervously in our yard, bouncing up and down on my toes as I stared off into the distance in the direction he'd run. Eventually, I saw a person walking across the field towards the house. It was Kem and I breathed a big sigh of relief to see my brother looking unharmed.

"Why were they bothering you?" Kem asked as he got close to the driveway, finally having me in earshot. "Do they always pick on you? Did they call you names? Did you try to fight back?"

"No," I answered his last question, my voice quiet and hollow.

Kem shoved me so hard I staggered back and hit the dirt. Stunned, I climbed back to my feet and dusted off my hands and pants.

"Why did you push me?" I asked, feeling a little wounded.

"If you ever get bullied again and you don't at least try to defend yourself, I'll beat you up every time," Kem said.

This was one of the many invaluable lessons my brother shared with me, to stand up for myself and not let other people dominate my emotions. My brother always gave me tough love and in doing so, he encouraged me to be smarter, he pushed me to be faster, quicker, and tougher. He understood what made me tick and pushed those buttons at will in order to help me grow and improve. At times, I didn't understand whether he was in my corner or not, because it seemed like he was just being hard on me because he was my older brother and that's what older brothers did. But as I got older, I saw that everything he did was for my benefit. Where my father was not, Kem filled those spaces for me and taught me to be better, and he became my benchmark for everything. For example, if I could beat him at basketball, I felt sure that I could beat anyone.

One day, when I was about nine or ten years old, Kem and I were getting ready for school. I had coarse hair that required some attention…actually, lots of attention. I made an attempt to let it grow out like Kem's, but my hair wasn't as manageable as his and my hair would become so nappy and tight that it would hurt to comb it out without some assistance. I needed some activator to wet and soften my hair thoroughly, and we typically used Sta-Sof-Fro afro sheen that helped tremendously. On that particular morning, we were out of Sta-Sof-Fro and I didn't feel like going through the agony of combing out my hair because of how much it would hurt. Kem, being the neat freak he was, couldn't stand the idea of me going to school looking like that and he decided to take action.

My mother drove the head-start car used to pick up some of the local kids for school, and she had about a thirty-minute drive to work in Saluda, a neighboring town, so she would leave before us in the mornings. Kem would drill me on looking my best, ensuring my clothes were ironed properly and my appearance was neat and my head was groomed. That morning was no different, and he warned me to comb my hair.

"I will," I told him, exasperated.

"Do it now, because it looks bad," Kem said.

"Leave me alone!" I exclaimed as I continued to put on my things and prepare for school. We crossed paths several times throughout the morning, which was to be expected, as there was only one bathroom, one sink, one toilet, and one mirror over the sink.

"You are embarrassing me, man!" he said. "Go comb your head or I'll do it for you."

"Don't rush me!" I yelled.

Back then, Kem was a little stronger than me and he had had enough of my mouth. I understood and saw that my hair needed attention, but I couldn't take him pressuring and yelling at me. As I searched for my pick, I also had to place my belt around my waist and thread it through the loops of my pants. I started to take care of the belt first when I noticed a pick near my bed. Kem never wanted me to touch his hair picks, as if my hair was not fit for his personal grooming accessories.

"Don't touch my pick!" he warned. "Find your own!"

This only served to further anger me, fueling the perfect storm that was brewing. As I began to thread the belt through my pant loops, Kem grabbed me as if to put me in a headlock and then took his pick, raking it through my hair. With no activator in place to ease the pain, it felt as if someone had grabbed a chunk of my hair and yanked on it like a game of tug of war.

"Stop!" I yelled, my belt still in my hand.

"You can't go to school with your hair looking like that anymore!" Kem insisted. "You're embarrassing me!" The words stung worse than the raking and I snapped. I had already coiled some of the belt around my hand and arm, leaving the belt buckle exposed. "You need to look better and you're not walking to school with me looking like a bum!"

As Kem shouted, I had already made the mental leap from my hair to my face. *You're ashamed of me?* I thought. I wrestled loose and as Kem hurled the last insult at me about my nappy hair, I swung that belt towards him with all the force of the anger that was boiling inside of me.

"Don't talk to me like that!" I yelled as I let loose at my target. I made contact on my first swing and Kem clutched his head where the belt buckle had connected with the top of his head.

"I told you to leave me alone!" I shouted. Kem's hand began to fill with blood as it streamed through his fingers and down his face.

"You hit me with a belt?!" he yelled incredulously before he turned and ran to the bathroom. My pain turned to fear as I watched him go, grabbing a towel to stifle the blood flow as he contemplated his options. I remained silent, although I wanted to apologize. I could've killed him.

We had a rotary phone mounted on the wall in the kitchen. Kem walked in there and I followed him silently, awaiting my fate as he dialed the number for the Henman house. Our mom usually stopped by the Henmans' house to pick up Ursula for Head Start; she was the same age as Lynnette and they were in the program together. I watched the wheel on the phone spin as Kem selected each number, each rotation bringing me closer to my fate:

six…eight…five…Kem's dialing was slow and methodical, and I couldn't do anything other than wait and watch.

"Can I speak to my mom?" Kem asked when Mrs. Henman answered. Her reply was audible from where I stood in our quiet kitchen.

"Hold on," Mrs. Henman said. "Rose? Kem is on the phone!"

There was a long pause as I continued to watch the blood trickle down my brother's face. Fear had begun to show in Kem's eyes; I saw it as I stared at him.

"What is it?" I heard our mom ask irritably on the other end of the line. "You're going to make me late for work."

"Foots hit me with a belt!" Kem exclaimed.

"What?"

"I'm bleeding badly!"

"Put Foots on the phone!"

Kem held out the phone to me and I took it, starting to speak before I'd even finished lifting the receiver to my ear.

"He was bothering—" I tried to say but she cut me off.

"You don't hit *anybody* with a belt! Are you crazy?"

Am I crazy? I wondered.

"I am on my way back home," my mom said before she hung up the phone.

Kem and I waited quietly for our mother to return, each with our own fears. I knew I had seriously wounded him because he hadn't tried to fight me back. I wanted something from him, anything to know that he was all right. I needed some kind of retaliation from him to justify me striking him, but nothing came. Instead, we just waited until we heard the van pull up to the house and shortly after, the door banged open.

"What is going on in here?" my mother demanded. Her eyes fell on the blood that had spilled onto the kitchen floor. "Let me see your head, Kenneth."

I knew this was a big deal because she only ever used our full names during serious, emotional moments.

"You need stitches, boy," she said. "Go get your things and get in the van. I need to drop these kids off and take you to the doctor." Then she wheeled on me. "Are you crazy, Foots?" she asked as she stared at me in horror. "You could have killed your brother!"

I said nothing. There was nothing I could say.

We all loaded up in the van and as soon as she saw him, Lynnette started to bombard Kem with questions as he continued to hold the towel to his head. He ignored her, choosing instead to stare out the window. The elementary school was within walking distance from our house, but my mom dropped me off as they headed to Saluda to take care of Kem's stitches. I found it hard to focus on school that day, my brain looping through terrible thoughts as I wondered if I was some kind of monster. Was I just like my father? What if I had killed Kem? My emotions swung from pity to anger at Kem for initiating the altercation. Why me? Why do I have the difficult hair on top of these scars? Okay, God? You couldn't have given me something to work with? Was I a monster like my father? Did I have that crazy gene or had Kem just pushed me too far? Kem was my own brother, and yet I had swung that belt with intent. I had known where the buckle was and I had aimed it, lashing out at Kem with bad intentions. I couldn't wait for the bell to ring to see if Kem was all right. I had to just sit there in my thoughts, grappling with the possibility of truly being my father's son. Did I inherit my father's mental self-destruction gene? It was agonizing.

When the school day finally ended, I ran across the field towards our house. I headed down the street, past my friend Stanley's house, looking towards our home with anticipation of another round of "why's" from my mother or Kem. As I approached the screen door of our house, I took a deep breath, steeling myself for what I might find inside. I opened the door and saw Kem sitting on the couch.

"Man, you tried to kill me," he said by way of greeting, a grin on his face. He eased my anxiety immediately as I tentatively returned his smile.

"Are you all right?" I asked.

"I'm cool! I had to get a couple of stitches, but I'm cool," Kem said. "But you still need to comb that nappy hair of yours."

I laughed with relief because Kem had made it all right for me. My mom never mentioned the belt to me, but she didn't have to—I got it. That event changed me in unimaginable ways. Kem knew me and still knows what I'm capable of, and he'd warn me of the anger within.

"One day you're going to blow, man!" he'd tell me. "Be careful."

I knew how dangerous anger could be. If I'd struck Kem in the temple, he could have died. I analyzed that morning in my head over and over again. I promised myself that I would never attach something to the end of my natural hands to strike someone in anger. After that, I never approached a fight with the idea of placing a weapon of any sort in my hands, whether it be a knife, a gun, a rock, or a stick, in order to strike another human being. It wasn't so much the idea of harming another person, but I didn't want to wound them to the point of killing them and find myself in jail or prison like my father. I didn't want to be him, so I did everything I could to avoid situations like that morning when I faced off with my own brother and lashed out.

If I was capable of striking him, the brother that I loved, I feared doing it to someone of whom I thought less, so I took that element away. I had knives pulled on me and I once even had a neighborhood friend hit me with a bat after a basketball game gone wrong in his backyard, but a weapon of any sort was out of the question for me after I hit Kem. Instead, I just had to deal with the consequences if I was unmatched during a squabble. I learned to channel my anger through sports at some point, and found I really enjoyed boxing and releasing that built-up anger in a punch. My friend Chester's dad lived on the next block and built a legitimate boxing ring to train him. I enjoyed stepping in there when I had the opportunity because it felt good to punch anything or anybody, win or lose.

Kem and I got into a couple more fights after that, but it was more controlled because he would lay out the ground rules beforehand, which was, in hindsight, hilarious.

"No hitting in the face and you can't pick up anything," Kem would say. It was never a real fight because of the rules, but I got it. I hated weapons of any sort. Even when I joined the army, I still hated firing my weapon. I did enjoy blowing stuff up, and, strangely enough, I liked being close to fire, which seemed completely counterintuitive to me. Barn fires during 4H Camp in Aiken each summer sparked my interest and I loved the warmth of it. I would stare at those flames and be drawn to it, like I was daring it to burn me again. I figured the fascination with fire had to be some type of traumatic syndrome, but I didn't think about it too deeply. I got into some scuffles, but I had my rules and no one—with the exception of Kem—understood why. I kept my emotions as pinned up as possible, hoping I wouldn't just explode on someone and harm them without thinking. That has always been my biggest fear, so I've done my best to avoid drama throughout the years. However, Kem still reminds me of the belt buckle incident every so often, poking me like big brothers do.

"I warned you to leave me alone," I always say with a smile.

At one point, my mom purchased a set of boxing gloves for us—my brother's idea. Kem loved boxing, which meant I loved boxing by default. He always had all sorts of big ideas, and once we got the boxing gloves, he decided to create a boxing club and build a mock ring in our backyard like Chester's father had done in theirs. Of course, I became target practice for him—I think most, if not all, little brothers are familiar with this sort of situation. Kem wanted to teach me to box and said that he felt the best place for me to learn was inside our bedroom.

"The small, closed-in area will make your reflexes quicker," Kem insisted. However, he and I both knew that our bedroom would give me little wiggle room to run as he unloaded on me. We would spar and he would coach me.

"Keep your gloves up!" Kem would say as he showered hits on me. *Pow! Jab! Pow! Pow!* "Use that left hand!" he'd say as the rain of hits became a downpour. *Jab! Jab! Pow!*

After a few minutes of abuse, I would throw off my gloves, enraged at the beating my brother dealt me. I would yell for our mother, who would simply instruct us to go play outside. Kem would smile and tell me to quit crying like a little baby. I'd suck back the tears, sniffling them into submission, and we'd head outside. Once in the yard, Kem always had a way of conning me into another round of boxing, this time outside the confines of our bedroom.

"You're getting better," Kem would insist. "Stay tough. We're from the streets of Philadelphia."

This always got to me because I loved our city roots, as did my brother. Kem always reminded me how lucky we were to have had the best of both worlds by being born in the city and raised in the South.

Kem joined the army immediately upon graduating from high school. It was a major adjustment for me, because the one male

I looked up to was gone. At this point, my mother was dating the man who later became my stepfather, but she kept him at arm's length from our family. We knew him, of course, but she wanted to raise us herself. So, with Kem gone, I became the man of the house. Kem had always bailed me out whenever I got into a tough spot, but now it was up to me to take care of things. I had more responsibilities around the house after Kem left, such as cutting the grass, taking out the trash, looking after Lynnette, and so forth. I had thought it would be cool to have my own room until Kem left and I realized I had to clean it myself. In an odd way, I missed Kem yelling at me to clean the room. It felt so empty without him there, too quiet. But there was no time for me to feel sorry for myself due to my added workload, because my mother needed me more than ever before. So while I missed Kem dearly, I did my best to step into this new role he'd left for me.

CHAPTER 8

Champions

As my brother began his first tour of duty in Germany, I began my eighth grade year of middle school. It was great to be an eighth grader because it meant we were the big kids of the school. The younger kids looked up to us and we set the standard for what was considered cool: the dress code, the slang, even the way we walked. Most importantly, we led the way in sports. Sports were my world and everything centered around them. I knew I had to make good grades to play sports, as per my mother's rule, so I made good grades. My eighth grade year was very memorable because it was truly a breakout year in sports for me; I led the team in points scored and we won the middle school area championship. This was also the first year I served as the team captain for both football and basketball, positions I held all the way through high school.

Kem would call home on Sundays to get an update from me on how I was progressing in sports. He was tough on me and always wanted me to do more on the football field or score more on the court. Our conversations were brief due to the cost, so I had to give him my stats quickly and listen to him lecture me about performing better each time. He pushed me because he wanted me to be better and he believed I had the talent to eventually get our family out of our financial situation. He sent a lot of his military money home to our mother to ensure we had food to eat and clothes on our backs. I eventually filled this financial role by working in the peach fields during the summers to help support our family. But first, however, I had to suit up for sports.

It was football season and I was eager to show off my skills. All the speedsters like myself wanted to be running backs. There were a handful of fast guys, but only three spots available: fullback, tailback, and wingback. Therefore, the only way for a hopeful player to separate themselves from the pack was through reps, drills, and wind sprints. I desperately wanted to show the coaches that I wanted and deserved the honor of the first string position of tailback. Getting into my uniform, shoulder pads, and helmet made me feel like I was transforming into a superhero. I could hide behind them, hide some of my pain, and the opposing players and coaches had no idea of the extent of my burns. Football was an escape for me, a positive escape from the realities of being badly disfigured and the harshness that came along with it from other people. Although the accolades from scoring touchdowns felt good, they weren't what drove me. Sports were the area in which I excelled and I wasn't just normal, I was exceptional.

That year in eighth grade, we had a basketball team that only lost one game that season, a nearly perfect record. Coach Stowe was a tall, lanky man with golden-brown hair. He looked totally out of place in Ridge Spring, like one of those seventies-era hippies you'd see hanging out on the beach in California with a Winnebago. Coach had run track at the College of Charleston and subsequently believed one had to be physically fit to play any sport. As a result, we were in better condition than the other teams in the area because Coach Stowe required us to run—a lot. I'm sure that during tryouts we completed some drills with the ball in order to make cuts, but they were few and far between the suicide and baseline drills. Coach opened the doors of the gym and we ran down the hallways, past the front office, and down the wall of lockers before circling back towards the gym, completing the loop inside the gym for one lap. We ran ten.

As the cuts for team members began, Coach Stowe lengthened the runs by having us go outside. He had a deep, but non-threatening voice as he instructed us on the course.

"Okay, down the hill towards the elementary school playground, around the swings along the fence line, up the hill towards the elementary building by the front office, and back to our gym."

I thought Coach Stowe was nuts, but I loved it all the same. I always wanted to finish first, not only for myself, but also for Coach. I needed to hear "Good job!" but only once. I needed to hear it for that boost to fuel me to push myself harder. When I initially got to practice, I just wanted to shoot the basketball, but I figured Coach was going somewhere with this workout regime of his, so I stuck it out. My body felt absolutely drained after the laps, but I didn't want Coach Stowe to read that exhaustion on my face, so I held my expression as tight as I could, holding in what I was feeling. I persevered, hoping I would be rewarded for my efforts.

Finally, Coach Stowe made the announcement that he would post the final cuts for the team on the board the next morning. If your name wasn't on the list, you weren't on the team. I knew I'd made it, I could feel it, but the night before, I still felt nervous. What if I was wrong? What if I'd misread Coach's reactions to my performance, what if I hadn't made the team? I spent a good portion of the night before the team roster was posted going over my grades in my head, calculating my GPA to make sure that wouldn't be a factor that could keep me off the team. But despite my fears, I felt certain I'd finished in the top three each time we ran laps or suicide drills. I felt anxious, both nervous and happy variations, and I couldn't wait until the next morning.

As I entered the gym to check the team roster, there were some disappointed faces walking towards me. A couple of seventh graders, an eighth grader or two. I didn't have to ask what happened because their look said it all. There was one seventh grader I was certain would make the team, a kid by the name of Ricky Brunson. He was an incredibly talented player who came from a poor family that lived in the Bottom, a neighborhood that lay in the lowest area of town. He was tough, though, like me, and we would gain great admiration for one another throughout the years in sports, and eventually through military service as well. Ricky made the team, along with my eighth-grade buddies: Dexter, Robbie, Boogie, Steven Hartley, Billy Elders, and of course, my man, JB. A couple other guys, Rodney Hammond and Ricky, rounded out the team, along with me.

Once the team was finalized, we began our conditioning in earnest. Coach wanted to teach us the importance of conditioning, because if you were in shape and understood the fundamentals, the game became easy. Coach had us run five-on-five drills as he worked his core players to prepare us for our first game. Little did I know, that for the most part, Coach Stowe already knew each of our basketball skills from observing us, either during gym class, free play, or during lunch break. He already knew who could "ball," so to speak, but he wanted to get a jump on conditioning us before the season began. I felt faster each week as we began to conduct those five-on-five scrimmages. We typically played shirts versus skins, since this was back in the days before there were scrimmage jerseys, and Coach began to form the starting five in his mind without officially announcing it. He would mix it up a little during scrimmages, which left a little ambiguity in our minds in regards to the starters to keep our edge on the court. Coach Stowe always saved the official announcement of who was starting right before we left the locker room for tip off. We were ready.

The first game of the season was a home game. The gym had only one set of bleachers, which were typically packed at every game because they seated both home and away fans. Thursday evening in a small town isn't usually a big hub of activity, so most people looking for something to do drifted to the gym. All day before the game, I was so excited and I made a concentrated effort to avoid doing anything stupid in class that might get me in trouble and jeopardize my opportunity to play. When I got home from school that day, I reminded my mom about my first game. She wished me well, but sports were secondary for her and she reminded me of what was still to be done before I played: The trash still had to be taken out, clothes still had to be hung on the line (we didn't have a dryer back in those days), and my homework still had to be completed prior to my leaving the house for the game. I had a reprieve from the dishes that day, as I sometimes got when my mother was in a good mood.

I rushed to complete my chores—after all, I still had to watch *Little House on the Prairie* before I left for the game. It was only a ten-minute walk to school, and I had a little bit of a time buffer between the girls' game and ours. As I approached the gym, I began to get very nervous. My heart was running in my chest, faster than my feet had run all of Coach Stowe's drills. I walked into the gym and saw all of those people in the bleachers and I immediately started to sweat. I hated crowds. At the time, I had to be the shyest person in school. Maybe because of my scars, maybe not. But either way, I hated the idea of people watching me. Sports later became my one exception, but for my first game, I didn't feel that yet.

As the third quarter of the girls' game concluded, the boys' team walked towards the locker room. When we entered, we saw that our uniforms had already been laid out by the manager. I knew that drill all too well from my former days as a manager. But now I was on the other side, ready to put on the uniform instead of just laying it out for someone else to wear. I had gotten to pick out my own number and there it was, number forty-two, waiting on the bench for me. As soon as I saw my uniform, my nervousness transformed into excitement and anticipation as Coach Stowe began to go over the game plan. He told us that he wanted us to run and press the team, and he announced the starters: James, JB, Ricky, Boogie, and Billy. Four eighth graders and Ricky! I was so happy for Ricky and I know how thrilled he was for this chance to shine on the court. I was so excited for the game to start and I felt as if my heart was about to jump out of my chest.

Then, it was time. We entered the gym floor and started the layup line. I looked around the gym at all of those people with amazement; they had come out to see us! Their cheers were intoxicating and only served to further heighten my excitement. The officials called for the captains before tipoff and Coach Stowe pointed at me to walk to center court. I didn't show it, but I was beaming inside, because Coach had not directly mentioned to me before that I was team captain. That nudge of confidence gave me what I needed, not only for the game, but in my life. This was it, sports could give me what I needed, what I felt I'd been lacking, what I'd been looking for. We jumped out on that team and beat them like they were a peewee league. That was only the first of many games in which we demolished teams, winning left and right until we earned a spot in the championship.

As it turned out, Coach Stowe was right; as a result of our training, we would absolutely destroy other teams. Our skills and strength gave us confidence and a swagger, boosted by the way we would drop a load of points on opposing teams to the point of embarrassment. It was so fun for me as a player, and my teammates and I established a reputation that would carry on to high school. Coach Stowe eventually pushed to another championship season, this time in track, during my sophomore year in high school. He was an inspiring coach and excellent at his craft.

However, no matter how well I played, what happened after the games became a quick reality check to remind me of the way things were. After football games, I would remove my helmet and I immediately drew stares from our opponents. The questions were, of course, always the same.

"*What happened to your face?*"

I hated that question with a passion. I didn't understand why they couldn't just look away and not say anything. Why did they always have to interrogate me? What gave them the right to know my story? This constant questioning made me pull away from people because they made me feel like I was the ugliest person on the face of the earth. I wanted to figure out how to take the focus away from my burns, and ultimately I realized that the only way I could possibly do that was by running faster and being quicker and better than everyone else, excelling at everything I did.

Despite the probing questions, I can't emphasize enough how much sports saved my life. They were so transformative to me, because you couldn't tell a kid's income or background from a team photo unless you looked at his shoes. But really, no one ever inspects footwear in a team photo—you're looking at the players themselves. In that way, sports were really an equalizer for me. They also offered me a release because I could take all of my frustrations and disappointments, all of the insults and stares from others, and channel everything into a game. Finally, I had a real outlet for everything I was feeling. During a game, I felt free from all of the negativity, free to not just perform, but excel in my element, on my terms, and it was amazing for me. My self-esteem, usually so fragile and broken, was rebuilt, piece by piece, by the cheers and adulations of the spectators.

My mother didn't like or understand sports so she never came to my games, and with Kem in the military, he was obviously unavailable to as well. But my baby sister, Lynnette, was always there to cheer me on and for me, that felt like enough. I understood my mother's focus and love for me just like I knew of my brother's sacrifices, so it was okay that they weren't at my games. I was never angry towards Kem or my mother about that, but I did harbor a lot of anger towards someone: my father. It was his fault that my family was in this situation. He had scarred us in more ways than I could ever hope to fully express. Through this anger, he became my nemesis, which drove me to work that much harder. When I was younger, I thought that one day I would make it to the professional league in one of these sports and wipe those tears away from my mother's eyes for good. I imagined that my father would one day read about me in the newspaper, after I'd sunk the game winning basket or rushed in the final touchdown, and all of the pain he'd caused my family would be instantly transferred back to him. He'd know what he'd done, what he'd missed, and it would no longer be our burden but instead be his.

Finally, it was time for the championship game. We had earned enough wins to own that title outright were we to win that final game. A loss would give us a co-championship with Saluda, a team we had beaten once during the season, but that game had been their one loss. For that final game, we played them in their gym to a packed house. We jumped out with a quick lead, but they fought their way back, keeping us neck and neck. It was a nail-biter all the way to the end, and when the clock hit double zeros, our fate was decided: We had suffered our first and only loss of the season.

We were co-champions with Saluda, but at the time we didn't feel much like champions. We all received our trophies after the game, which softened the blow a little, but the nicest part for me came after that. My favorite cousin, Sandra, and her future husband, Larry, had made the trip to watch the game and had wished me luck beforehand. After the game, Larry gave me a dollar for my efforts and told me I'd played well. I thought that was so cool of him, and in the wake of what felt like a terrible loss, that dollar meant a lot to me.

Despite the loss in the championship game, I realized that I'd gained so much from this first season. I had found my confidence in sports, both on the court and off. I discovered that I had leadership capabilities and my peers respected me. I understood that if I worked hard, my coaches and others would recognize my efforts without me having to make a fuss about it. I already knew that life wasn't perfect—I'd experienced so many imperfections already—but through this basketball season I'd learned that it was okay that things weren't perfect. We'd lost a game, but we were still champions. Later, I saw my name in the local newspaper in a write-up about the game and our season alongside the title of MVP. Seeing that gave me such a feeling of euphoria that I carried within me. I was elated; it gave me so much joy to see that recognition for all of my hard work. When other people mentioned the article to me, I played it down a little to keep my ego in check, but privately, it fueled me. I couldn't change my appearance or go back in time to alter the events I'd survived, both physically and emotionally, but I could control how I handled those aspects of my life going forward, just like how I could control how I played on the field or on the court. That realization felt so good, like I was finally able to reclaim my life back the people who had taken it from me.

CHAPTER 9

Country Living

There is nothing that really expresses the sense of freedom like living in the country. Acres of space, open air, and a feeling of expansiveness. There appeared to be less noise and chaos in the South, despite the irony that my family experienced a very violent and horrific ordeal down there. But despite that ordeal, things still felt much slower and more peaceful. There were no cars racing down the streets or sirens blaring at all hours of the night like they had in Philadelphia. People spoke slower, and with less of a bite behind their words.

The train that divided Ridge Spring served as the only real recurring noise, but even the wail of the whistle can be incorporated into the white noise of a town, so that after a while, it's as common and uneventful as the rustle of the wind in the trees. Despite the train's division of the town in both a physical and social sense, I didn't identify it as something negative, because even that racial divide between blacks and whites in town allowed me to dream. The train was almost rhythmic and therapeutic as it rolled through town, and it reminded me of something or someone going somewhere, a journey that promised excitement and adventure. Sometimes I'd let my mind wander on just such an adventure and allow myself a small mental escape from reality. I thought maybe one day I could hop on the train and ride off into a land of opportunity, somewhere I could make all of our dreams come true. At the very least, I wanted to wipe away a few of my mother's tears by making her dreams come true.

The serenity of the country allowed me to take that mental vacation to indulge in those fantasies, whether I was listening to the sound of a train, climbing a tree, or sitting on top of the school building. Sometimes, I would go for walks in the woods and feel like I was smack in the middle of one of Tolkien's stories. Other times, I would play in the field behind our house and imagine I was a superhero with special powers. I'd make my own world, where I controlled my own destiny. This feeling was sometimes difficult to hold onto in my real life when I felt so much of my life was dictated by someone else's choices. But out in the country, I was able to be free, at least for a little while. Personally, I don't think I could have dreamed or imagined so freely in the city. The buildings would've somehow overshadowed or blocked my ability to look out amongst the clouds and dream those big little-boy dreams.

We kids used to hold barefoot races, challenging each other and pushing ourselves to run faster and farther. For some reason, we were convinced that we could run faster without the aid and protection of socks or shoes. Of course, we couldn't, but that didn't matter, especially during the warm, hazy days of summer. When I was about nine years old, we started to hold weekly football games in our backyard, epic bowl games that drew kids in from miles around to participate. There were certain areas of town where kids naturally congregated to play certain sports. Outdoor basketball was typically played on the elementary school playground because there were two baskets, so we could play with a full court. A neighbor on the next block over from us had a real outdoor boxing ring. Football, however, was played behind our house on Sundays.

Our backyard wasn't huge, but it was level and clear. Many of the backyards in the area had tree stumps, flower beds, junk cars, or other types of decor, making our yard unique. We didn't have a fence, which allowed everyone to just walk right up to the yard. Our house was also centrally located, so people could easily travel from different areas of town. My brother, Kem, was very popular in the neighborhood and he always had friends over to the house, but even so, I'm still not sure how the Sunday games originally started. However, once they did, our house was the place to be on Sundays for everyone in the neighborhood. Everyone would line up in formation, no pads, and face off with our mouths set in hard, determined lines. A crowd would gather to watch us play, including cute girls who cheered us on when someone made a spectacular play.

The games didn't start until we arrived home from church, and there was no certain time to be dismissed from a southern black church. The service could go on forever, but typically we were home by about one in the afternoon. Sometimes we'd come home to find kids waiting on the curb for us. My brother would immediately put me to work and instruct me to get on the phone to call his friends and let them know we'd arrived home from church. As they filtered over to our house, the excitement in the air always rose like an electric current. There would usually be around twenty to twenty-five kids in our backyard, with music and side games and lounge chairs like we'd all gathered at the beach or something.

Most kids there were older than me, closer to my brother's age, but I got to play because my brother would insist I was tough enough on the field to earn my spot. That, and it was our house, and as hosts, we made the rules. My mother didn't mind the games, as long as we stayed outside, there was no profanity, and we didn't leave the garden hose running, wasting water. Sometimes there were scuffles and fights amongst the kids, but never anything serious. There were no set scores or time limits; we just played until we got tired. Eventually, the games would end as the sun sank lower in the sky. We'd talk about the awesome runs or hits we'd made, talk a little trash, and each of us would go home and look forward to the next Sunday.

Our summers were a kaleidoscope of go karts and bicycles of all types: chopper handlebars, ten speeds, mountain bikes, high clown bikes, and the works. I had several bikes growing up, but one in particular stands out in my memory. One Christmas, my mother was able to scrape up enough money to buy me an Evil Knievel bicycle. It looked like a replica of the real motorcycle, white with bands of stars wrapped in blue. As soon as I saw it, it was love at first sight on Christmas morning. I rode that bike all over town with my friends. I loved being able to ride my bicycle without the fear of getting hit by a car, and rules were simple for us back then: stay outside until dinner time and be inside before the streetlights came on.

We played outside and created games until the sun went down, and bike riding was one of our favorite pastimes. We made homemade ramps and jumped them like Evil Knievel without a single thought for our physical safety. But, then again, what kid worries about a possible broken arm when you have a shot at glory amongst your friends for clearing an epic new jump? Sometimes, we placed a clothespin and playing card in the spokes to make it sound like a real motorcycle. Some kids went to the extreme to make their bikes stand out amongst their friends by adding accessories, like mirrors on the handlebars or hanging streamers from the handle grips. Others would cut up colorful drinking straws and place them on the spokes of their wheels to add a flash of colorful flare when they rode down the road, or experiment with different styles of handlebars.

The coolest trick any of us performed was "cat walking," which meant popping a wheelie on your bike and seeing how long you could go without dropping the front wheel. We had some talented guys in our neighborhood that could cat walk for almost the whole block. I tried, but my talents lay elsewhere. There should've been more broken bones in our neighborhood than there were, but I guess we were built a little differently. Either that, or we were just very lucky. We had a ball in the neighborhood as we switched from bikes to skateboards to roller-skate and back to bikes. We played and laughed and rode and rolled, and living in the South, in the country, allowed us to go on these adventures in a way we never could have in the city.

PEACH TREES

The smell of peach tree blossoms is sweet in the spring, but the flavor of South Carolina peaches is even sweeter in the summer. Despite Georgia's declaration as the Peach State, South Carolina is actually the leading producer of peaches in the South. Of these peach growers, three families reigned supreme: the Forrest family, the Watson family, and the DuBose family. As of this writing, Matt Forrest is the current owner of Dixie Belle Peaches, the third generation on both sides of his family to uphold the tradition of growing peaches that began in the 1960s. The second family, the Watsons, own Watsonia Farms in Monetta, about four or five miles away from Ridge Spring. They began growing in 1918, but their first cash crop wasn't peaches; it was asparagus. Joe H. Watson planted the first asparagus in Monetta, which later became known as the asparagus capital of the world. Seven years later, Watson got the five leading farmers in the area to start planting peaches, sixty acres each, and in doing so, he kicked off the commercial peach industry in that area. Lastly, but certainly not least, is the DuBose family. They have grown peaches in Ridge Spring and Monetta for seventy-five years and the current owners practically grew up in the fields, now growing thirty-five varieties of peaches each year.

At the age of sixteen, I began working in the peach-packing shed. There were three sheds, or factories, within a twenty-mile radius. They were owned by three prominent families who were all millionaires, the aforementioned Forrests, Watsons, and Duboses. They owned thousands of acres, and the land was a major cash cow, not only for them, but for the town as well. The crops changed with the times, from cotton to corn to the current crops consisting of organic yellow and white peaches; yellow zucchini and winter squash; pickling and slicer cucumbers; bell peppers; asparagus; eggplant; slicer and grape tomatoes; sweet potatoes; collards; strawberries; plums; persimmons; nectarines; and muscadines. All of these crops are profitable, but peaches are king. I worked at the Dubose shed, which seemed to be the popular spot for workers. Mr. Clark Dubose was a tall, bear-shaped man, and very intimidating. I was told that he would fire you at the drop of a hat if you got out of line. Some fireable infractions included showing up to work drunk or late, harvesting non-quality peaches, or insubordination. He demanded excellence, but in return he paid good wages, and as a result, everyone wanted to work there.

I spent several summers working amongst the peach trees, and to this day, when I bite into a peach with the juice running down my fingers, I'm reminded of those times. My day in the orchards would start around five thirty in the morning when the grass was still slick with dew, and the foreman would drive through the neighborhood in a pickup truck with a large camper top covering the bed of the truck. We could usually fit about eight to ten of us in the back of the truck, with two or three people squeezing together to ride shotgun in the front. My mother would wake me up in the morning with a sandwich wrapped in aluminum foil to take with me for lunch. I would slip on a long-sleeved shirt to protect my skin from the peach fur and head out of the house to meet my friend, Stanley, in front of his house before the truck arrived.

Stanley was a year older than me and a little more mature. I learned so much about life from him. He gave me tough love at times, but I owe him a lot for allowing me to tag along. I drank my first beer with Stanley, a shared Old English 800, or as we called it, an Eight Ball. He brought me along to participate in organized softball tournaments and insisted that I was added to the roster. I was a lefty and would often play with a right-handed glove, until I found out that one of Stanley's classmates, a guy named Craig Burton, owned a left-handed glove that he was looking to unload. He agreed to sell it to me for eight dollars, and had you seen my excitement, you would've thought I'd just purchased big blocks of Apple stock at bargain prices. I no longer had to catch a fly ball and take off my glove to throw it to the infield. It elevated my game and I owed my improved performance to Stanley; at least, I gave him credit for setting up the transaction for me.

Stanley would also take me along to other towns for high school basketball games or to the skating rink on Sundays. He indulged in some activities that I didn't care for, but I took away what I needed in life from him, both the good and the bad, and used what I learned to deal with some of the older guys at the peach orchard, especially the hustlers that would try to take advantage of youngsters like me. Stanley, along with the older ladies, also taught me the ropes at the peach orchard. He showed me how to put baby powder under the long-sleeved shirts we wore to protect us from the peach fuzz. The peach fur, combined with a little sweat when exposed to bare skin, would itch relentlessly. It reminded me of the old insulation one would find in attics. Stanley also showed me how to pick the ripe peaches and would even share a sandwich with me during our breaks if I hadn't brought one from home.

Junior was my best friend during those days. He was a year behind me in school and didn't really take picking peaches very seriously. Junior's passion in life was working on cars, and he was good at it. He learned from his father and was driving me around before he even had a license. Junior taught me how to drive a stick shift in his orange super Volkswagen Beetle when he was fourteen. It was one of those "only in the country" moments, for sure, that never would've flown in the city. Junior was a lighter version of JB with striking good looks, and girls *loved* him. He came from a working-class family who worked long hours in the fiberglass factory in Aiken for many years. He was so outgoing and said whatever was on his mind to absolutely anybody. Junior was about twenty pounds lighter than me, but he carried a Charles Barkley-type mentality into any argument. Part of why Junior and I got along so well was because our personalities were polar opposites, and we worked together at the packing shed.

There was one job that paid much more than the assembly positions in the packing shed: driving the tractor in the fields. Once the peaches were harvested and loaded into the containers, which typically sat on the trailer connected to the tractor, the driver would haul the peaches from the field to the packing shed, empty the bends, and return to the field. This was dangerous work because you had to be pretty skilled at driving a gear shift tractor with an attached trailer, and able to maneuver through the field along tight paths and turns. Additionally, on the main roads, cars would zoom past you and push you to the shoulder of the road, causing you to swerve. It was a tricky job, and Junior was aiming for one of those coveted spots—and he convinced me to the do the same.

At the time, my mom was dating a very kind man across the road from where we lived named Mack, who later became my stepfather. Mack was a quiet man, who worked the fields and on the farm for most of his life. He had served a tour in Vietnam and had used his money to buy a few acres of land for him and his mother after returning home from war. He was the lead foreman and trusted hand in the fields, and would often bring the equipment home from work to use in his own gardens, including the tractor. One Sunday evening, when Mack came over to our house to visit my mom, I summoned up enough courage to ask him to teach me to drive that tractor.

Kem and I were implants to the South. There was no faking it with us, especially me, because I didn't meet any of the criteria. I didn't eat grits or eggs; I didn't eat lima beans or black-eyed peas, liver poutine, turtle soup, possum—none of that foreign stuff. I didn't hunt, I could barely change a tire, and I had to figure out that whole jumper cable thing with the positive and negative terminals. I loved the country, but the country was not in me. I had to figure it out, like a stranger in a foreign land, but despite my southern shortcomings, I was up for the task of learning how to drive that tractor. Mack agreed to teach me, and one day after work, he took me to the field across the street and showed me how to work the tractor.

When he allowed me to sit in the driver's seat of the tractor by myself, I looked over at him and Mack had a look on his face as if he would never see that tractor in one piece ever again. Mack looked like he wanted to change his mind, but needed to save face with my mom, as if she'd paid him to teach me. Under his direction, I drove the tractor slowly around the field until I figured out how to shift and turn, moving faster with each pass. Mack allowed me to practice for about thirty minutes before he waved me in for the evening. I thought I'd conquered the tractor, but Mack's face was not beaming with pride the way I'd expected. He immediately began to hit me with warnings.

"You know, these tractors can be dangerous out on the road," Mack said. "People act crazy around tractors, so you better make sure you really want to drive one of these."

Had he seen something I hadn't? Because I thought I'd killed it! When we returned to the house, my mom asked Mack how I'd done, and of course, he said fine.

"Well, all right!" my mom said with a smile.

Fine? I thought. No follow-up? Either way, I was moving forward towards my goal of driving a tractor in the orchard and I told Junior I was ready to go down to the packing shed to sign up for the tractor job with him. Sure enough, we did our dry runs in the field and we both landed those coveted spots. I was thrilled and couldn't wait to start.

About a week or two into peach season, I was down in one of the peach rows, hanging out with migrants on my tractor while I waited for my bins to be filled. It had rained the previous day so the rows were a little wet, the soft ground littered with the footprints from the pickers' shoes. The peach pickers liked to joke around with Junior and me, teasing us about being so young and not being able to handle the tractors. Sometimes we would show off by pulling out quickly or just firing back our own jokes to keep up the friendly banter. I had been warned about the mud when I started my tractor job, but on that particular day, I was feeling a little cocky. As the bins filled, the guys gave me the signal that I was ready for return. I started the tractor and drove up the row. As I pulled out and began to round the corner, the wheels began to sink into the mud. My heart began to pound and I panicked. I stopped and tried to back up, but the wheels sank deeper and the other workers began to scream for me to stop. I yanked the gear forward in one last-ditch effort to get the tractor out. Instead, I bottomed out in the mud, axle-deep. There I was with four bins full of peaches, completely stuck in the mud, with an orchard full of migrant workers staring at me as if I had run over the only cow in the pasture.

"The man is going to fire you over this," one guy said, surveying my predicament.

Actually, I hadn't even thought about the man yet. Instead, I had only been able to think about the one person who would be more disappointed than anyone else in the world: my mom. I really wanted to make her proud, and I was so new to this job; it seemed far too soon for me to have made an error of this magnitude so quickly. Then, I considered the guy's words and thought about the man and all those peaches, just sitting there. I could hear the other workers behind me, increasing my anxiety as they talked about the hot sun baking the peaches and ruining them.

"Is that even possible?" one man asked, eyeing the bins.

"Oh, sure," another said. "All those peaches, wasted."

Someone else chimed in to say that the boss had been radioed and he was on his way. I saw everyone else surveying the tractor and hoped they were looking for some idea about how to move the tractor and get me unstuck, but I knew that they probably just wanted to see this play out, one way or another. I had screwed up big time and it was more than just the sun's heat that was making me sweat.

"Mr. Dubose himself is on his way!" someone exclaimed.

Oh no! I'd had no idea that's who they were talking about when they said someone was coming. I could feel my anxiety climbing higher and higher. This was it. I was definitely going to be fired.

A few minutes later, a huge four-by-four Chevy Blazer came roaring through the trees. I knew immediately it was Mr. Dubose. When he got close, he hit the brakes and popped out of the truck in one fluid motion. He was a huge, brawny man who stood at about six two. Mr. Dubose wore a folded, weathered hat like the ones Brett Favre wears, and he also wore a pair of overalls, one strap unfastened and thrown back over his shoulder. He walked right up to the tractor and stared at the tires for a moment before looking back at me with a steely glare. In actuality, he only stared for about five seconds, but it felt like it lasted for at least four times that length. My pulse thrummed in my ears as Mr. Dubose walked around the tractor, shaking his head in disbelief, never saying a word. Finally, he turned to one of the onlookers.

"Get Tommy down here and get this mess taken care of," he said before turning his gaze back to me. "Get in the truck."

I did as Mr. Dubose said and climbed into the truck. While I waited for Mr. Dubose to join me, I glanced out at the other workers in the orchard who were all looking me as if that would be the last time they'd ever see me alive. Mr. Dubose and I drove back to the shed; I felt like I was riding with Bill Gates and I had just crashed one of his prototype computers. As we drove, Mr. Dubose didn't say a single word to me. He didn't even look my way. I wanted to just jump out of the truck and take my chances with a tuck-and-roll, but he was driving too fast.

When we arrived at the shed, Mr. Dubose finally acknowledged me.

"Let's go."

I obediently got out of the truck and followed him. I figured he was going to walk me to the main office and tell the office administrators that I was officially fired, but we walked past the office. I was confused, but I kept following Mr. Dubose. We walked through the assembly line in the shed and all eyes were on me. I'm sure I had a dumb, confused look on my face, but I couldn't do anything but continue to follow Mr. Dubose. We moved down the line towards the loading dock in the back, where we finally stopped. Mr. Dubose told me to stand fast while he discussed something with the lead loader. I watched the two men talk briefly before Mr. Dubose motioned for me to join them.

"Listen to everything Mr. Earl says and be on time," Mr. Dubose said before he turned and left me alone with Mr. Earl. I was in a state of disbelief. He didn't fire me! But why? He could and should have, and yet there I was, still with my job.

I was taken off tractor duty and moved to the loading docks. The story of me bogging down that tractor traveled faster than Mr. Dubose's Blazer through the peach orchard, and the jokes and clowning went on for weeks. However, I didn't even care, because I still had my job. It wasn't the one I'd started with, but it was still a job, and that was enough to save face with my mom. On that first day, I felt numb with shock as I learned my new gig at the peach orchard. When I got home, Junior was there to greet me and he had the biggest grin on his face.

"I heard you bogged that tractor down to the axle!" he exclaimed.

I was embarrassed and felt mad at him at the same time for clowning me, but I hadn't expected anything less from him. He was my best friend, but Junior wasn't about to give me a pass for screwing up something as big as that. He laughed so hard that he rolled on the ground, which in turn made me chuckle a little. Eventually, my embarrassment over the tractor incident eased a little and I settled into my truck-loading job at the packing shed. Ultimately, I realized that maybe this was for the best; at least I got a chance to see the girls inside the shed.

Those who had licenses took turns driving to the shed each morning. As we approached the shed, we passed the Dubose plantation. We would all look over at that house every time we drove by because it looked like it'd been dropped from heaven. The estate was a fairytale built with long white columns in the front. We could see the pool entrance from the side and the long walkway leading to the front door. I had seen something like it in the movie *Gone with the Wind*, but it didn't seem right on the outskirts of Ridge Spring like that. We had other plantation houses, but nothing of that stature that looked like Scarlett O'Hara would come swirling out the front door at any moment. From that house, we knew that peaches made money—lots of money. I knew I couldn't afford a house like that for my mom, but a young man could dream, which is exactly what I did each time I looked over at that mansion.

The other workers and I complained about the hours, but we spent the days joking and laughing the time away. We talked about the cute girls and made small talk on our breaks. We talked about the clothes we wanted for the upcoming school year and discussed the approaching football season. We also talked about how much money the owners probably made off of those peaches, especially if the Dubose house was any indication. We knew we were cheap labor, but we didn't really care because we were sweating and laughing and laboring the day away together.

During our sophomore year, we suffered a major tragedy. Fabian, our classmate, was riding with two of our other classmates, Chris and Michael, in the backseat on the way back to the shed from break. We typically received about a forty-five-minute break during lunch, so time went fast. They had driven to town to grab a bite and were rushing to get back in time so as not to be late. Chris was driving a little too fast, maybe way too fast, when he lost control of the car and hit the shoulder of the road. The car hit the ditch and flipped over a few times, tossing Fabian from the back seat. He wasn't wearing a seatbelt and died as a result of the crash. The others survived the wreck, and because they were all our classmates, we didn't want to blame anyone, but we missed Fabian so much.

Fabian's younger sister worked at the shed with us as well and we were all heartbroken for her. Sadness hung heavily over all of us when we attended Fabian's funeral. We didn't blame Chris and tried to show him that we still loved him, too, but it was tough on him. We all did our best to pull together in our community and support one another. This was the late eighties and there was no division amongst races that we saw as kids, and the times and music were good. We were all country built, with the same dreams of trying to make a couple of extra dollars, hoping that would eventually help us carve out a better life.

During the summer, most high school students worked the assembly lines, no doubt because we were cheap labor. The process of peach cultivation began in the fields, where laborers would field big satchels of peaches in the orchard before dumping the fruit into large square bins that were hooked to the back of a tractor. Each tractor pulled a line of three bins, which could hold hundreds of peaches. The tractor driver would then haul the bins of peaches to the packing shed, or factory, a few miles away and empty the bins of peaches onto a conveyor belt. The peaches then slid down the belt and were sprayed with water to wash them. Workers seated on each side of the conveyor belt would sort through the peaches and throw out any noncompliant, subpar fruit. After that, the peaches that passed inspection would head down another, smaller conveyer belt, where boxes awaited them. The belt fed into several chutes that led down to the waiting boxes, quickly filled by pristine, juicy peaches. A worker stood behind each shoot to ensure the boxes were filled properly and evenly before placing a lid on the full box and replacing it with a new one.

The completed boxes were then pushed down the line to the guys who were waiting to load them onto crates. Each wooden crate could hold eight boxes as a base, stacked five high, for a total of forty boxes per crate. The crates were then loaded onto an eighteen-wheeler truck with a trailer. We could load the crates two abreast and about ten to twelve rows deep in the trailers. It was backbreaking work for the loaders, but some of the other high school students and I found it kind of fun, because we used the loading work as weight training—the old-fashioned way. Everything was in preparation for sports; that's how I often viewed it to help me stay focused during the day.

But spending my days in the factory was kind of fun; not because I found peaches especially thrilling, but because most of my high school friends worked in the factory, so we laughed and joked while we worked. There was no set end time for our work days, we simply kept going as long as the peaches flowed, and took intermittent breaks throughout the day. Sometimes we worked until five or six in the evening, and other days we were there until eight or nine.

Working in the actual orchard was grinding work due to the blazing-hot sun, and the temperatures pushed up into the eighties and nineties on a daily basis. We started our days early, but the sun would always quickly join us as an often unwelcome companion. The work was hard, and certainly not meant for people who weren't used to working outside. The owners demanded perfection because they delivered these peaches to customers across the country—their brand was at stake and the peaches had to be flawless.

We were typically given a row of trees to follow in the orchard. The other workers and I would line up along the columns and would go down the rows, working one tree at a time. The older ladies were the best at filling their baskets with high-quality peaches as they moved efficiently down the line. They had a rhythm to their peach picking, almost like the people of old working in the cotton fields. Some would hum a tune, some would crack jokes, and still others were silent, but everyone had a way of moving down the rows with ease to fill their baskets. Once a basket was full, we would place our assigned number between the handles of the basket to get credit for our work. Basket accountability was all on the honor system, and no one dared to replace their ticket with someone else's basket; tickets meant money and everyone depended on this money to feed their families. Although this was just a summer job for me, it was real employment for others, their way of financial survival. Living in the country, it was pretty normal for us to work alongside our elders as we earned money for school clothes and food.

During the beginning of my tenure in the peach fields, the older ladies kept an eye on me, stopping occasionally to toss the peaches from my basket that weren't up to the orchard's standards. The ladies were patient with me and incredibly helpful, but they also warned me that I needed to learn quickly so I wouldn't slow their own work and negatively affect their income. With the assistance of the ladies, I soon got the hang of it from watching Stanley's basket, and before long, I was powering through my trees like a pro. Eventually, I began to work those trees like it was a competition, racing to move faster than anyone else. I never could beat those veterans, but my weekly wages increased alongside my productivity. I didn't really enjoy the work all that much, but I loved the money because I knew I was lifting a financial burden off of my mother. The peach baskets we filled were for local sales at produce stands, but the higher levels of peach picking were reserved exclusively for the veteran employees, including the migrants that came up to South Carolina from Florida. They were the ones who had the huge satchels with the release strap at the bottom. The peaches picked mainly by the migrants were used for larger markets across the country, the ones that were sent through the peach sheds and packed into trucks by high school kids prepping for the upcoming sports season.

DRIVING SCHOOL BUSES

Another great part about living in the country was the responsibility given to young people. We were allowed to work at an early age, and one of the jobs available to us was to drive school buses immediately after receiving our drivers' licenses. For a few of us, it was a dream from an early age to have the privilege of driving a bus as we matriculated through school because it represented a certain level of prestige to have your own bus as a high schooler.

My older cousin, Vernon, lived across the street from us, and when he was in high school, he had his own bus. He was two years older than Kem, and like my brother, Vernon was a great mentor to me. Sometimes on the weekends, I would go over to Vernon's house to help him clean his bus. Having a clean bus was of the utmost importance. The student drivers all took painstaking measures to ensure their buses were immaculate, shining the tires with Armor All and spraying silver paint on the rims to make them stand out, and Vernon had one of the best looking buses around. I was fascinated by Vernon's bus, and on one of those Saturdays when I helped him polish up his bus like a new penny, he told me that one day I could get my own bus if I kept my nose clean and stayed out of trouble.

"You'll also need to keep your school attendance tight and keep your grades up; the selection rate is tight," Vernon warned me. I took his words to heart and made sure I did exactly as he said until the opportunity presented itself for me to get my own bus. I couldn't wait!

There were only about twelve to fourteen buses available and in order to drive one, you had to meet a strict list of requirements. You had to have good attendance, decent conduct in school, and you had to pass both a written and road test for the bus. Sometimes, this was easier said than done, because driving a large boat of a vehicle with a stick shift was not an easy thing to do. The person administering the road test was tough; he replicated scenarios you might encounter while driving the bus, such as kids yelling or standing up. Each time he tried to distract me, I had to diffuse the situation and tell him to please take his seat or remind him of the correct speed of buses. There was also a specific procedure we had to use when crossing railroad tracks. First, we had to come to a complete stop at the crossing. Then, we had to open the door and glance left, then right to ensure a train wasn't approaching. Then we could drive forward, keeping the door open all the while, until we crossed the tracks and could then slowly close the door before proceeding down the road.

The tester yelled as I approached the tracks to try to throw me off the procedures to see if I could handle the pressure, since a busload of kids isn't likely to sit quietly just because you're approaching a railroad crossing. The tester also did this because he wanted to place us in real situations to see if we were mature enough to deal with our peers and the younger students who would be our passengers. Vernon had warned me about the yelling, but I was unprepared for one situation during my road test. The test administrator wanted to evaluate my skill in backing up a bus about a hundred feet using the rearview mirrors. I was more nervous than I could ever remember being in my life, even more than before I ran out on a basketball court before a big game. I put the gear shift in reverse and began to slowly drive backwards.

"Straighten up the bus!" the tester suddenly yelled.

Before I could process what was happening, I was immediately jolted hard against my seat belt, the straps biting into me, as the bus backed into a ditch. The tester flew from one side of the bus to the other with a thud.

"*Stop*!" the tester screamed.

I immediately did as he said and stopped. Then I shifted to first gear and tried to pull out of the ditch, the motion throwing the tester back to the opposite side of the bus.

"*Stop the bus*!" he yelled again.

I stopped and watched as the tester raced up towards the driver's seat in horror. He ushered me out of the seat and took my place at the wheel, pulled us out of the ditch, and he began the drive back to the school. I sat down, embarrassed beyond comprehension. I didn't have to ask; it was clear I hadn't passed the test. When we were maybe half a mile away from the school, the tester glanced over at me.

"Do you really want to drive a bus?" he asked.

I wanted it so badly that I was shocked by his question, but I gave him my best pitch on how much it would mean to me to drive a bus, not just for me but for the extra money for my family. As I finished my impassioned plea, the tester pulled the bus back into the school parking lot, parked, and opened the door.

"All right," he said. "Go on back to class."

I disembarked, devastated at the loss of my dream of one day getting to drive a bus.

Towards the end of the school year, I was summoned to the front office by the bus coordinator. She asked about my bus experience, and I reluctantly told her about what had happened with my test and how the bus had ended up in a ditch, rather than on the road where it was supposed to have been. To my astonishment, she told me I would be retested the following week.

"What?" I asked, shocked. "Really?"

"Yes, really," she said with a smile. "I need dependable drivers for the following school year and I think you deserve a second chance."

I thanked her effusively, and a week later, I proved her right for believing in me and I passed my second road test with ease. At the end of my sophomore year, I began substituting for drivers, which earned me my own bus route as I started my junior year of high school. A typical day on the job involved driving my route to pick up students and dropping them off at their respective schools, before I parked the bus at the high school and went to my own classes. At the end of the day, I simply reversed my route and parked the bus at the curb in front of my house, before starting the process all over again the next day. It was normal for us and I thought this was typical of schools all around the country until I later shared my bus-driver stories with my army buddies as an adult.

"Wait, they let students drive the buses?" they asked in astonishment.

"Yeah, why?" I asked. They were shocked that the administration would trust students to drive school buses, but for us, it was just our normal routine. To accommodate us so we wouldn't miss out, football, track, and basketball practices wouldn't start until we drivers had completed our afternoon routes. I had no idea other school districts didn't operate the same way!

The bus drivers were responsible for picking up all the school-aged kids, with the exception of the special education students, who had a separate bus due to different start times. Each driver had a specific route, most often determined by where they lived in relation to the students. Those of us who drove the buses would often boast to each other about who had the fastest or cleanest bus. We'd talk about who had the most entertaining bus and compare stories from in the trenches. Best of all, drivers earned between $150 to $200 per month, depending on the length of the route. That was big time money then, especially for a high school student.

CHAPTER 10

Girls

I always wanted to be with the prettiest girl in school, someone who would love me and shield me from all the negativity and criticism and questions that followed me. However, most of my experiences were not quite as I'd hoped. I would notice a beautiful girl staring at me and I would think that surely, she saw something she liked when she looked at me. She would check me out with her soft eyes framed by long hair, accentuated by brown skin and a curvaceous body. I would imagine that she could see past my scars, the deep burns and deformed arms and hands. By the time she would approach me, I already felt like I was falling in love. But then, when she got close, her mouth would open and I would once again hear the question, that same question that I could never quite escape like a dark shadow: "What happened to your face?"

In that moment, my fantasy would shatter into a thousand pieces like broken glass and I would come back to reality. My affection for the girl would dissipate and I would feel the slow burn of anger. This fantasy girl, the one who would love and understand me, was someone I could hope for, but I felt like I could never realistically have her in my life. The chance for a relationship felt like just one more thing that had been taken from me by the fire.

Nevertheless, I ended up having girlfriends throughout my high school years. I believe my issue was that I was too much of a serious guy; I was always thinking about a wife instead of just living in the moment. I ended up purchasing some type of friendship ring for each one of them, from my freshman year to my senior year. I didn't mess around, spending well over a hundred dollars for each one of those rings. I didn't even ask for them back after the breakups. Charles Ingles would have never done such a thing, so neither did I. I would date someone for about a year before we would break up, but then we'd end up becoming really good friends. I guess that's what we did in a small town, because once you were no longer in a relationship, you couldn't avoid your ex. Besides, our mothers all knew each other, so no matter who was to blame for the breakup, both parties just had to suck it up and be friends. At least, that was my approach once I stopped feeling sorry for myself and blaming everything on my burns each time. And anyway, I figured I would make it to the pros or become rich and they'd want me back, which gave me a little peace of mind. It was easier to cope that way when I saw that each of my ex-girlfriends seemed to move on immediately after our breakup.

My baby sister was extremely protective of me and would give all of my ex-girlfriends the evil eye. She was used to dealing with people staring at my mom at the grocery store. Kem and I didn't go with our mother, but Lynnette would always tag along with her, and as a result, Lynnette built up a rather large resentment towards anyone staring at our family. Even at an early age, she could give you a death stare as if to say, "What are you looking at?" Lynnette told me that our family's experiences made her very sympathetic towards people with disabilities or scars over the years, but it also made her like a mother hen. Maybe that's why she always showed up to my sports games. She was always there, even though she knew so little about sports. Whether instinctively or planned, she was always there, cheering me on from elementary through high school, sitting on the first or second bench, watching and cheering and giving the evil eye if needed.

Growing up, I spent a lot of time with my sister and my mother. Kem had toughened me up during my adolescent years, but as I reached my middle school years, Kem had begun to hang out with his friends, never letting his baby brother tag along. He kept me away from his world, protecting me in the same way he had while running out of the burning house years earlier: stay back, stay away! He dealt with his pain differently and didn't want me to charter my way down that path. As a result, my sister became my buddy. She shielded me, and, in turn, I protected her. I had already become a mama's boy, but I really bonded with my sister. Kem began to spend more summers away in Philly without me, and once he joined the army after high school, I was left to be the man of the house. I saw Lynnette as a reincarnation of our mother, as if our mother was growing up again, without the burns, and I had a chance to protect her. As a result, I felt a need to shield her at all times because she was perfect from what I saw on the outside: perfect skin with the cutest dimples (hence her nickname) and a contagious smile that would just light up a room.

We had a few pictures of our mother from before the fire, and Lynnette was my mama's daughter. My sister could have been a model, with strikingly beautiful features and the height to match. My mother enrolled Lynnette in all of the programs designed to enhance her charm, with dance classes, specifically ballet, and I really loved my sister dearly. I confided in her and trusted her more than anyone, and I felt like I could truly unmask while in her presence. She and my mom really shaped my perspective of what I thought about women, and the way I treat my wife and daughter is a direct result of my relationship with Lynnette and our mother. I had a balance with my siblings, between Kem giving me that edge and Lynnette giving me that unconditional love. *What would Lynnette think about her?* I would always wonder to myself when meeting someone new. I needed my sister's approval, even more so than my mother's. Our connection reminds me of twins as I think about her and ache when she is going through anything difficult in her life. Lynnette really became my guardian angel in the flesh. She didn't play when it came to protecting me, and she could be piercing with her eyes to anyone who tried to hurt me, or hurt us, with their words.

My sister escaped the fire physically unscathed, but her scars were unseen. My father pulled her out of the fire after the rest of us had escaped so her skin remained perfect, but internal scars can keloid and be as dangerous as the external ones. Lynnette didn't come out as whole as we had originally thought. One thing I have learned from my life is that there is no relationship quite like that between a mother and a son. However, there is also a strong bond between a father and a daughter. Maybe God planned it like that, and when those relationships are damaged or altered, it can affect a person in a negative way. My sister only knew the prison version of my dad; she never met him in person, not really. The last time he ever held her was when he pulled her from the flames, and that was only at the pleading request of our mother. Lynnette spoke with our father on the phone in prison throughout the years, but those conversations were not pure. He always needed something. He tried to persuade Lynnette and gave his warped version of the truth, which was unfair to her. She needed a relationship with him, just as I did, but I think about my daughter and I now understand the anguish Lynnette felt and may still feel. He betrayed all of us and we were left with this fractured life. Looking back, Kem and I owe her an apology for not realizing how she suffered; we owe her so much for being so strong for us. Lynnette is my hero and is the standard bearer for dealing with invisible scars. Her mental and emotional weight was and still is just as heavy as ours. Through it all, Lynnette is our mother's daughter and still remains protective of us all.

My junior year in high school really flowed for me. I had my in-school buddies and my main man, Junior, after the bell rang. I played all the sports and drove the school bus. During football season, all the players who drove buses would drive their normal routes and drop students off at their homes before returning to practice, which didn't start until we had all finished our routes—a luxury of country living. Junior and I always hung out after practice and we would often drive to the neighboring town, where a lot of his extended family lived. There was no doubt that Junior was a ladies' man, especially in high school, when he met a young lady, Victoria, in Batesburg, where his cousins lived. Sure enough, one of Junior's female cousins, Maxine, and his new girl were best friends, and then Junior and I were best friends, making us an ideal foursome. Junior was the talker, so he asked the girls to go out on a double date with us.

"I need to ask my momma if I could go out on a date with y'all," Junior's cousin, Maxine, said.

"Me, too," his girlfriend added.

In my mind, that meant no, so I immediately gave up the idea.

"I'll be right back!" Maxine said before she headed into her house. A few minutes later, Maxine called us into her house, where her mother was sitting on the couch staring at me. She knew me because I'd made so many trips with Junior to Batesburg, but this was different.

"What is this I hear about you and Junior wanting to double date?" Maxine's mother asked. All eyes were on me as I surreptitiously looked for a window to jump out of. It was the ultimate interrogation setup, but I pulled out an answer very quickly.

"We want to go see the new *Ghostbusters* movie and thought it would be fun if we all went together," I said. Maxine's mother knew Junior was a Slick Willie, but I played the shy role. It was kind of natural for me, but she still gave me a look like she knew I was more like Junior than I was letting on.

"You guys can go as long as it's okay with Victoria's mom," she said. "I'll give her a call and tell her that you're a nice young man. Tell your momma, Rose, I said hi."

Junior was shocked that I'd gotten her blessing and we laughed about that one for years, but at the time we still had to pull off the date and we knew absolutely nothing about dating. At that point in my life, I had had about two girlfriends and we'd mostly spent time together at school. Very seldom had I ever gone to my previous girlfriends' houses, and when I did, we could only sit on the porch and hold hands. A serious relationship to me was talking on the phone for about an hour with your girl while listening to slow jams in the background. We had a radio station that was really popular in our area called the Big DM on 101.3 FM. They played slow jams at a certain time every night, and the one-hour time slot was called "The Quiet Storm," where they played all love songs, and if you had a girlfriend, you would probably have that station playing in the background. Some of the favorites that lit up the airwaves included, "Rising Desire" by Stephanie Mills; "Adore" by Prince; "Do Me, Baby" by Melissa Morgan; "Baby, Come to Me" by Regina Belle; "You Give Good Love" by Whitney Houston; "Gotta Get You Home" by Eugene Wilde; "Lovers and Friends" by Michael Sterling; and "Turn Out the Lights" by World Class Wreckin' Crew.

At this point, the girls didn't see my burns, or at least react to them, because we had all grown up together and I was just James, or Foots to the locals. But this double-date situation was very different and complicated and it took some major planning on the part of Junior and me. We were dating girls from out of town, so we felt the need to impress them. We told our parents, and they treated this movie date like we were going to the prom. I had the driver's license, but Junior had the car, his orange Beetle, so our plan was to have me drive away from the house towards Batesburg and then switch drivers, since Junior drove stick shift much better than I did. Our driver switcheroo went off without a hitch and we headed over to pick up the ladies.

We arrived at Maxine's house and both she and Victoria were waiting for us. Junior and I greeted the parents before all of us piled into the car and headed off to the movies in Aiken as planned. Everything was going smoothly, except for one problem that Junior and I didn't really pick up on because the two of us were so used to hanging out together: Junior and I were sitting in the front seat and the ladies were in the back...and we didn't see the problem. We were rookies, sitting in the front and laughing it up, while our companions sat in the back, freezing. There was no heat pumping into the back of the Volkswagen, but Junior and I were comfortable because of the hose that ran up through the front, warming us just fine.

"We're freezing back here!" the girls complained.

"It should warm up back there once we get going," Junior said nonchalantly. The girls should've demanded to be dropped off back at home, but they didn't and we made it to the theater. We enjoyed the movie and ate popcorn and when it was over, we were prepared to return home, when Junior came up with a devious plan. Back then, we had the Star Center, which was like a modern-day multiplex where they hosted all types of events, including dances. That particular night was Saturday and there was a dance happening. The only problem was that Junior had to be back home with the car before his parents went to work on third shift at the fiberglass plant in Aiken. They left for work between eight thirty and nine at night, so our brilliant plan was to drop the ladies off at the dance, go home until Junior's parents left for work, and then sneak back out to the dance.

Once again, we showed a complete lack of chivalry as we dropped Maxine and Victoria off at the Star Center. At the very least, we gave them some money to get into the dance before we returned home where we waited until Junior's parents left. My own mother was pretty liberal in regards to going to the dance for a couple reasons: one, she knew I couldn't dance and would just stand around and head home as soon as I got sleepy; two, she thought we had already taken Maxine and Victoria home for the evening.

Junior and I crept back out to make our getaway. In retrospect, I'm not sure why we were being so stealthy, because once you started the engine to that bug, it woke up the neighborhood. However, stealthy or not, we hightailed it back to the Star Center to meet the girls, and to our surprise, they were still sitting outside in the cold where we'd left them.

"We didn't feel comfortable going in there without you two, so we stayed out here to talk," Maxine said. "Do you think you all can take us home?"

Junior and I were zeroes and we knew it. We took them home, and amazingly, both relationships managed to survive that night. Maxine and I dated for about eight months before she broke up with me, but we remained friends. Junior and Victoria broke up around the same time, and it retroactively served us both right for screwing up that double date as badly as we did. I learned that night that it's much cooler to sit beside your significant other during a double date instead of your buddy; it makes for a much more special evening. My daughter is almost the same age as Maxine and Victoria were back then, and just thinking about someone going on a double date with my daughter makes me sick to my stomach. However, by the time a young man finished enduring my interrogations, he would probably insist that Trinity sit in the backseat just the same—but for very different reasons. Times are different these days, anyway, with the ability to track my daughter's every location, along with constant Facetime calls just to see how things are going on the date.

I love technology.

CHAPTER 11

Military Moves

When my brother came home from boot camp, he was in great shape, better than he had ever been when we used to box in the backyard. He shared story after story of the bonds he'd made with his platoon buddies and showed me the way his drill sergeants had trained him to do push-ups. It seemed like he could do a million of them! I was so hooked on his stories, because there was something about them that reminded me of part of what drew me to sports. I wanted to be a part of something special, something where I belonged, so I set my sights on joining the military when I came of age. During my junior year of high school, I really started hearing those "Be All You Can Be" commercials on TV and it felt like they were speaking directly to me. The army was drawing me in and then I saw a commercial for the National Guard: two weeks out of the year and one weekend per month, with the promise of the GI Bill. It sounded like a no-brainer to me, a complete win-win. I could get some money for college, get in shape for my senior year of football, and do something honorable like Kem. All I needed to do was get my mother to sign the papers for me since I wasn't yet old enough to do it myself.

My mother had wanted all of us to attend college. My brother, to my mother's dismay, had opted to join the regular army upon his graduation from high school. She wasn't happy about his decision, but she nevertheless supported him. Knowing this, I was a little nervous as I prepared to discuss my plans with her. I rehearsed what I was going to say and when I felt I was ready, I went to her room and gave her my pitch.

"No way!" she exclaimed. "I thought you wanted to go to college?" she asked, her voice flooded with disappointment.

I explained to her that by signing up for the National Guard, I had the option to complete my training during the summer months when school wasn't in session. I emphasized that the GI Bill would lessen the financial burden on our family for my education, and she bought it…kind of. She made me promise that I would complete college and I readily agreed.

I had no idea what I was getting myself into. All I really wanted out of the deal was a conditioning regimen like my brother so I could return to school in the best shape of my life. I got the training I wanted, but I got it alongside a whole lot more. It was a decision that changed my life forever.

My brother introduced me to the army, but a guy named Stanley Frazier introduced me to the National Guard. Ridge Spring was a town full of Stanleys. Stanley Williams, my main man, lived across the street from me and we worked together in the peach orchard. Stanley Patrick lived one block over and stood about six four, a classmate of the first Stanley. Stanley Roland lived in the Bottom, across from the fish market and laundry. Our neighborhood sat on a level plain stretching out some distance towards the middle and elementary schools. The land just past the schools gently sloped down and out by the playgrounds and down to the roads. The homes down there sat on slopes that flowed down to the laundry and beyond down to the pool hall. There was one home that sat beside the pool hall and beyond that, ran the spring. The Ridge Spring flowed down even further, past a few more houses.

We called the whole area "The Bottom." It always seemed overcast down there, but there were good people and good times there, as well. The pool hall was mainly reserved for adults, but my best friend, Junior, and Stanley Williams and I would go down there from time to time and shoot a game or two of pool when a table was free. We thought we were good, but we were nothing compared to the old-school guys who hung out in the hall. Those guys could really shoot a game of pool, trick shots and all. They would make major bets on games of Eight-ball, and we would watch like it was a prize fight, while the pool sharks circled the tables, looking for their next mark.

Also in the hall were card games, men clustered around lobster-backed cards as they pressed their luck while the jukebox played on. While in the pool hall, you could witness a fight or two when someone got liquored up, but the crowd there was mostly harmless. Someone would occasionally threaten to go get their shotgun, but it never happened and cooler heads always prevailed. The guy who threatened to get his gun would be given a ride home and the next day, when the booze had worn off and a good night's sleep had dulled their anger, they'd be right back at the pool hall as if nothing had ever happened. My mother got her hair done in the Bottom by Ms. Lucille, which sometimes presented a problem for me. I was not allowed at the pool hall because my mother would kill me if I set foot in there. As a result, I knew I had to be careful and avoid that area on hair day, which occurred every two weeks or so, just in case my mom rounded the corner just as the crew and I were slipping down to the pool hall.

The Bottom really offered a lot, and everything was black-owned. Mr. Rivers owned the laundry and the fish store, a co-owner of the pool hall, and he even sold used cars in an open lot by his property. Mr. Coleman was a mason, in addition to serving as the

Boy Scout master for our troop when we were kids. Mr. Coleman bricked most of the buildings in the area as well, as he taught masonry at the high school. Also in the Bottom was a funeral home and the Masonic lodge. We had a lot going on down there, and my friends and I would ride our bikes down the hill from the main road in town towards the Bottom. If we picked up enough speed, we could coast all the way down before beginning our ascent towards the Star Center, the original high school for blacks that was later converted to the multipurpose center for dances, Boy and Girl Scout meetings, talent shows, and whatever other community events needed a home.

I hung out with each of the Stanley's from time to time, so my mom really didn't know which side of town I was on if I said I was going to hang out with Stanley. My fourth Stanley was Stanley Frazier, a young man three years my senior and a long-distance track star in and out of high school. He won a local race during the Harvest Festival, leaving one of the local bullies in the dust and infuriating the boy's father while Stanley made himself a sort of hometown hero for the rest of us. Stanley was untouchable in long-distance running, especially in the one-mile race, through all four years of high school. Then, after graduation, Stanley joined the National Guard. He continued to showcase his running prowess, blowing away his fellow soldiers in the two-mile run and we'd often see him run around town.

One day, Stanley allowed me to work out with him. I had run the eight-hundred- and four-hundred-meter races during my freshman and sophomore years in high school, but I needed some pointers, which Stanley was more than happy to provide. Man, he could really run like the wind! My friend Michael and I ran behind Stanley and were able to keep up for maybe the first quarter of a mile before Stanley began to pull away. Fortunately, Stanley had given us the route so we knew where we were going, and when we finally reached the end point, Stanley was waiting patiently for us.

After we ran, Stanley told us stories about how he smoked the other soldiers during basic training and advanced individual training. He loved the National Guard and told us the most legendary stories about soldiers, annual training trips, and parties. He painted amazing visuals with his words, accentuated by his big eyes that would pop during the exciting moments in his tales. He pulled us into the stories so deeply that we weren't entirely confident we could tell fiction from reality. Then again, we didn't really care, because Stanley made us laugh until our stomachs hurt. The more I listened to Stanley's stories, the more intrigued I was by the National Guard. Between Stanley's and my brother's stories about the military, I was completely hooked. I joined 122nd Engineer Company CSE (Combat Support Equipment) on February 20, 1987, during my junior year of high school. I signed up for a lot of reasons: finances, physical conditioning, curiosity, and honor, but I had no idea exactly how much my decision to enlist would change my life.

School let out for the summer on June 2, 1987, and a few days later I was on a plane headed to Fort Polk, Louisiana, for basic training. I had signed up for the National Guard with my buddy and classmate, Robbie, so I wouldn't be so alone. My mother drove me up to the National Guard unit in Saluda, South Carolina, where we waited for the recruiter to get the van ready to drive us to Columbia Airport for the flight. I had to really put on a strong face in front of my mom because I could tell she was already starting to cry. I joked with Robbie in an attempt to avoid my mother's eyes until we got ready to get into the van. I turned to my mom to say my goodbyes and she was already soaked with tears. It was hard to say goodbye, but I hugged her tightly, told her I loved her, and got into the van. As the vehicle pulled away, I watched my mom through the window. This was the first time we'd really been apart since our respective hospitalizations, and although I was ready for this next step, it still made me sad to say goodbye. The drive to Columbia Airport was an hour and a half long and I spent most of it sitting in the van, watching South Carolina speed by my window.

When we arrived at the airport, we received our instructions from the recruiter, who told us to hang tough and stick together. We boarded the plane, and after a short flight to Louisiana, we disembarked and made the long bus ride to the military post. The bus was packed with recruits and the shades were pulled down over the windows, so we had no idea how long the trip would take or where we were going. The bus was enveloped in total silence, the only sound coming from the rumble of the vehicle rolling down the road. Fort Polk had not instructed basic training since the Vietnam Era, but that summer it had reopened for recruits for the first time. Sitting on the bus with us were two soldiers wearing Smokey-the-Bear-style hats, exactly like the drill instructors I'd seen in the movies. I'd expected them to yell at us or something, but they were silent, which was almost more disarming, like the calm before the storm or the eye of a hurricane.

We rode on that bus for what seemed like a country day until the bus temporarily came to a stop. I later found out that we were passing through a checkpoint, and then the bus started again, carrying us a little further until we came to our final destination.

"Everyone on their feet!" the drill sergeants suddenly shouted.

We were all startled and my heart jumped at the sudden influx of noise. All of us recruits obediently got to our feet and exited the bus. Suddenly, all hell broke loose. There were drill sergeants everywhere yelling at us like we had stolen their grandmother's church hat. The Louisiana air was hot and sticky and my heart was racing. I was used to the heat, but this Louisiana heat and humidity were something different altogether. As I surveyed the mess of drill instructors and recruits, I was told the drill instructors couldn't hit us, but I couldn't exactly tell at that point because recruits were falling down everywhere, tripping over their bags as well as their own feet. The drill sergeants screamed at us and called us maggots, scumbags, and everything in between. In the midst of their yelling, they divided us into platoons. I was looking around for Robbie to give me a little comfort, when I noticed we were being divided alphabetically. Robbie's last name was "Bettis," which felt like miles away from "Scott." We were still in the same company, but we ended up in different platoons, which felt at times like we might as well have been in different zip codes. Being in separate platoons, we were housed in separate barracks, and I felt like I had temporarily lost my support network. Even the chance for a friendly glance or a half smile was gone, and I felt like I was on my own.

As all of us recruits started to get situated; the dust finally began to settle from the chaos outside the buses and we started to get into the routine of things—if you can refer to getting called scumbags and dropped for push-ups for moving around in formation as routine. It wasn't until the end of the first week that I realized my mother was actually just as tough as the drill sergeants, if not more so. It was a trade-off with cutting grass and hanging out clothes or doing push-ups and sit-ups; getting grounded or beat with a belt or getting grilled by the drill sergeant.

The part that really caught me by surprise was that no one cared how I looked. I'd spent so many years being stared at, whispered about, and asked endless questions about my scars. But in basic training, none of that mattered because we were all maggots. They didn't care, or appear to care, about my burns at all. I was just one of the twenty-five to thirty soldiers trying to make it through basic training. For the first time in my life, I liked blending in instead of standing out. I found I enjoyed every aspect of army life, especially saluting the flag and marching. I felt so patriotic and special as I paid my respects to the Stars and Stripes. Being in this world was so foreign to me, but it felt like a rite of passage, and I was more than up for the challenge.

I didn't show it, but I used every opportunity as a conditioning session to mentally get through the punishment. I hated long-distance running, but I would imagine myself running long touchdowns as the drill sergeants looped us around the installation. We would go to these old World War II buildings and receive instruction on first aid, drill and ceremony, PRC 77 Operation, and many of the other common tasks for everyday army life.

PRC 77, called the "Prick 77" by those of us who had to use it, was our primary means of communication in the military. We all had to learn how to set it up, place it in an operational state, and transmit radio communications. An AN/PRC 77 radio set is a portable VHF FM combat-net radio that provided two-way communications and was first introduced during the Vietnam War in 1968. AN/PRC stands for Army/Navy Portable Radio Communication, because the army is nothing if not very literal and to the point. The PRC 77 was able to be used in the field and to use it, you had to connect a long whip antenna to the radio, and the antenna was screwed together and could easily be packed away as well. Today, the PRC 77 has been mostly replaced by SINCGARS radios, but PRC 77s are still capable of working with most VHF FM radios used by the ground forces of the US and their allied forces.

Being in the buildings felt like torture, because even though they had large industrial fans blowing on us, it was hotter than hell in there. If you've ever been to Louisiana during the summer, you know a fan is practically useless against that kind of swampy humidity. Due to the heat in the buildings, combined with a lack of sleep, privates sometimes dozed off during the lessons. The absolute last thing one wanted to do was fall asleep during instruction at basic training because there were always drill sergeants lurking around, waiting for eyelids to drop so they could swarm in like angry bees, stopping an inch away from the sleeping private's face.

"*Get up!*" the drill sergeant would yell.

The private would jerk awake, while the rest of us glanced nervously at the victim as if they were headed to the slaughterhouse.

The drill sergeants always asked the same question: "Were you asleep, private?"

"No, drill sergeant," the private would say, desperately blinking the sleep away from their eyes.

"Yes, you were! Get up!" the drill sergeant would yell.

The private would hop up to their feet as quickly as they could. Then, we watched as the drill sergeant escorted the private to the back of the room and tortured them with a round of side straddle hops or wall squats. The rest of us would try to turn our attention back to the lesson at hand, each of us attempting to fight against the elements so that we wouldn't be next on the wall.

We began to advance through the weeks, learning drill and ceremony and how to fire our M16s, and I could feel myself transforming into a real soldier. I felt my body changing and adjusting to the military's schedule. When we had been in for four weeks, we started to feel the anticipation of making it out of basic training. Four weeks down, four to go!

I only saw Robbie in passing, usually when we trained as a company or did company runs, but we'd only be able to get close enough to briefly check in with each other.

"How is everything?" one of us would ask.

"Everything is good!" the other would reply, and that was the extent to which we could chat. There was no real chance for us to hang out, but that was okay; we were both focused on the experience at hand. The apprehension on each of our faces when we started basic training shifted to "we got this" by week four. We had both lost some weight, but I could feel and see muscles forming in places that I hadn't previously had. I could call cadence and run farther without getting as winded as I used to. Speaking of cadence calling, it was the one motivation factor that carried us through many tough situations. Our drill sergeant must have sung in a choir in a previous life—before the army with all the swearing and colorful language—because he could blow a tune like no other. He made a soldier feel like marching a hundred miles and back again. It was uplifting and glorious and a major part of basic training. During my senior year of high school, I took some of those cadences home on the bus trip during football games. Between the two of us, Robbie and I had the bus rocking with those army songs. We had another teammate, Andre, who had also completed basic training. Andre had gone to Fort Benning for his training, but he was a comrade all the same and he would always join in on the cadences. He was loud and could carry a tune, and between the three of us we would get the rest of the bus involved. Our other teammates would figure it out after a couple of rounds of listening to us, but they had no idea what the cadences meant, nor did they fully understand our passion behind the singing. These songs were the tunes that carried us through marches and long runs; they were the songs that eased our minds and gave us pride and joy as we pushed forward.

Mama, Mama

Army Running Cadence

Mama, Mama, can't you see,
What the Army's done to me?
They put me in a barber's chair,
Spun me around, I had no hair.
Mama, Mama, can't you see,
What the Army's done to me?
They took away my favorite jeans,
Now I'm wearing Army greens.
Mama, Mama, can't you see,
What the Army's done to me?
I used to date beauty queens,
Now I love my M16.
Mama, Mama, can't you see,
What the Army's done to me?
I used to drive a Cadillac,
Now I carry one on my back.

We Are Marching By

Army Marching Cadence

Let 'em blow, let 'em blow,
Let the four winds blow.
Let 'em blow from east to west,
The US Army is the best.
Standing tall and looking good,
Ought to march in Hollywood.

Hold your head and hold it high,
Platoon is marching by.
Close your eyes and hang your head,
We are marching by the dead.
Look to your right, and what d'ya see?
A whole bunch of legs, looking at me.
Dress it right and cover down,
Forty inches all around.
Nine to the front, six to the rear,
That's the way we do it here.

They Say That in the Army

Army Marching Cadence

They say that in the army, the chicken's mighty fine.
One jumped off the table and started marking time.
Oh, Lord, I wanna go,
But they won't let me go home.
They say that in the army, the pay is mighty fine,
They give you a hundred dollars, and take back ninety-nine.
They say that in the army, the coffee's mighty fine.
It looks like muddy water, and tastes like turpentine.

Those last couple weeks of basic training seemed to drag and my emotions ebbed and flowed, a mixture of homesickness and an eagerness to complete this arduous training period. There were three different phases of basic training, broken down into the Red, White, and Blue Phases. Throughout the different phases were milestones we had to complete, including: Nuclear Biological and Chemical (NBC) training (the gas chamber), basic rifle marksmanship, individual tactical training, drill and ceremonies, basic military communications, and map reading. The objective was, of course, to pass and advance. I was not a hunter by any means, and I was really nervous about firing a weapon for the first time. To qualify and receive a passing score, you had to hit at least twenty-three out of forty targets, with twenty rounds shot from the foxhole, and the other twenty from the prone, unsupported position. Again, I was not a weapons guy at all, and, at that point, I hated firing my M16, so this particular test was completely traumatic for me. It seemed ironic, but there I was, this rough and tough high school football player who was scared to fire a weapon. We had trained using many methods to perfect our shooting, and the drill sergeants even had cadence calls designed to go over shooting methods, such as the "Breathe, relax, aim, and squeeze." Even with that extra help, qualification week was very stressful for me. It was like being terrified of public speaking and having a teacher tell you that you had to give a speech in front of your entire eighth grade class.

Finally, the day came when I had to walk the line with my weapon. Each of use was handed our two magazines of twenty round clips and walked to our foxhole. I lowered myself into the hole and set my sandbags to the proper height, adjusting my position until I was comfortable. I waited on the targets to appear at various distances, the first at twenty-five meters, as the range officer instructed us to watch our individual lanes. My heart pounded as I waited for my target to appear over the ground. Suddenly, there it was, and our guns all exploded in a chorus.

Bang!

As the dust settled, we gathered our empty brass rounds. I know I missed a bunch of my targets, but I knew I'd hit a couple, too. But had I hit enough? I wasn't sure. We waited patiently at the base of the tower as our scores were called out by our drill sergeant.

"Lane four, Scott! Twenty-four!"

I was so thrilled that you would have thought I had won the lottery! I had qualified as a marksman, just barely, but I'd made it. To me, it was equivalent to finding out on the day of your high school graduation that you'd passed a difficult class and would be able to march with your friends. I was at the bottom of the shooting rung, but I had passed and could move on to the next phase. Pass and advance!

I had made it to the final phase, the Blue Phase. I had passed all of my common tasks, and all that was left was my physical training test. I wasn't worried, because if I had a strong point, it was definitely physical fitness. I was young and conditioned and felt the best I ever had in my life. The only thing that could deter me was my push-up form. The Army is very particular about how you perform your push-ups and sit-ups. There is a manual that describes the form, and a demonstration is given prior to administering the test. If you violated the form, your test could be terminated and you would fail. While I felt good about my fitness, I was nervous I'd go too fast on my push-ups and be terminated. To pass, a man between the ages of seventeen and twenty-one had to do at least forty-two push-ups and fifty-three sit-ups in two minutes each, and run two miles in less than fifteen minutes, fifty-four seconds. A woman in the same age group has to do nineteen push-ups and fifty-three sit-ups and run two miles within eighteen minutes, fifty-four seconds. My push-ups went off without a hitch, and I breezed through the rest of my PT test. Once I passed, I knew I was officially a soldier and would be marching across that parade field for graduation.

We had time to reflect after we completed our PT tests, a few days before the graduation ceremony. We spent that time cleaning and getting fitted for our uniforms. There was a mixture of active duty, National Guard, and reserve soldiers in training with us, so during this few day period, they had to get their orders cut to process to their next training station. I was a split option soldier, which meant I had the option in my contract to complete my basic training between my junior and senior years in high school, followed by advanced infantry training (AIT) after my senior year of high school. Once our orders were set, we finished up the rest of our loose ends. We took our end-of-cycle basic training photos. We shined our shoes and brass for our uniforms, we starched our shirts and buffed the floors. We joked and imitated the drill sergeants as we waited in endlessly long lines to out-process. Out lines were the same for all of us, but the paperwork was not, with all of our differing orders and destinations. We updated our medical records and Servicemembers' Group Life Insurance (SGLI) forms. We scheduled our flights to our next destinations, which meant going home for me. I loved being a soldier, but I was so eager to get out of there.

In 1962, Fort Polk became an Advanced Individual Training (AIT) center. A small portion of the base is filled with thick vegetation that, combined with Louisiana's humidity, is akin to permanently sitting in a steam room, which made it the ideal place to train soldiers for the Vietnam War since the conditions mimicked those of the jungles of Southeast Asia. This area of Fort Polk was given the nickname "Tigerland," and for the next twelve years, more soldiers were shipped to Vietnam from Fort Polk than any other American training base. As a result of this history, people have always looked at me strangely over the years when I tell them I attended basic training at Fort Polk. This is due to the fact that, as I mentioned earlier, the army stopped training soldiers there after the Vietnam War. However, from June to August of 1987, Fort Polk opened its doors for one summer to six hundred recruits, myself included. They haven't trained basic trainees there since that summer, which makes it that much more prestigious to me. During basic training, the drill sergeants reminded us often of the Vietnam vets who trained there before of us, some of whom never returned home. For me, that added a level of honor to my military training and service. It made me want to press forward, push harder, and become this warrior of a soldier and everything that being a soldier represented.

Our ranks had thinned through the weeks, some leaving due to a lack of physical fitness, others because they couldn't shoot, or there was an illness, a death in the family, or they had a bad attitude. A few went AWOL, although I couldn't understand the point because I had no idea where you could escape to in those Louisiana woods. But I was still there in the ranks, only a week away from graduation, and feeling as proud as one could be about the upcoming ceremony. My battle buddies made their plans for family members to attend the graduation, but I knew the trip was too far for my mother to attend. While I missed her, it was okay she couldn't attend because I knew my purpose there and I was entirely focused to ensure I didn't make any bonehead mistakes to screw up my graduation. The drill sergeants had begun to relax a little around us, and during a quiet moment, my drill sergeant asked about my scars and what had happened to me. I gave him the short version, leaving out my father's involvement and just describing it as an accident, and kept moving. My drill sergeant looked me over for a moment, examining my demeanor as well as my face.

"You're a good soldier, Private Scott," he said.

I could feel that he really meant it, and to this day that remains one of the best compliments I have ever received. After so many years of military service, all a soldier wants to be remembered as is a good and decent soldier. Even thirty years removed from basic training, I can still see those drill sergeants shouting in my face that first day when we stepped off the bus. It never leaves you. I had the opportunity to serve as a company commander of basic training at Fort Leonard Wood, Missouri in 1998, and when I arrived it felt like I'd come full circle. Although I was in charge of the drill sergeants at Fort Leonard Wood, I still marveled at their presence and admired their ability to train and mold civilians into soldiers, just like mine had done with me years earlier.

The night before the ceremony, I spent a lot of time reflecting on the time I'd just spent at Fort Polk. I thought back to the conversation I'd had with my recruiter about the possibility that I might not be able to join due to my burns. Serving in the military was an honor, not a given. I had worked so hard to cross this major hurdle and I was so proud to be where I was. I felt different. I thought about my friends back home in Ridge Spring and how surprised they were going to be at how conditioned I was. I thought about all those "Be All You Can Be" commercials and the recruiter telling me I probably wouldn't be accepted by the military. We had spent all day marching across the parade field and passing the review stand, saluting. Eyes right! We snapped back forward, marching in step, and I loved every second of it. I couldn't wait for the actual ceremony. It felt like the night before a home football game, and the anticipation was almost unbearable. I thought about my brother and my mom and how proud they would be of me, and the thought made me smile. A big reason why I'd wanted to sign up for the army was to get into great physical shape for football, but I didn't feel like I'd expected I would. Maybe it wasn't about that conditioning program, after all; maybe it was deeper than that. I felt more patriotic than I felt like Mr. Football, but mostly I just felt grateful for this whole experience.

I ended up not getting much sleep the night before graduation; none of us did. We were all jittery with anticipation. We got up before the crack of dawn like we always did and headed into the mess hall for breakfast. We gobbled our food quickly, although we had no reason to since we were not pressed for time. Basic training had taught us to eat quickly—there was no time for leisurely meals—so we did as we'd been told; no need to break tradition now. We returned to our barracks and eventually began to put on our green dress uniforms. Everyone was walking around with huge, cheesy grins like they were war heroes or something, but we did have reason to smile. It was our day and we were so excited to graduate. The drill sergeants came in to inspect us and their demeanors were erratic and unpredictable, jumping from joking to snapping at us if we got out of line or too loud. As we prepared for the ceremony, our drill sergeant gave us a speech about standing tall in formation and not locking our knees. He then told us how proud he was of us and to look sharp. We felt so pumped up and then, finally, it was time to march to the field and the drill sergeant gave the command to form up outside into a platoon formation. We were minutes away from showtime and my heart was racing.

The ceremony began promptly at 1000hrs. We were all on the parade field, and at that point, had been there for an hour rehearsing and waiting for the graduation to begin. People began to fill the stands about twenty minutes out from the start as we formed into our platoons. Fifteen minutes out, we went to our parade rest stance as the leaders arrived to begin the ceremony. Finally, the narrator announced that the ceremony would begin in two minutes as the adjutant, a military officer who acts as an administrative assistant to a senior officer, brought the unit to the position of attention. We had been previously told to not lock our knees to avoid fainting. The heat grew quickly in Louisiana and that, combined with standing at attention for a period of time, could easily send a person crashing to the ground. Not a good look, especially on graduation day.

"If someone faints, just step to the side and stay locked in!" the drill sergeant ordered. *Holy smokes!* I thought. *No mercy!* The military did not have time for fainting spells or "heat exhaustion."

"Parade rest!" came the command.

The chaplain recited a prayer and an officer gave an eloquent speech as we fought the heat on the field.

"Attention!"

Finally, the National Anthem began to play and then it hit me: I was graduating basic training; this was really happening. In that moment, I was overcome with pride at the realization that I was now a true soldier. It was real and I felt every note of the National Anthem strike in the core of my being. I'd heard the song before—of course I had—but this time the song carried more weight than it ever had before. This was it for Robbie and me—we had done it! I knew I wouldn't be able to explain what this meant to any of my classmates back home, because what I felt was unexplainable to people who had not experienced it. Robbie and I were the only representatives from Ridge Spring on the parade field that morning, and we carried a town full of a lot of hopes and dreams with us that day as we marched with pride. In completing basic training, I felt like I had done something honorable and erased the bad legacy of my father, and for me, the National Anthem celebrated my personal achievement.

"Right face!" the drill sergeant commanded. "Forward March! Column left March!"

We were conducting our final pass in review in front of the grandstand for the senior officers to see and witness us, a ceremonial final inspection.

"Column left March!" the drill sergeant called as we neared the grandstand. "Eyes right!"

We rendered the hand salute we'd been taught, turning our heads to the right, passing by the grandstand, and finally snapping our heads back forward and dropping our hands to our sides, marching in unison. It was done! Basic training was complete!

Once we left the field, we said our farewells and grabbed our duffel bags. We made promises to keep in touch and maintain our newfound bonds, but basic training was finished. We boarded the buses and made our way to our destinations. I was a soldier now and this felt like the culmination of all of my efforts. I had fought my way up through the sixth grade into the higher education track, proven myself on the football field and the basketball court, and earned my money in the peach fields, but this was different. The army fatigues had somehow even managed to camouflage my scars and battered past, lifting me up into this honorable environment filled with a blend of people from all walks of life. It was like wearing basketball uniforms where we all looked the same and you couldn't tell who was rich or poor just by looking in the ranks. My burns didn't matter in this world; I was a soldier.

When I arrived home after basic training, I was a changed young man and my body felt amazing. I hadn't even had so much as a soda in two months. I woke up at five thirty without being prompted, no alarm clock needed. I made my bed without my mother having to yell at me twenty times to get it done. I hung my clothes out on the line just because the chore needed to be done, not because I'd been asked. Who was this guy? I was more mature, taking more initiative, and evolving into the person I wanted to be. I ran around town like Stanley Frazier for about two to three miles at a time, and while I still couldn't run as fast or as far as the greatest of all time, I'm sure he would have been proud of me all the same. In the afternoons, after football practice, I'd run through more drills, wanting more exercise and training like I'd gotten in basic. I was hooked.

There were three of us in all that experienced a trip to basic training that summer: my friend Robbie, a guy named Andre, and me. Our changes were imperceptible to us, but others saw them like neon signs. They'd hear us chant our cadences while we ran or used army terminology and phrases. We pushed ourselves harder, sprinted faster, and the three of us huddled together during breaks to talk shop about the army. Basic training also brought out a much more patriotic side of myself. I didn't play around with the flag and would berate someone for clowning around when the National Anthem was being played. They'd respond by telling me to loosen up, but they'd see the look in my eyes and know I was serious. I drank the Kool-Aid, all of it, and I loved every drop.

I had always enjoyed walking in the woods, which turned out to be a good fit for me when I went out to field exercises. During my very first field exercise, I was paired with one of the specialists in my squad, Specialist Wideman. We had to dig our fox hole and the dimensions were grave standard, chest high of the tallest soldier. We sketched the outline and began to dig and pull weeds from the base of the ground. Because I was the rookie, Specialist Wideman decided to give me the instructions and then take a break and disappear for a while. I was young and didn't mind the physical labor. I began to sweat profusely, the perspiration stinging my eyes, but I continued to dig, and after a while, the fox hole began to take shape and was looking pretty good. I was making good progress when Specialist Wideman returned. He walked towards me and surveyed the scene with his hands on his hips.

"Where are your gloves?" Wideman asked.

"Oh, I'm good, I don't really need them," I said, feeling tough and a little proud of myself. Specialist Wideman glanced over at the discarded pile of weeds before turning back to me.

"Well, you know that's poison ivy, right?" he asked, one eyebrow raised. "I sure hope you haven't been touching that with your bare hands."

I looked down and realized that my hands had begun to swell, as had, unbeknownst to me, my face. I was in pain and Specialist Wideman thought my ignorance about poison ivy was the funniest thing in the world, and he kept calling me a Krispy Kreme donut. I made my way over to the medical tent and finally received some treatment for my itchy, fiery hands. This particular anecdote of my introduction to the National Guard went around the Guard for years.

"Tell them that time when Wideman had you pulling those poison ivy weeds!" they'd say. But I learned a lot of life lessons from those old soldiers in the National Guard. We still had some soldiers who had served in Vietnam and they were legendary. They were the hardest workers and the hardest drinkers. They taught me how to drive a dump truck and to operate a grader. I learned how to properly shine my boots and earn respect from elder statesmen.

Since I was still in high school, it was kind of strange to play in the high school football games on a Friday and then attend a Drill Weekend on a Saturday and Sunday. It was different, but it was my new normal and I just rolled with it. I had strong boundaries on all sides of me because it was imperative that I maintained my physical fitness. I couldn't use drugs and I had to show up for my monthly drills and annual training because it was the law. I was committed. These boundaries were limits I needed to keep me on the straight and narrow. I was by no means a saint and I had my vices, but I understood that if I could stay focused on this path, the military could assist me with my dream of playing professional football or take me somewhere else entirely that I couldn't even imagine yet. Either way, I enjoyed the soldier life and it was a great fit for me.

THE FLAG

I enlisted in the Army National Guard while still in high school at the age of seventeen between my junior and senior years of high school. My mother had to sign a waiver for me to enlist, and as a result, I have served either in the military or as a federal employee for my entire adult life. The flag and what it represents to me go hand in hand with my service to this country. It is instinctive for me to stand up and salute or place my hand over my heart, and prior to recent controversies, I would look cross-eyed at those who weren't standing. We have movie theaters on almost every military installation, and prior to the start of each movie, the National Anthem is played and we stand when it's played. The first time I experienced it as a young lieutenant stationed in Korea, I thought it was the coolest thing ever. Fast forward twenty years later, my family and I had the opportunity for a permanent change in station (PCS) to Korea and we went to a movie on post as a family for the first time. My wife and kids had never experienced the Anthem being played in a theater before, and as I stood up, they were slow to move.

"Get up and take your hat off!" I told them. The boys did as I said and my wife and daughter followed suit, understanding without needing any additional elaboration. The flag carries a different meaning for me than it does to them, maybe because of the sacrifices military members have made for their families and the benefits and the opportunities the military has afforded us. With that said, I have willingly made those sacrifices serving so many years to give my kids options, choices in life to become anything or to choose any profession they want. They enjoy certain luxuries and so many great experiences of living abroad and traveling to different countries because of the sacrifices my wife and I have made for them.

My kids have lived a sheltered life, but they're also Black Americans who may face injustice at some point in their lives due to the color of their skin. They may have to take a stand for an injustice that may occur to either themselves or on behalf of people who don't feel like they have a voice. We have raised all of our kids to be respectful, but to also be courageous, and if that means taking a knee to save one life—including their own—then kneel. I can't speak for all veterans, but I believe my thirty years of federal service have afforded my seeds the right to make that stance. I could personally never kneel, but I'm a different type of soldier.

CHAPTER 12

Senior Year

For most people, sleep is peaceful. It's a respite from the day, from worries, from everything. But for others, nighttime is a dark and torturous place. For me, it was the latter. Nights were exhausting and far from restful. As I slept, my head would bang vigorously against my pillow as if I was having a seizure. A horrible metronome, *thump, thump, thump*, pounded my head over and over as I drifted in and out of a restless sleep. As happened most nights, my mind would replay the events of the fire, and once more, I was four years old. Each time this happened, I would start my nightly routine of fighting against the painful memories of my father setting our house ablaze.

So often when tragedy strikes the African American community, we either pretend like nothing ever happened or we treat it as normal. My family had gone through a major tragedy with the fire, but we never received any counseling. We had never discussed the circumstances leading up to that tragic day, which left each of us to sink or swim with our own individual mental issues. In the black community, we try to pray it away, drink it away, or smoke it away, but we never come together to discuss the problem or tragedy to cope with it as a unit. Instead, we just deal with things in our own ways and try to wash away the problems the best way we know how: alone. Such was the case with the Scott family. I never asked my mom what happened, I never asked Kem how he felt about that day or what it was like having to live with other family members. I never asked my mother about her own physical and mental pains that she endured. Lynnette, having been so little at the time of the fire, never probed about that night, and in turn, I never asked what it was like for her to grow up with another family for part of her life. It was somewhat taboo in our community to visit a shrink, and we probably couldn't have afforded one anyway. Left without any other options, we just moved forward, putting one foot in front of the other.

Although we never discussed it, Kem understood my inner struggle, largely due to the fact that he had his own demons to fight, but he let me fight this battle on my own. Sometimes, when you're in the thick of it yourself, it's difficult to reach out and help the person suffering beside you. So, each night when we were younger and shared a room, Kem would lie quietly in his bed while I began my turbulent lullaby. I thought about my father and what he'd done to us, and the angry, hurting questions poured through my mind. "Why did you do this to me?" *Thump.* "What did I do wrong?" *Thump.* "Didn't you love me?" *Thump.* "How could you do this to me?" *Thump.*

Eventually, I'd drift off into a restless sleep. But never for long.

The next morning, I would awaken, drenched from embarrassing night sweats. However, I would feel relieved that I had defended myself against the evil thoughts that plagued me for one more night. For one more night, I escaped long enough to sleep a little. Every moment of rest, a moment without a thought of my father and his violence, however small, was a victory. I would climb out of bed, stretching my arms as I walked to the bathroom, reveling in my temporary peace. But that peace was short-lived, and vanished as soon as I looked into the mirror. Each morning, there was an absurd hope at the back of my mind that wished fervently to wake up and find my face to be normal. Instead, I was reminded of my reality, my scarred and disfigured reality. In the mirror I saw the same reflection over and over again, the truth shattering my few moments of fantastic hope at the beginning of each day.

Once, when I was seven, I couldn't wait to go outside and play on a Saturday, same as always. From my backyard, I could see my friend Junior and his father over at their house a few doors down from ours. On that particular day, Junior's father was teaching him how to shoot free throws.

"Remember to follow through," Junior's father said, his voice just audible from where I stood watching. I was jealous, my gaze envious as I watched the bond between father and son. I felt the hurt tears prick at the corners of my eyes, so I turned my thoughts inward and lost myself inside.

There are only ten seconds left in the game. We're down by one, and I have the ball—of course I have the ball. I'm driving hard to the basket, my feet pounding on the court. Although my father has been absent from my life for years, he's present now, cheering from the stands. His voice is louder than all the others and it pushes me to play harder. Defenders are collapsing, but I'm too quick. I cross over one defendant and pull up for the mid-range jumper. As the ball leaves my fingertips, the horn sounds. Everyone watches for those tense seconds, waiting to see what will happen. In? Or out? The ball swishes through the net and the room explodes in a wild cacophony of cheers. "Good shot!" my father calls, grinning proudly at me. "Thanks, Dad!" I call back to him, glowing in his admiration.

Suddenly, my mother's voice broke my daydream and pulled me back to reality.

"Get in here and clean your room!" she called to me from inside the house.

I turned obediently to head inside, but I paused for a moment, looking back at Junior's house. His father looked over in my direction and I immediately turned away. I didn't want to interrupt their time together, even for a second.

My father tried to kill us that night, but he did not win. I repeated this to myself often. What didn't kill me made me stronger, and while I feared no evil, I still feared something: failure. That's why I trained so hard, ran so fast, and studied so hard. I had overcome so much, fought so hard, and I couldn't let myself fail, not now, not after everything.

It was my senior year of high school and the football team and I were preparing for a big game. Not only because of our own drive to be the best team, but because it was the night the scouts were watching. I knew I had to perform as well as I could, because my mother couldn't afford to send me to college. Football could be my ticket; the fulfillment of the plan Mrs. Peterson had set for me by putting me in track 7-1.

After school, the rest of the team and I showed up for the pregame preparation. The coach was Coach Strickland, who was inducted into the South Carolina Football Hall of Fame after having won over three hundred football games, including several championships, and had coached at a few different high schools in South Carolina. Ridge Spring had the distinction of being his first head coaching job for football. Strickland, along with Coach Dale Rodgers who coached the defensive side of the ball, were master motivators. Our geography teacher, Coach McCormick, also served as the offensive coordinator for the coaching staff. Coach McCormick and I had a great relationship for two reasons: One, he had also served in the National Guard; and two, I never saw him have a bad day, and his positive energy was contagious. He encouraged me, even when I made some bonehead play or missed an assignment on the field.

As it turned out, Coach McCormick experienced something life changing after the football season ended that year. One night, he was riding in a car with some friends when they were in a serious accident. Coach McCormick was thrown from the car and paralyzed from the waist down. I used to think about him a lot, especially during long runs when I entered active duty military. In fact, I made it through many of those runs using him as my motivation, thinking of his positivity and drive. Coach McCormick still teaches at Ridge Spring as of this writing, and in spite of everything he has endured, his spirit has not changed since the football days.

Coach Strickland was born to be a coach. It was evident in his presence and demeanor, the way he talked to and inspired us. Before each game, he'd start by reminding us how fortunate we were to be able play football and represent our town.

"Play like champions tonight," he said. "Play for your families, play for the town, and—most importantly—play for each other. The time to play this game will pass in the blink of an eye, so try to cherish the moment. Let's play like Trojans tonight!"

That was all I needed to hear and the light bulb would click for me. I was ready to play.

"I need at least a hundred yards out of you tonight, James," Coach Strickland would tell me.

"Okay, Coach!"

It was the way he looked at me with those blazing eyes that made me want to run harder. The whole team would leave our gymnasium and head down along the outer entrance of the stadium that led to the main entrance where the attendees paid before entering. We had a war chant we'd shout while hitting our hands on our thigh pads twice before a clap. As a team, we made the walk past parents and visitors alike, walking deliberately towards the field, feeling like we were entering the Coliseum in Ancient Rome. Once we hit the field, we formed a circle with the captains in the center. Then, we would enter a countdown from ten, running in place and stopping on each number with one knee up, holding it for a second, until we counted all the way down to one. The surge of adrenaline was such a thrill, and Coach was right—those days did pass by so quickly.

We would run through a couple offensive plays, and after Coach had seen enough, we'd go through some defensive plays led by Coach Rodgers. Coach Rodgers had one of those strong coaching voices and reminded me of Bear Bryant, the legendary Alabama coach, in both style and appearance. He was tough on us, we had immense respect for him, and we would have rather walked through a field of thorn bushes than piss him off. His son, Mark, and I served as the inside and outside linebackers during our senior year and we were as close as brothers, nicknaming ourselves the "Ebony and Ivory Hit Squad." Mark understood football schemes, whereas I mainly played off instinct, and I learned a lot from him. At times, he could see what was coming and he'd let me know if they were coming to the right, or if I should watch the pass. Mark eventually became the head coach of Ridge Spring's football team, coaching them in the school's first and only championship game to date. We lost that game, but I was still awfully proud of Mark. I was actually in attendance for that game, and told him so when it was over.

On this particular night, the stands were filled with spectators and I felt myself shift into my zone, my game-time zone, and I funneled the crowd's energy into my own. I'd been on this field, just like this, so many times before, but that night was different. As I surveyed the stands and listened to the roar of the crowd, I made a mental phone call. I had opponents on the field, but on that night, it was my father that I played against in my head. It was between him and me.

You're like a nightmare, I told him in my mind. *You can't hurt me here in my space, on my field, because in this place, I call the shots. This is a special place God has given to me, my sanctuary away from you and what you did to us. I can hear the roar from the crowd, but I'm not here to prove myself to them, not even the scouts. I'm here to prove to you what I can do, not because of you, but in spite of you.*

I know it's not healthy, but I fed off of my father's negative energy. Thinking of him was like a smelling salt to get me hyped for the game. And for this game, I needed all the hype I could get.

I will pay you back for all the pain you caused us, I silently told my father. *I will take your negative energy and let it fuel me. Now the lights are on, and it's time. I'm the featured running back tonight and I won't be stopped by you.*

Coach was talking, but his voice was background noise to the call I was making.

"I need a hundred yards from you tonight," Coach told me. I nodded, but I was only partially listening. Instead, I was looking out at the stands, picturing my father sitting in the middle, and it made me angry. I was ready, because every yard I ran, every tackle I made, I knew all of those would help me slay my father.

You didn't destroy me, Daddy, I told him. *You made me stronger.*

When the game ended in a victory for us, the crowd went wild. The coaches from the opposing team jogged onto the field, and I pulled off my helmet so I could shake their hands. The coaches were smiling as they came towards me until they got close enough to get a proper look at my face. Then, their expressions shifted in a way that was so familiar and still so painful to me. Suddenly, my 120 rushing yards and ten tackles didn't matter anymore. The opposing coaches couldn't see past my face. After I shook their hands, I saw them whisper to one another. I couldn't hear their words, but I didn't have to. I knew they were wondering about what happened to my face, where my scars had come from, and so on and so on. Everyone is curious and everyone is unoriginal, asking the same thing over and over like a broken record. But

I didn't have long to think about the coaches because suddenly there was a reporter standing before me, pen and paper in hand, ready to record my answers. Seeing the reporter made my game winning high fade, like the Incredible Hulk changing back into Bruce Banner.

"Great game tonight!" the reporter exclaimed.

"Thanks," I said, suddenly shy.

"To what do you attribute your success?" the reporter asked, pen poised and ready. "You were playing like a man possessed!"

"The coaches really prepared us this week and the line did some excellent blocking," I replied, feeling shyer by the second. I always feel nervous when I talk in front of people, especially if they're holding a pen and a notepad in their hands, or worse, a video camera. I always feel so awkward, like I just want everyone to turn around and stop looking at me. Whenever I was interviewed, I did my best to keep my answers short to speed up the dreadful process.

"Well, I'm sure your parents are proud of you," the reporter said with a grin as he jotted down a few notes.

"My mom is," I agreed. I thought of my mental phone call to my father before the game. *You're not invited to this part*, I thought. *You don't get to share in my victory I earned in spite of you.*

"Well, good game," the reporter said, flipping his notebook closed. "Stay healthy."

"Thanks," I said, grateful to end the conversation, and I headed towards the locker room to join my team.

CHAPTER 13

The College Years: South Carolina State

I applied to and was accepted to one school, South Carolina State College (now University). I had gone there once to visit with my girlfriend during our senior year in high school. SC State is a historically black college and was only an hour by car from where I grew up, which was perfect for me so I could stay close to my mother. Although I had not been offered an athletic scholarship, my dreams of playing football still had a flicker of hope when SC State offered me an invitation to walk on the team.

However, things didn't work out with football, and after only three weeks into my freshman year, the weight was too heavy for me. The thought of not being a part of the football team, Ronda and me facing our relationship and deciding to be the best of friends instead, and the contrast between military and college life had left me feeling confused and unprepared for the college experience at that point in time. I didn't make a list of pros and cons or seek out some mentor, because there was no one I felt I could turn to in order to help me make my decision. I just felt a certain way and reacted. I packed up my stuff in our old burnt-orange Dodge Aspen that my mom let me drive after she married my stepfather, and I didn't look back.

I probably had about forty or fifty dollars to my name, so I dropped about twenty dollars in the tank and headed down towards the entrance of campus. I passed Dukes Gym and headed up slowly past the student center, avoiding anyone I might know. I glanced to the right as I slowed for the speed bump, passing Bradham and Manning Halls that housed female students, including Ronda. I'd told her I was leaving, but I'd said it was due to my financial aid mix-up. I knew differently, and she probably did too, but she didn't contradict me. I looked upon some students with envy at the energy and excitement in their faces over the possibilities of their futures. Was I making a mistake? Probably.

I eased past Washington Dining Hall where all the kids hung out. I looked over briefly, but turned my gaze back towards the front. I was almost off campus as I passed the infamous Lowman Hall that housed the male students. If there was any dorm on campus that compared to *Animal House*, it was Lowman Hall. They had their own social club, with Low Phi Low shirts to boot. I smiled briefly as I passed the MLK Auditorium on my right, and then I arrived at the entrance. I stared at the bulldog statue for what seemed like the final time, and drove off the South Carolina State campus, leaving behind my hopes and dreams, as well as those of my mother.

Ridge Spring was only an hour away from SC State, but the drive from Orangeburg in that old car felt like it took forever as I found myself lost in thought. I was worried how I would be perceived by people back home and I felt like a failure inside, a feeling that left me numb, like the first time I'd failed my driver's license test.

"Did you pass?"

"What happened?"

"I thought you knew how to drive?"

However, if I'd thought those questions had been difficult to face, they were nothing like what I expected to experience upon returning home from college, my degree unfinished. My mom was not one for pity parties, so I knew I had to come up with a plan, and quick. I'd initially left home with some superlatives, speaking at my high school graduation about the possibilities of our futures. I had gone from completing my military training with dreams of playing football for SC State, but there I was, back in my home town without a solid plan. But we do what we know, and I knew how to work, so I knew I'd have to find a job.

After I arrived back in Ridge Spring, I headed to the post office to check for our mail and I happened to run into the bus superintendent from my high school.

"What are you doing home?" Ms. Fullham asked, surprised. "I thought you were in college."

I felt humiliated as I scrambled for a plausible excuse.

"I decided to take a semester off to get my head together," I said, blurting out the first thing that popped into my mind.

"Well, I need a bus driver," she said. "Would you like to drive your old route and make a little money until you decide what you want to do?"

"Sure!" I accepted enthusiastically, grateful to have some kind of plan in place for myself.

Driving the bus again didn't fill my days, but it did give me a lot of time for reflection, as well as time for my new pastime: watching *Days of Our Lives*. I was enthralled by the romance of Bo and Hope. I would never let on to my friends that I was an old-school, hopeless romantic type of dude who wanted to have the kind of love that Bo and Hope portrayed. It reminded me of my *Little House on the Prairie* days, in the way that if the guys knew I was holed up in the house watching soaps, my street credit would have been in a deficit. I now know that there were many undercover male soap watchers, but I didn't at the time. *Days of Our Lives* was my drug of choice and I was caught up in the fairytale life between those two characters. Hope was beautiful, and to me, she just jumped off the screen. But it was more than that; watching soaps took my mind off of the realities of my life, if only for the duration of an episode. Once the credits rolled, I still had to face the fact that I was a bus driver and that this would be my full-time occupation until I came up with a plan.

I also had to deal with the comments people made when they saw I was home and driving the bus instead of sitting in class at SC State. Junior was my best friend, but he was also my biggest critic when it came to driving that bus.

"You were the football star, and now you're driving a bus, man?" he'd ask. I didn't want to admit it, but his words stung. Some of the parents in town who had watched me play sports also made comments.

"I thought you were going to play sports or something in college," they'd say, either in church or just in passing around town.

"Not right now," I'd reply.

No one ever said it around my mother because they knew she'd rip them a new one. I took it all in, the positive and the negative, good advice and snarky comments, and I eventually used it all as fuel for my life.

These four months turned out to be some of the most pivotal of my life because I learned so much about humility. I often thought back to the conversation my mother had had with me when I was a kid in the car on that day on the side of the road. I'd been feeling sorry for myself because of my burns and my mother had put a stop to it. *The world doesn't owe you anything, James! You are burned and you wear those scars, but so what? What are you going to do, quit on life?* Those words echoed through my mind every day as I dealt with my peers ridiculing me for driving that bus again. *Quit on life?* I thought.

I reflected on my mother's life and the struggles she'd endured, the sacrifices she'd made. She had been a teenaged mother who had witnessed domestic violence in her own childhood. As an adult, she had experienced more domestic violence and wore her scars as daily reminders, just like I did. My mom had lost so much, including her own mother, and on top of that, she had to deal with the pain of watching me and my struggles. I couldn't quit. Was I being selfish with my thoughts and doubts? I realized that maybe this journey wasn't even about me as much as it was about ensuring that my mom's sacrifices didn't fall on broken promises.

Over the course of my childhood, I'd witnessed my mom on her knees, praying to God for what seemed like hours. I'd seen the tears she'd cried and my hope was to change the emotions behind those tears. I wanted that waterfall to transform from sadness to joy. I needed to do that for her, and the only way I could do it was by channeling whatever that prayer was that she sent up every morning into my life's goals. I asked God to give me her list and show me the way. *Give me strength,* I asked of Him. *My mom has already challenged me so many years ago not to quit, so help me. If you are real, take this journey and put that weight back on me when I'm ready.*

My shame and disappointment during those first few weeks began to shift into introspective thought and motivation. Being out of school, I now had time to look around my town—*really* look at it—and talk to some of the elders, such as Mr. Mobley, who shared stories with me of the really tough times. Mr. Mobley was a veteran who knew I'd joined the Guard, and he decided to give me some advice. I'd told him that I enjoyed the military, but I didn't know what I wanted to do with my life and I hadn't decided to go back to college yet. He didn't mince words.

"Get your butt back in school and don't ever come back, except to visit."

I thought that was stern and maybe a little harsh, but I could see the seriousness in his face. I also talked with some of my brother's former classmates who now earned a living in the factories or working different trades, like the barbershop. The barbershop had always served as a place much larger than just getting a haircut; it was a place to talk politics, sports, relationships, and just life in general. Windell Davis owned the local barbershop, his second location within a twenty-mile radius, and one of my brother's friends, Reggie, worked there. Reggie was a family friend on whom I could lean for advice. I had the type of hair texture that needed a weekly haircut, which served me well because it gave me an opportunity to laugh and get my weekly education about life. I would listen to stories from those either coming off shift work or getting ready to report to the factory. They'd share with me the stories of falling asleep at the wheel after a twelve-hour shift from being so tired, or working a dead-end job for very little pay. Some of the guys wanted do-overs, but they had families of their own and needed those jobs, meager though they might have been. The guys joked about their work anecdotes, but they were serious in their advice to me and other young people as they stressed to us the importance of education.

Another of my brother's closest friends, Kenny Leaphart, still lived in the area. He would always tell me to go back to school and get my education.

"Don't stay around here," he'd tell me.

I loved my hometown, but I was starting to understand that I couldn't hold on to what it used to be for me. My days of playing high school football and basketball were over, and I could no longer live off of the high of those cheering crowds. That chapter had closed and it wasn't about me anymore. It never was, as I came to realize. It was time for me to grow up. As I digested all this information, I spent my free time talking to people, reading books, and attending high school sports games on Fridays.

Right after I graduated high school in 1988, my little brother Maurice was born, and my mother married my stepfather, who lived literally a stone's throw across a field from our old house. The truth of the matter was that my mom had begun spending most of her time over at my stepfather's house during my senior year, but it became official after the wedding. She moved in with him, and Lynnette had to go as well, which she hated, but she was only in ninth grade and had to toe the line. Their moving out left our old house empty, which meant I had it all to myself. I was self-sufficient, and had been for many years because my mother had taught us all how to cook and clean and iron our own clothes, but I still spent time at both houses—which meant double chores at times. She was still my mom and, besides, I had a new baby brother and I needed to see him and spend time with him.

Maurice was a complete joy to me. I was eighteen at the time and our age difference was great enough to where Maurice could've been my son, but it was so cool having a baby brother. I couldn't wait to teach him how to play basketball and nurture him and mentor him. It was just so fun and new to have him around. He was different in so many ways from Kem, Lynnette, and me, and the way our childhoods had played out. Maurice had stability with a mother *and* a father. He had three older siblings who would support him in all aspects, including financially. He wouldn't have to carry the same emotional scars that were etched on his siblings' hearts, and times were different, even in Ridge Spring.

When Maurice got older, he joined the school chess team. We played a lot of checkers growing up, and there was our baby brother, on the chess team! His life was different than ours had been and I was happy about that for him. I wanted to shield Maurice from the unnecessary things in life, just as I do for my own kids. Kem and I spent time in the streets of Philadelphia during the summers and we hung out in the country with different folks. Maurice never experienced that life, and that's exactly the way I wanted it. Kem, on the other hand, believed in toughness and thought the only way to truly get it was from the streets. I thought that the streets could kill you and I didn't want that for Maurice. I spent as much time with him as possible, and despite the questions and lingering stares I got from folks in my hometown when they saw me driving a bus, I loved being with my baby brother.

My mother, however, was less than enthused by my current choices and began to challenge me in ways that only a mother can by making it a little more difficult to sit around the house and get too comfortable.

"Take out the trash."

"Wash and dry the clothes."

"Cook for yourself."

"Pay for your own food."

"Don't take long showers and run up the water bill."

"Don't talk on the phone for too long."

Finally, I felt I had to talk to her and ask what was going on.

"What's going on, Mom?" I asked. "Don't you love me anymore? You trying to kick me out?"

I had been half joking, but she didn't answer. My mother saw my scars, and yet she didn't. She always wanted to toughen me up and prepare me for the real world and she pushed me like no one else did. She never said it out loud, but I knew she was disappointed that I was home from college. I later understood that the way she pushed me was fueled in part by preparing me for the next step in my life, as well as by frustration with my choices. I started thinking about my mom's attitude towards me since I'd returned home, along with all of the comments I'd heard from childhood friends and adults about me quitting college. This wasn't the right place for me.

During the spring semester of 1989, I re-enrolled at SC State. I packed up my belongings on that cold January day and headed back to Orangeburg. I parked behind Bethea Hall, the same dorm I'd left a semester earlier, and headed inside. Just inside the main entrance, the same head resident assistant from before was standing there, watching me walk in with my stuff.

"You back?" he asked. At first I was surprised he recognized me, but then I remembered that I had an unforgettable face.

"I told you I was coming back," I said, giving him the Ridge Spring grin.

"Welcome back, bulldog!" he exclaimed, matching my smile. I beamed with pride because I knew that although I hadn't begun taking classes again yet, I was officially an SC State bulldog and I was here to stay.

When I restarted my matriculation at SC State that spring, I majored in business management with the laser-like focus and maturity of someone who had seen some things and experienced life a little, and there was no turning back. Football was still in my system, a lingering bug I couldn't quite shake, but my attention was turned elsewhere. When I'd visited the office during registration, I'd noticed an ROTC sign and decided to go check it out. As soon as I entered the building, I felt like I'd found kindred spirits.

Army people all speak the same language, and at times it can be weird to hear grown men talking to one another and saying words like "hooah" and "tracking" and know exactly what they're talking about. The term "hooah" is universal army speak that all soldiers know, a battle cry that means "anything and everything except no." The mannerisms and the uniforms just do something to a soldier. I knew I was in the right spot, and enrolled in ROTC at my first opportunity. It felt good to be in an environment that was relatable and measurable, although there were still unknowns about becoming an army officer. There was another guy from the neighboring town of Edgefield by the name of Bruce Lee who began school with me. Bruce was a standout athlete and we were joined by another guy from Greenville named Hardtime.

"What's your real name?" I asked.

"Hardtime, but I go by 'Hard' for short!"

Our group was rounded out by Derrick, PJ, and EZ from Batesburg, and we all hung out together, young and green. We went to breakfast and lunch together as much as our class schedules allowed, we played basketball and Tecmo Bowl until the early morning, and we talked about girlfriends back home and the pretty girls on campus.

"What happened to your face, man?" Derrick asked once when we were all hanging out.

"I was in a house fire," I said lightly, giving my standard answer. Broad details only, nothing overly specific.

"I bet that was hot," one of the other guys said, and we all laughed, using the humor to keep the conversation moving and from delving too deeply.

"Yep, it was hot," I agreed. "But I survived."

"Cool," Derrick said, not one to pry.

Bethea Hall was full of athletes of all kinds, mainly freshmen and sophomores; football players, basketball players, and ROTC cadets. The dorm wasn't exclusively athletic, but athletes did make up the overwhelming majority. There were regular guys, too, but no women, as we didn't have co-ed dorms at the time. As a result, a bunch of young men in one place could only result in one thing: madness. The saying went that if you could survive Bethea Hall, you could make it anywhere. It was obviously the first time most kids were away from home without adult supervision and it really showed. During my time at Fort Polk, I'd become accustomed to the pristine military life with waxed floors and corners on the bed sheets, clean toilets and showers, the works. Bethea Hall, on the other hand, was…different. Especially on the weekends. Stray pizza boxes and beer bottles were the least of it. Once, I remember some of the guys came into my room, laughing uncontrollably. In between guffaws, they gasped that I should come out to the hallway. I'd heard a scream a few moments earlier, but I'd assumed someone was just clowning around as usual. As it turned out, someone had squirted baby oil on the floor at the entrance. One of the guys in the hall had been heading down to the shower when he'd hit the slick spot and went ass up on the ground. He was cussing so loud that we wanted to find the culprit for him, but nobody was fessing up. The fall hadn't been soft and the guy was going to feel it in the morning, but the whole thing had been hilarious, and perfectly encapsulated what it was like to live in Bethea Hall.

In the hall, we played Spades, slapped dominoes around, and watched sports together. Amongst the residents were bootleg barbers that could cut as well as the professionals for only about $2.50. Mike Tyson was the baddest man on the planet during those days, and we all watched *A Different World*. I felt like I'd found a new life and a new identity, with SC State as the perfect segue. The community was small and predominantly made up of African American kids from mostly small towns, but everyone from all over the country had congregated at this one place that felt like home. We became family and those guys accepted me as I was and treated me just as Kem and Lynnette treated me. We laughed, argued, and hung out like family. I managed to breeze through my first semester back before returning home for the summer break to work, which would turn out to be one of my toughest summers at home.

Around my area in Ridge Spring, we had chicken farms that sprang up and they paid good money. I decided to try my hand at working at the plants, and once I was hired, it was my job to clean up and dump the chicken heads into the truck after the other parts of the bird were processed. I wore rubber boots and gloves, as well as a mask, to quell the smell, but there was only so much I could do without strapping a Christmas-tree air freshener to my nose. I had grown up working in the peach fields and was used to hard labor, but working on the chicken farm was a whole other level. When I showed up to work every day, I had the distinct feeling that I didn't belong. It was like showing up to basketball practice and finding the dream team on the court—the original team with Michael, Magic, and Larry—and just feeling like you're in the way on the court. I felt like the other workers gave me looks that said, "You don't belong here, homeboy! I don't know who made you come here, but you don't belong. You don't know what you're doing; you are taking someone's job who really needs it, and you need to go home." In other words, I felt very unwelcome.

I had been pressing forward in my job for about a month, when one evening, I went to dump a load of chicken heads in the truck and the lip of the plastic can rolled off the edge of the truck. I hadn't gotten the can high enough to push it over and the plastic tub of heads spilled all over the floor. The other workers looked over at me, disgusted, as if I was costing them money by slowing their pace and dropping the ball (or chicken heads, as it were) on my phase of production. I immediately looked around for a shovel to start cleaning up the mess. As I scanned the floor, looking at the heads, it suddenly hit me what kind of work I was really doing and a wave of nausea washed over me. I swallowed it down and managed to shovel a little before I had to stop and go outside for some air. The rest of the cleanup continued in that fashion, shoveling a little before having to retreat outside for fresh air untainted by decapitated chicken heads. I completed my shift and after I clocked out, I found my friend, Ricky Brunson, who was also part of the crew, and told him I was done.

"Cool," he said.

"No, really," I insisted. "I'm done. Please tell the foreman that he won't see me back here again."

Years earlier, I'd been removed from my tractor job in the peach fields after getting stuck in the mud. Now, for the first time in my life, I had quit a job. I didn't want to admit it, but this job had bested me, and not only did I quit, I stopped eating chicken for a few months after that job. The smell of chicken made me feel nauseated, which was a little disappointing since I'd previously loved chicken. Eventually, I managed to get past the chicken heads on the floor to resume my prior eating habits, but that job also helped me to narrow my possible future professions down a little. Working on a chicken farm was definitely not for me. College, however, had opened up more options for me, and I decided that I would either give this football dream of mine one more try, or I would really dedicate myself to being a soldier.

I had been working out pretty hard with the hopes of walking onto the football team in the upcoming fall semester. I'd discussed it with the coaches prior to leaving for the summer and my goal was to report for spring ball. I still had my obligations to the National Guard, but I'd earned enough money from the chicken plant, as well as during my drill weekends, to sustain me. On top of that, I was also receiving my GI Bill check, so I had the time to really focus on conditioning before spring ball, which led me to get into what was the best shape of my life since basic training. I felt strong and fast, but I didn't really know why I wanted to play football anymore. I still loved the game, but was I passionate about it? No, not really, but I had to at least try to get it out of my system.

Therefore, I packed up my things in Ridge Spring and made the drive to Orangeburg to report to football camp. I checked into Bethea Hall, my old stomping grounds, but the head resident told me to report to the finance office. As it turned out, I had failed to leave a deposit for a room and didn't have a place to stay.

"You can stay with me until you get your stuff straight," one of the other walk-on candidates offered when I explained my situation.

"Thanks, but that's cool. I'm going home, man!" I said, feeling somewhat lightened.

"Are you sure?" he asked skeptically.

"Yeah, man, I'm good," I said. "I was waiting on a sign, and I got one."

He didn't understand, but I did. My football dreams were over, and that was okay. My heart wasn't in it anymore and I knew it. I'd missed my window of opportunity coming out of high school and probably would have gotten myself hurt trying to prove a point. Were there days after that when I wished I'd tried? Yes, of course, but I ultimately knew I'd made the right decision.

When I returned to Bethea again, I was stuck in between classes by taking that semester off, but it wasn't like high school, where your class level in school really meant something. I began to take ROTC seriously, and during my second semester, I was able to skip Military Science I (MSI) and jump ahead to Military Science II (MSII). MSI was an introduction to the army that covered topics like military courtesy, history, and basic skills, such as first aid, rifle marksmanship, land navigation, and so forth; pretty much all the topics I'd already covered during my training at Fort Polk. MSII really expanded on the topics of MSI, but the class also included topics like tactics, troop leading procedures, basics of operations orders, and ethics.

Unbeknownst to me, I was actually enrolled in one of the top ROTC programs in the country. The legendary SC State ROTC

Bulldog Brigade was known as the black West Point of the South and had produced more black generals than any other school. The program consisted of about four- to five hundred cadets during this time. I was majoring in business, but as my involvement increased in the ROTC program, it felt like if military science had been a major, I would have chosen it, or rather the program would have chosen us due to the time devoted to it. It was a natural fit for me because of my training, and due to that training, I was able to excel in the program.

My circle of friends remained the same until the second semester of my sophomore year in college. We all began to find our footing in school and started to take our own paths. Some dropped out, one found his soulmate for that year, and still others transferred or pledged different fraternities. We saw each other intermittently on campus because it was still a family atmosphere, but we each formed new circles. By that point, I had changed my major twice. I had begun as a business major with hopes of managing a business or running my own someday. However, my mom had a discussion with me about my possible opportunities in that field and convinced me to change to elementary education. Years earlier, I'd applied to work at a McDonald's in Aiken and they'd refused to hire me. When it happened, my mother had been much more affected by this than I had. She knew that the hiring manager would have had a problem with me standing at the counter and taking orders from customers because of my burns and that really pissed her off. As a result, she tried to shield me from the embarrassment of that episode again by steering me into a softer, more acceptable field, so I changed to elementary education. Then I thought about my passion in life and changed once again to physical education. I loved sports and understood the teaching aspect and figured it would be the perfect alternative if my military path didn't work out for some reason.

As part of our ROTC classes, we had to participate in a laboratory class where we learned the intricacies of the military structure to include drill and ceremony and common tasks. The purpose of drill is to enable a commander or non-commissioned officer to move his unit from one place to another in an orderly manner; to aid in disciplinary training by instilling habits of precision and response to the leader's orders, and to provide for the development of all soldiers in the practice of commanding troops. The primary value of ceremonies is to render honors, preserve tradition, and to stimulate Esprit de Corps. The Drill and Ceremonies (D&C) training included how to march, stay in-step, maneuver your squad of soldiers, and all the regular commands required of a military formation. The common tasks training included learning military chain of command, the use of military radios, combat life saver (first aid, buddy care), and marksmanship. These drills, lectures and classes were, for the most part, boring to me because I had experienced the real thing at Fort Polk, although not from a leadership standpoint. For one particular lecture, we had to report to the MLK Auditorium to listen to a guest speaker. We all marched up from the field to the auditorium and filed into the room to find our seats. We had been waiting for some time when someone called the room to their feet.

"Ladies and gentlemen, I would like to introduce one of our own. He is a fellow alumnus and graduate of the ROTC program at SC State. He previously served as the 21D commander, South Korea. Ladies and gentlemen, Lieutenant General Doctor!"

Most of the sophomores didn't understand the magnitude of what we were witnessing at the time. They really didn't understand the rank and were just standing there to earn those two credits, but I got it. I couldn't believe it! There he was, a three-star general, as well as a SC State graduate, in the flesh! I was shocked that our school had produced a three-star general and that he was taking the time to speak to us. I hung onto his every word as he spoke about his humble beginnings and what State meant to him. He discussed the importance of us training hard and giving our very best. He talked about commitment to the program and to one another. He challenged us to be at the forefront of leadership. I felt so proud in that moment! Before I heard about General Colin Powell, we had our own legendary hero in LTG Doctor, and he was there, speaking to us. It was the speech I needed to hear in order to turn that corner and fully commit myself to the military.

Going into my junior year, I signed my contract and I was 100 percent committed to the program. Finishing out ROTC and becoming a military officer seemed like the perfect fit for me. I had originally dreamed of working in a corporate setting at first before settling into education as a major, but becoming an officer would give me an opportunity to blend physical education with the world of leading and managing people. I knew from my experience of being an enlisted soldier that the military accepted me in spite of my scars. I would be evaluated based on academics, physical fitness, and my ability to lead; I was up to the challenge. I had found my career path, but I really had to dedicate myself to earning an active duty commission. It wasn't a given and we had a large corps of cadets competing for the same honor. Therefore, I knew that to be included in the program, I really had to devote myself to being the very best in all aspects of college. I had to be all I could be, so to speak.

I lived in Mays Hall between my sophomore and junior years of college and it was during that year that I had the great pleasure of rooming with a gentleman by the name of M. Christopher Brown II. Chris was no ordinary college student; he was a gifted individual with the ability to teach and lecture like a tenured professor as a college sophomore. We were an unlikely pair in many ways. For example, I lived like a college student in regards to the upkeep of my room. I at least made my bed in the morning, but Chris was different. His side of the room looked as if he expected a visit from the college president every day. He reminded me of Carlton from *The Fresh Prince of Bel Air*. Chris even wore silk pajamas with a burgundy bathrobe at night. He'd lecture me about cleanliness, structure, and order, but instead of telling Chris to mind his own business, I took note. He'd stay up late and prepare speeches, as he was often invited to speak at various events. I'd often awake to him reciting his speech and he'd have me critique a line or two in order to fine hone his oration.

"Sounds good to me!" I'd say.

Chris would glance over at me with his glasses perched on his nose as if to say, "Stay focused, young lad." I was impressed with Chris's abilities and knew that someday he would serve as president of a college.

"I like you, James!" Chris told me one day after a few weeks of rooming together. "You have a bright future ahead of you."

"Thanks, Chris," I said as if I was his pupil. The following week, Chris handed me an invitation for an event he planned to host on campus, a group talk for men—invitation only—and I, of all people, had been included.

I arrived at the event, which was held in a small conference room and consisted of about ten smart guys. I'd seen and knew a few of them from classes, but I felt completely out of place, like a football player in full gear sitting in the locker room at halftime with the basketball team. It was awkward. This was long before my official etiquette class I attended with my fraternity, so I wasn't prepared at all. Chris had sparkling wine and real wine glasses, cheese and crackers, the works. Chris began the discussion with a brief but eloquent introduction and then announced the discussion topic for the evening: the state of black men and the urgency and importance of higher education amongst minorities.

At this point, I was scanning the room and watching to see if it was time to grab a cracker and some cheese before embarking on a response or solution to a question that was surely coming around the room. It was the first time I'd delved into a critical thinking forum, and I watched Chris work the room, pulling out ideas from each person in attendance. I looked at him in amazement, wondering where he'd gotten such intellect at such a young age. There was no pretense as he jotted down responses, and he didn't try to put me on the spot, for which I was grateful. Afterwards, he shared with me that I must be able to blend into any environment and be prepared to discuss any subject.

"Reading and being well-rounded are essential to our success," he told me.

As the months and years passed, we both moved on to different dorms and eventually moved off the yard. However, I never forgot Chris and his lessons. He reminded me of Laddie Howard, who became my fraternity brother (or perhaps the other way around, since Laddie pledged before I did). Laddie had received a four-year Thurgood Marshall Scholarship and was destined for law school. Like Chris, Laddie was polished as well, and mature beyond his years. He dressed like he fell off the cover of *GQ* magazine, and had the thick Billie Dee Williams voice to match. I'd seen his mannerisms before in my childhood friend, JB, and I knew Laddie had experienced a different upbringing than I had. Laddie even walked cool; it almost seemed unreal for a person at SC State to move like that, but he did, and I noticed how authentic and genuine he was with other people.

I didn't own a scarf at that point in my life, but Laddie had a couple that he perfectly draped to compliment his sport coats in the winter. I believe I only had a black one, a blue, and maybe a gray suit during those days, and fortunately, I had my ROTC dress greens to round it off and keep me safe during some of the meetings. I was impressed that Laddie already had a wardrobe of different blends and threads. *It must be an upper crust thing,* I often thought to myself. Laddie was destined to become a lawyer; he had the DNA, and I admired his intellect. Between Chris and Laddie, I had these two figures in my space and it was like I had an opportunity to observe Denzel Washington and Wesley Snipes perform in their element, but it was no act. Chris Brown, the future college president, and Laddie Howard. The latter's name carried substance with the uniqueness of its pronunciation.

"Hi, I'm Laddie," he would say during an introduction with the confidence of Jim Brown, staring directly at you as he shook your hand with assertive firmness. It was as if one had to rehearse just to introduce oneself to Laddie, expecting a grade at the end. The saying goes that iron sharpens iron, and my dull edges began to take shape by the mere fortune of rubbing against these two metals of young men.

Laddie cast a vote for me, and I became his fraternity brother, allowing me the opportunity to observe him during functions and meetings. He was a natural and gifted speaker like Chris, but with Laddie it appeared to take less effort as he spoke with smooth, clear, concise precision. There wasn't a word out of place when he spoke, and I figured I'd better get a thesaurus or something in order to keep up. The concept of being well-rounded began to make sense to me, especially as a future officer in the US Army. In short, Laddie Howard impressed me. We as people often let jealousy or pride interfere with our growth, but I recognized that I needed Laddie, as well as so many others, as a guide to help me grow into the human being I was supposed to be. He unknowingly impacted my life and I need to acknowledge that. I felt a sense of pride at the fact that I was in the presence of these great future leaders and my compass was now set on a path of excellence as I rubbed shoulders with these men, studying them and leaning on them for advice and guidance. I came to SC State as an empty vessel and I left college with invaluable cargo to carry forward with me on my journey.

I was fortunate to have had these remarkable men enter my life at the right time, and although some may call it luck, I call it fate. As of this writing, Chris currently serves as the president of Kentucky State University. Before that, he was the president of the historically black land-grant institution, Alcorn State University. He was highly regarded during his time at Alcorn, with his efforts to increase enrollment, which grew to more than four thousand for the very first time in the college's history. Under Chris's leadership in 2013, Alcorn unveiled a statue of Medgar Wiley Evers, an alumnus and civil rights activist best known for serving as the first NAACP secretary in Mississippi. Evers worked tirelessly against segregation and for the enforcement of opportunities for African Americans, including voting rights. He was later assassinated by a member of the Ku Klux Klan, mere hours after President John F. Kennedy's nationally televised Civil Rights Address, at the age of thirty-seven. The construction of this monument during Chris's time at Alcorn State University was the largest of its kind in the world, and later that same year, the Center for HBCU Media Advocacy named Chris the HBCU Male President of the Year.

Laddie became an attorney and now designs high-quality leather bags under the L Howard brand. His gifts were apparent over twenty years ago to those of us who knew him, and his potential is still unlimited. I now understand the sentiment of how attending a four-year institution of higher learning can help one become well-rounded. The academic pursuit now seems a bit like an afterthought in regards to the total experience as a whole. The relationships of SC State, the family atmosphere, the idealists, all of us searching for and dreaming of a better life as we stood on the shoulders of our ancestors who prayed and sacrificed to make our journey possible—it all makes perfect sense to me now.

JUNIOR YEAR

My junior year really brought college into full focus for me. Football games were a treat, especially the halftime show, with the battle of the bands and the tailgating. Sporting events at an HBCU are like adding hot sauce to your fried chicken, spicy and full of flavor. We usually left the event feeling good inside, as if we had experienced one of our favorite artists live for the first time. SC State had become home for me. I spent less time traveling back home to Ridge Spring on the weekends and more time becoming fully ingrained in the college experience and everything it had to offer. I was never a big party guy, partially because I couldn't dance and partially because I didn't really like crowds very much. However, I still went to my share of parties and tried to slide a little bit.

There was something that intrigued me for some time throughout the years. Bonding had always been an issue, and I would never let anyone get too close to me. I had my lunch buddies and cadet network, but other than my core friends back home, I kept my circle tight at school. Fraternities and sororities dominated the scene at SC State and Greek life had begun to intrigue me. As with most historically black colleges and universities, there were numerous houses to choose from, and if you were so honored, one would accept you. I wrestled through my adolescent years, trying to rationalize how a father could harm his son. As a result, it affected my ability to bond and connect with other male figures over the years. However, there was a group of young men that intrigued me.

I had received my football recruiting letter from SC State years earlier, but it hadn't been in the cards for me. My football dreams faded away eventually, but still I yearned for that male bonding, and God smiled on me once again when I saw a particular group of men standing together on campus. I began to observe these well-dressed young men hanging out together, their conversations differing from those around them when they spoke of pursuits of excellence. They walked and talked with just a touch of swagger, and on Fridays, they wore black and gold. One of the guys, Derrick Corbett, and I had been friends throughout the years and he had pledged Alpha Phi Alpha a year earlier. I had admired his intellect and his ability to lead during ROTC training. I looked up to him and leaned on him when times were tough. I observed him often, both up close and from a distance, and he was the real deal.

All of the Alpha men possessed the same qualities from what I could see. I heard of their mentoring programs and how they volunteered at the Boys Club, I knew about the reading programs at the elementary and middle schools, and I saw them in classroom settings. I could see something unique about each of the fraternity brothers that I recognized in myself. They wanted the same thing in life as I did: to be great. I realized that I wanted—no, *needed*—to be a part of this group. However, first things first: My priority was my ROTC commission, along with excelling academically to maintain my standing in the program. I had goals of becoming an active duty army officer and I needed to train hard prior to summer camp. Summer camp was an ROTC advanced camp where I would go to compete against the best and brightest in the country. Our score at camp, combined with our academic standing and ROTC ranking, would determine whether or not we would receive an active duty commission. I really, really needed active duty. It meant so many things to all of us young cadets. It meant a full-time career with a real paycheck, traveling to see the world beyond the roads of South Carolina, and it meant a future that could change our circumstances and allow us to support our families. We all prepared ourselves accordingly.

We arrived at Fort Lewis, Washington, at different times, grouped according to rank. I had my strengths and weaknesses, but I still felt confident. We had a strong program full of talented cadets and we were trained by a cadre who prepared us as if we were going off to war. This was after Desert Storm, and our cadre instilled in us the seriousness of serving. I arrived there during the summer of 1991 and it was raining cats and dogs, which really set the tone for the conditions there. When I arrived, I expected to have other SC State guys in my cycle, but I was alone. There were men and women of what seemed like every race who were ready to compete during the six weeks we had to show that we had what it took to earn those butter bars and, ultimately, a commission.

We lost one or two of our group due to medical reasons, and a few during the PT test, of all things. *How could you fail the PT test?* I wondered. We were chosen for different leadership positions and evaluated on our performances. We went through obstacle courses and water survival training, we marched and trained in the field, and we patrolled and flew in helicopters. Lack of sleep and stressful evaluations led to some arguments throughout the weeks with peers, which was to be expected in the close quarters. Our cadre was always observing us, trying to find weaknesses or strengths, and finally, we concluded and were given our scores, one by one. I distinctly remember being called into the room before one of the cadre members. The scores were given by numerical value until the number three, and then they went in succession, starting at 3A, 3B, 3C, 4, and 5. The number five guaranteed an active duty commission, typically with your choice of army branch, such as medical service, infantry, etc.

"Relax," the cadre said, picking up on my obvious nerves when I entered the room. I nodded. "Do you want active duty, Cadet Scott?"

I thought it was a strange question, considering where I was and what we'd all been working towards, but I answered in the affirmative. He looked down at the paper and wrote the score as if he'd just made his selection and he hadn't already calculated it long before I'd walked into the room.

"3A, Cadet Scott. Congratulations, and I wish you well."

I kept my stoic composure as I thanked him before I left the room, and retreated to my bunk. I wasn't sure what to think of that score. It wasn't a five or four, but it also wasn't a 3B or C. Had I done enough to earn that coveted active duty spot? I wouldn't know until months later after I returned to campus.

I had volunteered to go to airborne school after camp, so I was immediately shipped off to Fort Benning for training. I knew I had to be crazy for signing up to jump out of airplanes, but there I was with a whole bunch of other crazy people, so I was in good company. I weighed about 180 pounds at the time and was a little thick in bones to be jumping out of an airplane. Little did I know that the five jumps would be the easy part. We ran all over Fort Benning that first week, and I had to call on God every morning to make it through those runs. No one had warned me about all the running because I probably would have just sat that one out and gone bare chested, but there I was, and pride alone kept me in those runs. And it wasn't like we were running over flat ground; there were towers and sand pits to simulate jumping and landing, over and over and over again. I knew then that I had to have some type of imbalance, because who in their right mind would have signed up for this? But I was ingrained in the army culture and I figured what the heck, why not try it? So try it I did, and soon I was sliding towards an open door of an airplane, waiting for the jumpmaster to give me the command.

"*Go!*"

I went out the door, looking out and counting down, *One thousand, two thousand, three thousand,* and I finally felt the tug and saw the canopy fully open above me. I was drifting back to Earth, soaring through the air, and it felt amazing. I couldn't believe I was doing something this crazy, and I wished the guys back in Ridge Spring could have seen me. My friends knew I was crazy, but this was an entirely different level. The ground came up on me quickly and my instincts kicked in: knees and feet together, tuck and roll. I hit the ground like a sack of potatoes, knocking my steel pot crooked as I landed, although I didn't feel anything pop or snap that wasn't supposed to. I had survived my first jump! Then I kept jumping, and all too soon, my fifth jump was done. I had done it! I was officially airborne qualified and it was time to go home.

Once again, the US Army had transformed me and I was a different person. I felt more mature and seasoned when I returned to college for my senior year, my last three semesters of college. I was kind of between year groups because I had been allowed to skip one of my MSII classes and complete my MSIII year, even though I was technically a second-semester sophomore. I had always been different, and figured my matriculation through college might as well be unique, too. Additionally, I was an education major, so I had to complete all of my core class requirements before student teaching, a requirement for all teachers prior to certification and meeting graduation requirements. I carried a full load most semesters and was used to it due to my workload in high school; driving the school bus, serving in the guard, and playing sports had prepared me to juggle many things at once. I had completed a major milestone with ROTC and it was pretty much a waiting game after we returned for our senior ROTC year.

I arrived on campus with the rank of cadet major. We had three battalions at the time, including the ranger battalion, the battalion of MSIIs, and a battalion for the MSIIIs. The top performer at camp, combined with his or her standing in the program, was selected for the coveted brigade commander spot with three diamonds on their hat. The battalion commanders held cadet LTC rank, primary staff officers held the rank of major, and we had captains and lieutenants as well. I served as the executive officer within the MSIII battalion and thought I was big time. We all thought it was a big deal to hold high rank within the program, and we ran the program as if we were already active duty officers.

It was an awesome sight to see a field full of cadets on Thursdays, standing tall and beaming with pride. We had a strong program and it really showed on those Thursdays. We absolutely were the black West Point and we trained with that in mind, holding ourselves up to the appropriate standard. I hit my stride in the program, but I had something else I wanted to do that I had held off for a while: join a fraternity. There was still that group of men I admired, and if I was ever-so-fortunate, the time was right and I could join them. I had met an Alpha while in airborne school and leaned on him for a deeper understanding of the fraternity, and he shared some of his stories with me about his experiences. He talked about some of the great leaders, such as Martin Luther King Jr. and other great Alpha men. I hung onto his every word and was excited about the possibilities that came with becoming a part of greatness.

My friend, Derrick, knew I was interested, but he waited for me to bring up the subject with him and I did. He agreed to sponsor me, and shortly after, I began the process of becoming a member by filling out an application and paying my processing fees. Afterwards, all interested parties were invited to a formal interest meeting where the fraternity members introduced themselves and explained some of their national programs and community projects. I didn't need any convincing, but this meeting further inspired me to join. Because my pledge process pre-dated Google, I turned to Derrick as my own personal search engine to learn as much as I could about the fraternity. From him, I found out that if everything checked out with my application, I would have to go through an interview process, and if I received the proper number of votes, I would move on to the next step of the process.

Many people showed up to the initial interest meeting, but only a few were chosen, including me. I received a yes vote, along with five other candidates. The six of us had never really hung out prior to this process, but out of necessity, we quickly bonded. We were given our numbers based on height and I became number three. There is an old saying that what doesn't kill you makes you stronger, and this was very true of the pledge process. We never had to do anything that put us in jeopardy of losing our lives, but there were some moments that made us lean on one another like blood brothers. We spent countless hours together, both early in the morning and late at night, studying and learning the history of our great fraternity. The big brothers gave us tough love while they shaped us into Alpha men, really pulling something out of us that we all already held inside of ourselves. We were like-minded, but unique in our own ways. We grew closer as the weeks progressed, learning the rituals as well as the importance of giving back to our community. Then, on October 13, 1991, I crossed the metaphorical burning sands and my life changed for the better forever. I remember the first time I put my black and gold shirt on with the Alpha Phi Alpha letters emblazoned across my chest and the pride I felt; I had become an Alpha man.

Within just a few very short years, I had become a soldier, gone off to college, begun my pursuit to become an army officer, and joined a fraternity. Was that enough to erase the past of my jailed father?

Could I finally redefine the Scott name and break the cycle of violence and prison? I didn't know if I'd done enough yet, but I knew I had to finish this journey. My grandfather had served in World War II, and I knew that this journey wasn't just for me, but for him, too. My brother, Kem, had sacrificed so much of himself as well and had planted the military seed in me, so I needed to finish this for him.

While I felt so much propelling myself forward, I couldn't deny that I had heard some of the naysayers' voices when I'd spent that semester back at home, driving the bus. I still also found myself staring at my face in the mirror. Sometimes I could forget about my scars, but the mirror always reminded me about the fire. No matter what achievements I'd earned so far, underneath it all I was still a scarred young man dealing with the guilt of being a victim of domestic violence. My father was still responsible for this, and I couldn't just change faces, so my goal was to cover it up or erase it with achievement. I saw each one as a step towards victory, to winning, to slaying the invisible giant one goal at a time. My army fatigues gave me honor and my Greek letters gave me status, but was that enough? I didn't know, but I was no longer alone; I had my brothers and we created a bond that still stands today.

SENIOR YEAR

I was officially a senior. I had only one semester of classes remaining, including my last ROTC course and my student teaching. Student teaching lasted for one semester and you were given a grade of either pass or fail. It was a big deal, and we had to apply and be accepted to a school back home or within the local area based on our major, working under a tenured teacher as we learned the inner workings of a classroom, or in my case, a gymnasium.

I was also nervous going into my last semester because we would find out our fate in regards to active duty commissions.

The process for all cadets who had completed their requirements for commissioning was called "assessments." Through these assessments, we would find out what military branch we would serve, such as armor, infantry, medical service, and so forth. Additionally, we would find out whether or not we received regular army, active duty, or reserve commissions. To this day, I still remember so vividly when we were all notified during class of our times to report to the colonel's office to learn our fate the following day. I had never prayed so much in my life. It was different times and different circumstances for most of us, I guess, because we all wanted active duty. We wanted it and really, we needed it, for so many reasons, the least of which was that an active duty commission guaranteed not just a job, but a career after college.

As I waited outside the door of the ROTC building on that fateful day, I saw one of my buddies exit. He was grinning from ear to ear as if he had just won the lottery.

"Active duty! Armor!" he yelled.

"Congratulations, man!" I said enthusiastically, although even I could hear the touch of nervousness in my voice.

There was one more person in front of me, a buddy of mine, and he headed inside the building. I waited anxiously because I was in the batter's box. It would only take a few minutes, and then I was up. I knew he was as nervous as me because he desperately wanted active duty, but his scores were not the best. Before assessments began, the top brass had given us one of those "hold-your-head-up" speeches in case things didn't work out the way we wanted. They had tried to soften the blow for those of us who didn't want a reserve commissioning, but there was going to be disappointment for some of us no matter what, speech or no speech. There were one or two of us who had other goals of going to law school or working in the corporate world, and didn't want the grind of serving full time in the military. However, most of us had to have it.

When my buddy left the building, he was already in tears. He paused for a moment to talk to me and he had already begun to try to rationalize what could have gone wrong. I tried to lift his spirits, but he wasn't in the mood for it.

"Cadet Scott!" Major Walton's voice thundered, calling me inside. He had to be the most intimidating major in the army inventory during those days, easily earning the nickname of "The Hammer." Major Walton even had a plaque displayed on the wall in his office that he had received at the completion of his company command with a miniature hammer inside of it. He would definitely drop the hammer on us during training exercises, but we had a lot of respect for him.

I filed into the office and Major Walton, along with the Professor of Military Science (PMS) and one of the captains, was sitting there, waiting for me. I thought that they would somewhat ease into the assessment, but it was like someone pulling out a loose tooth with a string, saying they'd pull on the count of three but then yanking out the tooth on one.

"Active duty! Corps of Engineers!"

Wait a minute, sir! I thought, confused.

"Active duty?" I asked.

"Yes, congratulations."

I was in shock and I just stood there, smiling.

"Get on out of here, cadet!" Major Walton ordered. "You're holding up the line."

"Yes, sir!"

Yes! Yes! Yes! I felt like Will Smith at the end of *The Pursuit of Happyness* when he got the stockbroker job, overwhelmingly joyful as he clapped his hands, realizing that he had achieved what he had worked so hard for. I thought back on my journey to get to this moment: basic training, AIT, field exercises, and morning PT; the sacrifices on weekends when my peers were hanging out and partying. All of it was worth it to hear those two words: active duty. This was the culmination of a lot of time and effort I had dedicated to military service, and I was proud of myself for reaching another milestone. Soon, the other active duty officers and I would leave SC State and our hometowns to go off to places unknown, some to other countries to serve our nation like so many had done before us, and we were ready. The cool thing about the Bulldog Brigade was, and still is, the long green line of excellence out there serving and waiting to greet you all over the world. Bulldogs from every call are standing at the ready, eager to mentor you. There are more than enough available for all who have entered the halls of the SC ROTC program, and I feel proud to be a part of that number.

I couldn't wait for my time to begin my active duty commission, but I had to complete my requirements. I pushed through my last semester of ROTC and completed my core curriculum requirements, so all that was left was my student teaching. I applied for a school on campus, Felton Laboratory School, which was a unique private school for students from kindergarten through eighth grade. I wanted to remain on campus partially for the convenience, but also because I was in love and didn't want to leave my woman. Fortunately, I got the spot and I had the opportunity to work with one of my mentors, Coach Martin, who served as the PE teacher at Felton. He had run track at SC State years earlier, and he really took care of the PE majors on campus. I often visited his office and was even invited to his house on occasion to hang out and play the game Taboo, which made him a fun, encouraging mentor to help guide me through this last phase of my college life.

I started my student teaching at Felton during the fall semester, and I found I really enjoyed it. I had an opportunity to teach little kids of all ages and to learn from Coach Martin, one of the best. However, there was one issue that had to be addressed after about three weeks of instruction: The kindergarteners and first graders had been staring at me. Coach Martin had been observing their behavior and he finally pulled me into his office at the end of the day. He started by talking to me about some of the superlatives I used when speaking to the little ones after they performed an exercise or followed instructions well, such as "Outstanding!" and "Fantastic!"

"Do you think they know what those words mean?" he asked. I told him I didn't. He explained that when I used bigger words like "outstanding," "excellent," or "fantastic," I ended up with a lot of blank stares because the kids didn't know what the words meant yet. Instead, Coach Martin explained I should say "Good job."

"And another thing," Coach Martin continued, "don't you hear them asking about what happened to your face?"

"Yes, I hear," I replied. It was a question I'd heard all my life, so of course I could hear the kids asking.

"Well, how are you going to address it?" he asked. "I'm not going to keep talking for you. You need to figure out how to address it, because this won't be the last time you have to do it. Come up with a plan and handle it the next time you arrive for PE."

I was used to dealing with adults after all these years, but I'd never had to address a group of kids about my face, at least not since I'd been a kid myself. But I knew Coach Martin was right; I had to face this situation head on (pun intended).

The next time the kindergarteners came in, I was ready for them. Coach Martin sat back and watched me work as I had all of the kids sit down in a semi-circle before I sat down in front of them. These were the days before my bad knees, and I could easily get down on the floor with the kids.

"What do you think happened to my face?" I asked. "Raise your hand."

"Fire!" one kid yelled out, his fingers straining towards the sky.

"That's right, I was in a fire," I said.

"How did you do that?" one of the other kids asked.

"My house caught fire," I explained.

"Why didn't you put it out?" another kid asked.

"Does it hurt?" asked another.

"One at a time!" I exclaimed. "No, it doesn't hurt anymore."

"Can I touch your face?" one kid asked.

"Sure, come up here and touch it," I said. The boy came forward and lightly touched the scars on my cheeks.

"It feels funny," he said observationally. "That don't hurt?"

"Nope!" I said. "And even though my face looks a little different, I'm happy to be here with you, and I can run and jump and play just like you." I surveyed the group and watched the kids take in my words. "Any more questions?"

"No!" the kids chorused together, already mentally moving on from our talk to the much more important business of playing.

"Okay, boys and girls," Coach Martin said as he took over the conversation. "Coach Scott is okay, and now you don't have to worry about him. Are you ready for some kickball?"

"Yes!" the kids shouted excitedly.

I learned a valuable lesson that day: Never assume that young people are comfortable with you and the way you look. Sometimes, they need an explanation. As a result of that experience while student teaching, I have shared my story openly with my nieces and nephews who had the same questions as those kindergarteners and first graders. My time spent student teaching with Coach Martin remains one of the highlights of my life. One of the most useful and important things he taught me was to teach to the grade level. I couldn't expected the same performance from first graders as I would from eighth graders when it came to jumping rope or hitting a ball.

"You have to meet students where they are in life," he said.

This was a valuable lesson for me. I had to remember that not everyone was an athlete and PE class was about much more than competition. It was about teamwork, motivation, movement, and having fun. Coach Martin also showed me the joy of molding young students and how best to approach them in order to connect with them and bring out their talents. He would bring me into his office from the very start of my student teaching tenure and break down the lesson plans in intricate detail, including seasonal sports and the approach to teaching them. He also showed me how to deal with behavioral problems based on ages and circumstances, an incredibly important lesson for any teacher. Coach Martin also taught me how to deal with parents and administrations; in every aspect, preparation was key, whether you were on the court or in a classroom. He taught me the importance of dressing up during parent teacher conferences—shirt and tie, not sweat suits. But above all, he taught me how to teach kids to stay fit through movement and how to have fun doing it.

Before student teaching, I'd thought PE was simple. I didn't remember my former gym coach putting much effort into classes, but Coach Martin taught PE with the same seriousness of chemistry class or algebra. Gym class was more than just rolling out a ball and allowing kids to play with no structure. Coach Martin showed me the balance between stern leadership and having fun with the kids. There were some days we had to stop a game and put the entire class in time out. Coach Martin had a technique where he would throw out enough hula hoops across the gym floor for each student in class. Then, each kid would have to silently sit in their own hoop, legs crossed, and they couldn't say a word until he gave the all clear sign. It worked like a charm each time! Coach Martin had the best discipline techniques, and the kids all loved him. I did, too.

"Scotty!" he'd say, his nickname for me. "Scotty, what would you do in this situation? What would you do in that situation?" He quizzed me constantly, holding court with me every day, and I listened to him and I learned a lot. That, combined with our friendship at the bi-monthly Taboo games at his house, really built a solid relationship between us. He made me feel good and capable as a teacher, and I really considered him to be a big brother.

I completed my student teaching in December of 1993, officially finishing college. Mission complete! My girlfriend and future wife, Yolanda, and I were discussing our future together, and I filled her head with promises of seeing the world with this active duty commission I had earned. I promised to take her to faraway lands and experience different cultures, and she was completely on board. Little did she know that we would end up about an hour and a half away from her home town for our first duty station, but you've gotta start somewhere, right?

CHAPTER 14

Meeting My Wife

I met my wife during an education class we took together during our sophomore year of college. I remember sitting in the classroom that had stadium-style seating and trying to make her laugh from across the room by making animated jokes about our boring instructor. I would make exaggerated yawning gestures when the teacher wasn't looking and Yolanda would crack up at my silliness, stifling giggles behind her hand so as not to be noticed by the instructor. At the time, we were both in relationships with other people and didn't really have any romantic interest in each other. Outside of my in-class jokes, we only saw one another in passing between classes, or through mutual friends. Then, as the seasons passed and we entered our senior year, we shared a mutual friend named Dezzaire. Dezzaire was one year my junior, as well as an ROTC cadet; she was athletic, articulate, and a real soldier. She reminded me a lot of a female Charles Barkley, the kind of person who spoke her mind freely, a real straight shooter. One day, Dezzaire came up to me after a training event. We stood alone, and without any chaser, she shot the question at me: "Boy, what happened to your face?"

Despite knowing her Barkley-esque personality, I was still kind of shocked at how blunt she was. At the time, I was a senior ROTC cadet over her, but when she asked me that question, I suddenly felt like a child who had been pulled aside by a teacher for a "chat."

"Well, are you going to tell me?" Dezzaire prodded when I didn't answer right away. She had taken time off from college when her National Guard unit was called up for Desert Shield/ Desert Storm, so she was a seasoned soldier and didn't have a whole lot of patience for hemming and hawing. I answered her question in a boyish tone as I ran down some of the details. I hadn't really been prepared to discuss my scars, but I was caught off guard by her frankness. When I finished, Dezzaire regarded me seriously for a moment.

"You're pretty cool," she finally said. From that moment on, Dezzaire and I became buddies. Having gotten through that initial barrier, it was easy for us to share stories from our lives.

When my senior year of college arrived, I had just recently given my life to God. To this day, I vividly remember one night during our annual revival back home when I was convicted by God. I usually sat towards the back when I wasn't performing my usher duties, never wanting to be the center of attention. In years past, I had always heard that quiet voice in the back of my mind when it was time for the invitation to give my life to the Lord and confess Him as my Lord and Savior, but that night felt different. The house was packed and I had some friends there from visiting churches, but it wasn't only different because of that. When I wasn't playing sports, I was extremely shy. My insecurity and nerves had always opened the door to let in my pride so it could stand in my way and prevent me from making that walk to the front of the church. But on that particular night, I didn't feel like that.

The singing felt extra special to me, as was the service leading into the sermon. I can't remember the message of the sermon anymore, but it tugged at my soul and I felt a deep pull when it came time for the invitation. Reverend Chandler instructed everyone to stand up and close their eyes, which we did. Then Reverend Chandler made the altar call. When he said those words, I began to feel a fire burning within me. God said, "Come!" So I came. This pull, this desire for God was stronger than any shyness or pride I might have had as I began to walk towards the front of the church. As I drew closer, I heard the first few claps, which grew into applause, even though all eyes were supposed to be closed.

My brother had made the same walk a few years back, but his experience was a little different from mine. On the day he accepted the invitation, he had just come off a rough night of drinking. As a result, his focus wasn't as sharp as it normally was and he misunderstood the pastor's instructions while his eyes were closed. The pastor had made a small change to the process, at the point when people who wanted to give their lives to God would usually raise their hands. The pastor would usually close his sermon with the alter call. We knew that two really good things were happening during the alter call: First, we knew that the sermon was done and it wouldn't be long until we were going home; and second, we knew someone would be saved. The piano player would begin to play gently, and usually one of my cousins would begin singing the sweet melody of some powerful church song. The song and voices alone were almost enough to bring you closer to God, but the pastor would go into his altar call as if this would be someone's last opportunity to make a commitment.

"All heads bowed and all eyes closed," the preacher would say as the music played. "If there is one out there who would like to give their life to the Lord, let them come." Sometimes, we would peek to see if there was anyone. The pastor would then talk about the struggles in life and the temptations, especially for the young ones among us. "Lay that burden down and allow Jesus to take control of your life! If there is one today, don't worry about what your friends would say. Just take that step! Raise your hands and the usher will guide you up. You don't have to make this journey on your own."

We weren't sure if Kem was raising his hand because he was agreeing or if he was just lifting his hands in prayer, but both Lynnette and I were peeking, and before we knew it, Kem's hand was up. My sister and I made eye contact and we looked at one another with mirrored amused, curious grins. We knew something wasn't quite right, but we weren't totally sure what. Kem read the Bible and was committed, just like most teenagers his age, but there was nothing that showed us that he'd caught the Holy Ghost in that moment, so we decided to watch this one and see what happened. Usually, when someone young made such a leap of faith and people saw them walking up, there would be an extra shout of praise and encouragement. However, in the case of my brother, Kem had always been the life of the party, and adults and peers alike knew it, so when they saw who it was, they broke out into one of those African dances. People were shouting and running down the aisle at the possibility of redemption.

Lynnette and I exchanged glances; we knew that him walking forward had to be a misunderstanding, but he'd already started to take the leap and there was no turning back. Kem couldn't say he misunderstood what was going on, so he just had to go along with it. Lynnette and I were grinning as we scanned the pews for our mother. She was already shouting and crying as well because she didn't see what we saw of Kem's accidental commitment, and she just figured that today was the day for Kem. Kem was up at the altar, and although Lynnette and I wanted to laugh, we didn't dare risk getting struck by lightning from God Himself for making a joke of the situation. For all we knew, it could have been the real deal, but, as his siblings, we didn't think so.

The pastor laid his hands on Kem and all of the ushers and my mom gathered around him in full prayer-mode while Lynnette and I looked on with bated breath. *Maybe he'll be nice to me for at least a week after this one,* I thought. Kem took it all in and everyone hugged him after church. Lynnette and I couldn't *wait* to get into the car so we could get the full details.

"Well, Kem?" I asked. "Did you mean to raise your hand?"

He started explaining that no, he hadn't, and we all began to die laughing.

"I knew it!" Lynnette exclaimed.

Our mom grinned, but she still believed it was the power of the Lord that had pushed that hand into the air. My siblings and I began to realize that our mom needed that moment, so we backed off on the joking—at least, until we got home and away from our mother for a minute.

"Well, Kem, you're a saved man now, and I guess the next step is a full preacher!" I said with a wide grin. He punched me in my arm, and I knew that he might have been saved, but he was still my big brother and would continue to treat me accordingly forever. We still laugh about that night to this day.

On the night I gave myself over, my experience was filled with a quieter joy than Kem's. When I walked forward, I felt something come over me. It was so peaceful and unlike any calm I'd ever experienced before. It was a summer night and we were having revival week. This is typical, especially in the South, where your home church conducts a week-long revival inviting guest ministers to preach. The week would begin on Sunday with a long service, and include a service in the evening of each day, starting around six or six thirty. I was home for the summer and had decided to go on Wednesday night, because there were always some cute girls from the visiting churches who usually sang with the choir. Typically, the visiting pastor would bring his own choir to sing a couple of songs, and this night was no different. I figured I would get a little spiritual healing while checking out some of the cuties at church.

I sat in my usual spot, one pew up from the back on the left-hand side. I could hear my cousin, Sandra, clearly from that spot if she decided to lead a song, and I could see everyone from that viewpoint. It was perfect for people watching. We didn't have central air during those days in our church, and we had to use those old fans with historical black leaders on the front, like MLK Jr. and Rosa Parks, with some advertisement on the back, typically for a funeral home. The ushers would hold them up for those who needed them and pass a handful down the pews until everyone had one. Sometimes the staples would fall out of the center stick that held the paper fan in place and you would have to ask for another one. Of course, if the men had their manners in check, they would give up their good fan to a lady and do without, or wait until an usher gave them another fan.

I was sitting there in the back, listening to the songs being sung and focusing on the preacher as he delivered the Word for the evening, and I began to drift in and out of my thoughts as I scanned the church, watching different behaviors and nuisances of the congregation. Southern Baptist preachers are different from other preachers in their delivery of sermons. They're much more theatrical, and we could usually tell when the sermon was drawing to a close. The preacher would hit the climax of the sermon, sweating profusely as he worked hard to bring it home. He would signal to the piano player and go into the cool-down period to wind it down, like an intense cardio workout. As the preacher wound down that evening, I figured we were almost done and I would have the opportunity to talk to some of the visitors my age, as well as a friend or two from school who were in attendance.

We went into the altar call as usual, and I was just standing in the back when something hit me. It was as if the pastor had received a message from God to talk to me personally. I didn't know what was going on with me, with my body. I felt a warmth and a gentle peace as the pastor sent out the request.

"Is there one person tonight that wants to take that walk and give their life to the Lord?" the pastor asked. "Come to Jesus."

I figured I was too cool for this during this time in my life. What about the cute girls? What would my friends think? *What is happening to me?* Suddenly, I felt an internal spiritual pull to go forward that was stronger than my mental and physical capacity to remain in place. Something had taken over my body, and for that brief moment in time, I experienced perfect peace as I walked down the aisle towards the pastor. I don't know what my brother experienced during his walk, intentional or unintentional as it had been. We all joked about it, but maybe he was too cool to tell us the real reason he'd walked that night or admit to his true experience. Maybe it wasn't a joke at all and he'd felt the same pull I was feeling that night, he just didn't share because Lynnette and I had made so many jokes about it. Nevertheless, I had that pull and it was the real deal for me. Ushers gathered around me and I received those same praises that Kem had when he'd walked.

"Do you want to give your life to Jesus?" the pastor asked.

"Yes," I said. There was no shame in that moment and I felt really good inside. I had never experienced that feeling before and I haven't felt that perfect peace since that night. My mom, of course, was overjoyed.

When I returned to school, I was filled with a love and a joy that I had been previously missing from my life. However, sometimes gaining a new part of yourself means letting go of something else. My girlfriend at the time didn't attend church, and after

I returned to campus and told her about my Savior, she couldn't understand. The bigger rift between us came when I told her that I couldn't do some of the things I had in the past. I felt confident in my decisions, but my girlfriend insisted that I was only going through a phase. Eventually, we went our separate ways, and although I was suddenly without a romantic partner, I was at peace because of my walk with God.

One day, Dezzaire showed me a picture of her best friend. When I looked at the photo, I was overcome with the sureness that I was looking at one of the most beautiful young ladies I had ever seen in my life. The young lady was wearing a white fitted dress decorated with a sequined pink-and-blue flowered pattern. Her hair was dark black and flowed down along her shoulders. Her smile was innocent and beautiful. She was standing inside her parents' home at the front entrance and it was evident from the photo that the house was very nice. It reminded me a lot of JB's house. More than anything, when I looked at the photograph, I knew that this was no ordinary young lady. She looked familiar, but I couldn't quite place her.

"Where is she from?" I asked, pointing at the photo.

"That's Lapetetra, stupid!" Dezzaire exclaimed. I later learned that "Lapetetra" was Yolanda's nickname in her hometown, just like how I'm known as "Foots" in Ridge Spring.

"Lapetetra, who?" I asked, still trying to place the young lady's face with the unfamiliar name.

"Lapetetra Barnes!" Dezzaire said, staring at me like she couldn't believe I wasn't making the connection yet. "She knows you!"

"That's Lapetetra?" I asked, the realization finally dawning on me. I had never seen her that way before, but the picture felt like it was practically glowing in my hand, as if God had shown me something important without revealing the obvious answer. "Can I have this picture?"

"Are you crazy?" Dezzaire asked. "I can't just give you my picture."

"Oh, come on, I'm sure you have other pictures of her, because she's your best friend, right?" I asked. Dezzaire grumbled, but didn't disagree. "Well, just let me have this one!" I pleaded.

"You're crazy, man!" Dezzaire said. "What are you going to do with that picture?"

"Nothing," I replied. "I just think she's cute in this picture and I'd like to have it."

Dezzaire reluctantly obliged, but I could tell she still thought I was nuts. However, I didn't really care. I knew this photo was special and I felt lucky to have it.

At the time, Kem was stationed at Fort Polk of all places, and had recently purchased a brand new red Honda Accord for his family. As such, he needed to do something with his old car, a silvery gray Nissan 200SX. When Kem purchased the Accord, the Nissan was at a bootleg mechanic shop in Louisiana and was in desperate need of a bunch of repairs, including new tires. I had a few dollars saved up from my National Guard checks, my ROTC stipend, and my summer camp check, and Kem had agreed to give the car to me if I paid for the repairs and found a way to head down south to pick it up. I made it happen during a long weekend shortly after I acquired the photo of Yolanda from Dezzaire, excited at the prospect of having a cool car in which to drive around campus—especially since I now had a picture of a drop-dead-gorgeous woman that I could keep in the visor of that car. For some reason, I didn't want to take the photograph to my dorm room. I still lived on campus at the start of my senior year, but I could have easily stored it in my drawer with my socks or something. Maybe I thought it too precious to leave unguarded in a drawer. Instead, I believed it served me best to be able to flip that visor down, especially when I was alone, undisturbed, and I could dream of the possibilities of sharing my life with a princess. The picture didn't have monetary value, but it needed to be protected like a gem. It definitely wouldn't be staying in my dorm room, and the visor served its purpose. When I picked up my new-to-me car from the shop, the first thing I did was safely tuck Yolanda's photo in the visor. Each time I drove after that, the first thing I would do before starting my car would be to pull that picture out and admire Yolanda's beauty. After a while, I realized what the picture meant to me, but I couldn't believe it.

One weekend, I drove home to Ridge Spring and spent some time with my best friend, Junior. Junior had joined the Marine Corps, but he was home at the time so we decided to take advantage of the opportunity to hang out. We were riding around in my Nissan and at one point during our drive, I flipped down the visor to grab the picture. I'd had it for about two weeks at that point, but I hadn't shown the photo to anyone else yet. I looked at the picture briefly and passed it over to Junior.

"Wow, who is this pretty girl?" Junior asked, marveling at the photo.

"That's my future wife," I said, unable to suppress a grin.

"No way!" Junior exclaimed. "How long have you guys been dating?"

"Oh, we're not dating yet," I explained, "But she's going to be my wife."

Junior waited for the punchline, but one never came. I was as serious as a heart attack. All the same, Junior gave me a smile anyway.

"Man, whose picture is this?" he asked. "How are you gonna marry somebody you don't even date yet? Do you even know her?"

"Yes, she goes to State with me."

"Okay, so you guys have been talking, but not dating yet?" Junior asked.

"Not exactly," I said, fully aware of how completely out there I sounded.

"Man, get out of here with that crazy talk," Junior said. "You have lost your mind."

I reached for the picture before Junior decided to do something crazy with my masterpiece. He slapped it back into my hands as if to say, "Give that picture back to its proper owner and quit pretending." I looked at the photo again, admiring her beauty once more before I placed it back into the visor. Junior was laughing so hard at the ridiculousness of my proclamation that he'd started choking. He was coughing and laughing, but it didn't matter to me because I knew I was right. Once Junior was able to breathe again, he and I eventually moved on to other topics, reminiscing on times past and enjoying each other's company. Junior was my best friend and I felt like I had to give him a heads up about what was ahead, and finding my future wife was big news.

The following semester, I moved off campus. I had pledged Alpha Phi Alpha and was living off the yard with my line brother, Thomas Hundley. We lived in a two-bedroom apartment that sat above a detached garage owned by an older lady named Ms. Robinson who lived on the street behind the SC State football stadium. Ms. Robinson was probably in her early seventies at the time and used the apartment rent we paid her to supplement her income. She lived alone in her home and treated Thomas and me like her sons, and in turn, we cut the grass and did other yard chores for her for free. Thomas and I were fraternity brothers as well as ROTC cadets. He had a baby face, and girls always went crazy over him, so he had no problems with the ladies. Thomas was from Mississippi, and in addition to being a smooth talker, he was very smart. We were like minded and got along well, making us two very easygoing roommates. It was a perfect setup for Thomas and me because rent was only $300 a month, including cable, which we split down the middle; $150 a month was still major money for a college student in the early nineties, but we still managed to turn it every month.

At the start of the semester, Dezzaire knew I was still infatuated with Lapetetra, but she had no idea to what extent. She called me up at my new apartment and told me that Lapetetra and her boyfriend had broken up over the summer. Since Dezzaire knew that I had split from my girlfriend as well over the break, Dezzaire asked if I wanted to go over to her house and watch TV.

"Lapetetra will be there," Dezzaire said, knowing that was all it would take to convince me.

"What time?" I asked.

"I'll pick you up around seven," Dezzaire said.

Thomas and I usually talked about everything, but this time I didn't tell him where I was going. I was so nervous that I was sweating, and even though I tried to keep my plans under wraps, he could tell something was going on with me.

"Where you heading, bruh?" Thomas asked.

"I'm going on campus for a minute," I said. "I'll be back."

"Okay, cool." Thomas was looking at me like he knew I was up to something, but he couldn't quite figure out what. However, I didn't volunteer anything, so Thomas didn't pry.

Back in my room, I searched for my favorite polo shirt and I felt like I was going on my first date or something as a kid. I finally located the shirt and ironed it until it was wrinkle-free. I did the same for my Levi jeans before I jumped in the shower and scrubbed like I was going to have to pass inspection. Why was I tripping? I was going to hang out with a girl I'd technically known for years. We'd laughed in class together, and I'd seen her on campus and at different events. Really, though, I knew why I was so nervous. I knew why this was different. The photo safely tucked into the visor of my car was why this was different.

When seven o'clock rolled around, I was already anxiously waiting at the window, frequently glancing out at the street so I wouldn't miss the car the moment it pulled up. Suddenly, I heard the horn blow. It was them!

"Who's that?" Thomas asked.

"That's for me! I'll be back!" I said quickly, reaching for the front door. Thomas gave me one of those smiles as if I was going to some hook-up, but this was no hook-up. He gave me a fist bump as I eased out of our apartment. I tried to look cool as I walked to the car, but I was incredibly nervous.

"Get in, boy!" Dezzaire called as I got close to the car, her grin as wide and knowing as the Cheshire Cat's. "We have to go pick up Lapetetra. You know her, right?"

"Of course!" I said, faking a confidence I didn't feel. "Hey, how are you?" I asked, suddenly feeling the need to pull out my best manners in preparation for seeing Yolanda.

"How are you?" Dezzaire repeated with a laugh, seeing right through my proper facade. "I'm fine, James, how are you?"

"I'm okay."

"What are you doing with that cologne on, man?" Dezzaire joked.

"Is it strong or something?" I asked, suddenly worried.

"No," Dezzaire reassured me, "but you don't usually wear that around me."

I knew she was trying to break the ice and ease my nerves, but it wasn't working for me. That, in turn, was hilarious to Dezzaire. She was helping me out by arranging this get together, but she was by no means above busting my chops.

When the car pulled up to Lapetetra's house, Dezzaire honked the horn and I immediately hopped out to open the car door for Lapetetra. Opening doors for ladies was something I got from TV growing up watching *Little House on the Prairie* and it always stuck with me. Lynette and my mother were used to me doing that for them when we were out around town at stores, but I wasn't in Ridge Spring and this lady was definitely not my mother or sister.

"Oh, thank you," Lapetetra said with a smile as I popped open the car door. Dezzaire, of course, took notice of this and made a joke about me opening Lapetetra's door. So, naturally, I walked around to the driver's side and opened Dezzaire's door with exaggerated politeness. Dezzaire raised her eyebrow and gave me a look that clearly said, "Don't overdo it."

"You done opening doors now, James?" Dezzaire asked before both ladies broke into laughter. I joined in, but I knew that this was no act for me. Well, maybe I was admittedly laying it on a little thick, but I was old school and traditional when it came to women from all the information I'd gathered by watching TV before all of my basketball games. Of course, there hadn't been cars on *Little House on the Prairie*, but good manners transcend time.

By the time we arrived at Dezzaire's apartment, my nerves had risen once more and it felt like the first day of school. What was different about Yolanda now? We used to joke in class and she was still the same girl from a couple years ago. The difference now was that my feelings had changed. I had pledged, what was in my opinion, the coolest fraternity on the face of the Earth, and we were considered the ice-cold brothers of Alpha Phi Alpha, but in that moment, I needed a higher power. I was more than ice cold, I was completely frozen.

We went inside Dezzaire's apartment and decided to sit on the floor of all places, despite the available chairs. It started with the two girls sitting down there with a boom box, searching for a cassette tape. I figured I would look odd sitting on the couch alone, so I plopped down on the floor as well. We sat in a triangle making small talk, and I felt completely stupid as I tried to figure out what to say. I knew that I only had a small window of opportunity to impress her, because a woman that pretty wouldn't stay on the market for long. Not like she was a BMW or something, but a beautiful princess just formed from the hands of God, waiting for some fortunate soul to be eternally blessed with magnifying beauty ten times over.

What do you say to a woman like that? I was typically witty and quick, but I was in quicksand. So, I did what players do: I closed my eyes ever-so-briefly and asked God to smile on me just this one time, to open up this young lady's heart and allow her to look past the scars my father had given me and see the man my mother had raised me to become. I asked God to give me something I probably didn't deserve because I was convinced this gorgeous woman was out of my league. Lapetetra and Dezzaire were preoccupied with the music so I had time to summon Him and wait for His reply.

Suddenly, I thought of something. I asked Dezzaire for a pencil as I reached for a stray piece of notebook paper on the floor. Both ladies glanced over at me as I ripped the paper in half and began to write. I was poetically gifted and began to stroke a line as they monitored me.

Do you like me?
__ *Yes* __ *No*
(Check one)

I folded the paper and handed it to Lapetetra and held my breath. She unfolded the note and read it quickly before reaching for the pen. Lapetetra marked her response, refolded the paper, and delivered the note back to sender. I opened the note, steeling myself for disappointment, but instead I saw she'd checked yes. I looked up at her, and she had the most beautiful smile a man could ever hope to see, so I went in for the kill.

"May I have your number to call you sometime?"

Lapetetra smiled again and wrote her number on the note. I felt so happy that I wanted to get up and run around Dezzaire's apartment, loudly shouting thanks to the Lord, but it didn't seem appropriate in the moment. I debated whether or not I should just shut my mouth for the rest of the evening so as to not mess things up and say or do something that might make her change her mind. I felt like I was dreaming. Was this really happening? This was so major! It felt like needing a passing grade from a professor to graduate college and he gave it to you, even though you know you failed that exam. It felt like I'd been pulled over on the interstate doing ninety mph in a seventy-mile-per-hour zone with no proof of insurance and expired tags, but instead of getting a ticket, the highway patrolman had let me off with a warning, just telling me to slow down. I kept asking myself over and over if this was real, but I knew in my heart that it was because of what I'd felt when I saw her picture that day. God had shown me my future wife and it was happening. From that night on, we were inseparable until I left for my officer course.

When I told Thomas I was dating Lapetetra, he couldn't believe it.

"Quit playing, James!" he exclaimed.

"Yep, we are dating, brother, and it's serious!"

He wanted all the details, so I told him I'd laid on some smooth lines on her and she was smitten. Thomas laughed, waiting for me to elaborate. Finally, I showed him the note.

"Ain't no way she fell for that mess!" Thomas exclaimed. We laughed, but I knew my life had changed because I was in love. I was in the kind of love where I wanted to take her home immediately to meet my mother—so I did. This was the kind of love that makes you forget to eat breakfast or put your shirt on backwards. When Yolanda called the apartment, I felt like I was in another world. I wasn't even thinking about doing my chemistry homework or anything else. This was a holding hands and "meet-me-at-the-Pit" type of love and I wasn't about to mess this up for anything in the world.

I told Yolanda about my dreams and goals and she believed in me. I discussed my plans of traveling and seeing the world with her, and for the first time, I had someone who saw me in the raw with my burns and my scars and accepted me as I was. She believed in the potential of the man I could become. I didn't have money and didn't come from a middle-class family, and she understood that. We talked about my childhood and my father and my siblings and she cried with me. Yolanda understood my limitations and my weaknesses and looked past them. She was a beauty queen and is still the most beautiful woman in any room, but she took a chance on me with all of my emotional and physical baggage and I am forever grateful God smiled on me that day in Dezzaire's apartment.

While Yolanda finished her last semester of college, I completed my basic engineer course at Fort Leonard Wood. I was allowed to return home for my college graduation in May, although my course didn't end for another month. This separation was the first time we had been apart for an extended period of time, and I figured I had better seal the deal on this relationship and put everyone else on notice that Yolanda was officially off the market. In short, I really didn't want to risk losing her. I'd never met anyone like her and I felt so sure that she was the person with whom I wanted to spend my life. We'd talked about a future together as well as some previous conversations about engagement ring styles, and at the time, I had bookmarked her comments in my brain for future use.

While I was in St. Louis, I remembered seeing a jewelry store in the mall and decided to purchase Yolanda's engagement ring there. I had asked one of my officer buddies how much you were supposed to spend on an engagement ring and he told me one month's base pay. Armed with that in mind, I went to the jewelry store and started to peruse the different styles and cuts. There were so many to choose from, but then I saw the one that I just knew would be perfect for her: a marquise-cut quarter-karat diamond ring. I knew the elongated style would lay beautifully on her finger and it secretly reminded me of a football, which somehow justified the choice in my crazy mind. It was part her, part me, and wholly representative of the two of us and the next step we were taking together. The other rings were gorgeous, but this one was Yolanda all the way. It was my first major purchase in my life and I felt really good about it. I didn't even have a car at the time, but I knew this would be an investment of a lifetime that I was ready to make.

I had decided to propose to Yolanda while I was at home for our graduation ceremony, and as I left the jewelry store with the ring in my pocket, I felt incredibly nervous. I really didn't have much of a plan outside of popping the question at my mom's house in Ridge Spring. Yolanda picked me up at the airport and I was simultaneously thrilled to see her and overwhelmingly nervous about what I was about to do. We drove to Ridge Spring, only an hour away from Columbus, and the drive passed in a haze of nerves. When we arrived at my mother's house, we were greeted by my family, and my sister immediately noticed something was different about me.

"What's wrong with you?" she asked.

I mumbled something about a long flight, but I had a huge lump in my throat as my mind raced and I tried to figure out how to go about this business of popping the question. I had seen it done on TV and in the movies, but this was real life, and at that moment, I would have rather sung the National Anthem during assembly in high school than go through a proposal. But before I could ask Yolanda anything, I knew I had to call her dad to ask him for her hand in marriage. Yolanda's hometown was two hours away from Ridge Spring, so I waited until Yolanda, my mom, and my sister were tied up in conversation before I slipped into the backyard with the cordless phone. I sweated profusely as I dialed and attempted to gather my thoughts. *Should I call him Reverend Barnes or Dr. Barnes?* I quickly rehearsed both options in my head as I began to dial his phone number. Finally, I just said, "What the heck," and hit the call button and waited anxiously through the rings until he picked up.

"Hello?" the Reverend asked. My nerves ran wild.

"Hello, Reverend Barnes, this is James," I said. My rehearsed speech was out the door, and there I was, just a nervous little boy asking this man for his daughter's hand in marriage. He bombarded me with questions, so many that I almost folded and I considered asking for a redo of this conversation when I was better prepared. But I didn't fold and instead, I told him I was ready for marriage. I felt like I sounded wimpy, and I knew we hadn't been dating for very long and he might have thought our relationship was only a passing phase, but he gave me his blessing all the same. Thankfully, this was before everything was so easily recorded so there is no audio file of my shaking, nervous voice to be found anywhere!

I felt happy to have Yolanda's father's blessing, but that was only part of what I had to do. When I walked back into my mother's house, I was so nervous that I could feel my hands tremble as I walked into the living room. My sister, who knows me better than anyone, had her eyes on me as soon as I entered the room. She didn't have to say a word; her face told it all as if to ask, "What in the world are you up to?" I knew I had to get this over with before my sister put me on blast in front of everyone, so I quickly asked for everyone's attention.

"I just got off the phone with your dad," I said to Yolanda, "and I have a question for you."

I dropped to one knee and took a deep breath.

"I knew you were up to something!" my sister yelled. I could feel the sweat all over my body and my hands shook, but my voice was clear and even.

"Yolanda," I said, looking hopefully into her beautiful brown eyes, "will you marry me?"

In that moment after I asked that question, I was more nervous than I had ever been in my entire life, even more than when I first tried for my bus license. As I waited for Yolanda's answer, my past fear and anxiety over the bus license seemed so trivial and inconsequential.

"Yes," she said, her face breaking into that beautiful smile that had captured my heart. As I kissed her, the first thought that ran through my head was that I had officially taken the most beautiful woman in the world off the market. Although my words had not been polished or poetic, I had done my best to propose to her the right way. I had used one month of my base pay as the price point to buy her engagement ring, I had called Yolanda's father to get his blessing, and I had proposed to my future wife in front of my mom. The most beautiful moments of our lives are rarely scripted or go off without a hitch, but that's part of what makes them so beautiful. We stutter, we sweat, we second-guess our words, but our best memories are messy and wonderful and, ultimately, exactly what we want.

I felt very fortunate to be able to attend my graduation at all, because I was in the middle of my training course, but my senior instructor had allowed me to go in spite of a pending major exercise. My senior instructor had initially disapproved my attendance...until my mother intervened. When I first approached him about letting me have the time off, my commander at Fort Leonard held fast on not releasing me for my college graduation.

"The military comes first. You should take your obligation to the military seriously," he told me. *It's not like we're at war or I'm missing something impactful,* I thought, but I still understood my commander's position.

There was an African American trainer assigned to our platoon in officer basic course who mentored us on various aspects of the military. She knew my situation and tipped me off on a plan to get released, but she warned me that if the commander ever found out that she'd told me, she'd pay me back. So, I decided to take her advice and did what she told me. There I was, a big time second lieutenant in the United States Army, and I did what soldiers did when times got tough: we call our moms. I dialed up my mother and told her that these folks didn't plan on letting me come home to march for my college graduation. I stoked the fire a bit, emphasizing how my hands were tied in this situation.

"Who do I need to call to get my baby home?" my mother asked. "Do I need to call the president or the senator?"

"Whoa, Mom!" I interjected. "It's not that serious! You can call my commander and talk to him."

The plan was set in motion, and if you know my mom or have learned anything about her from reading this book, you know she wasn't the one to play with when it came to trying to keep her son from marching on graduation day. She called my commander and cried on the phone as she talked about me being the first in my family to graduate from college, and she discussed our family's ordeals and what it would mean for me to be present at graduation.

I'm sure my mother laid it on thick and meant every word of it, and the next day I was called into the office to report to my commander as if I was in trouble.

"Received a call from your mother, Lieutenant Scott," my commander said. I stood there quietly, waiting for the punch. "I'm going to let you attend your graduation, but if you are even a second late upon your return, you will be punished. Do you understand?"

"Yes, sir!"

"Your mother will not always be there for you, so you must learn to fight your own battles."

"Yes, sir," I said. They were serious military people and didn't really understand the gravity of the moment for my family and me; they only understood mission first. However, he wasn't going to get any pushback from me on that day. As soon as I left his office, I called my mom.

"What day are you flying into South Carolina?" she asked. My mom certainly didn't play. I had been willing to accept my fate and not march, but my graduation wasn't really about me. My mom needed to see me march across the field in my cap and gown. This was for her, and I owed her that moment because it was due to her sacrifices that it was even possible for me to be able to wear a cap and gown. I didn't fully get it then, but I get it now.

Thanks to my mother, I flew into South Carolina and was able to march with pride alongside my fiancé at our college graduation. Governor Douglas Wilder, the first African American to be elected as governor of Virginia, as well as the first African American governor of any US state since the Reconstruction Era, gave the commencement address on that warm spring day in May. This was extra special because my graduation coincided with Mother's Day, which gave me time to reflect during Governor Wilder's speech about the journey my family had taken, especially my mom. We'd been through so much, survived so much, and not only that, we were thriving. I was a college graduate, already in a respectable career with the military, and engaged to the most beautiful woman in the world. Today was a celebration for my family in so many ways, and after the ceremony, we all headed to Yolanda's cousin Neecie's house in Orangeburg for a big party.

Although my future father-in-law had given me his blessing, he was far from finished with his questions. He got another opportunity to speak with me at Neecie's house when he and Yolanda's first cousin, Jamie, cornered me. There was a buffet set up at Neecie's, and after I got my plate of food, I was heading towards the backyard where tables and chairs had been set up when my future father-in-law motioned me over. There was one empty seat between Jamie and the Reverend.

"Have a seat, young man!" the Reverend said, gesturing to the open chair. I should have seen the ambush coming, but I was distracted and caught up in the flurry of excitement of the past few days between the engagement and our graduation, so I fell for it and sat.

"So," the Reverend continued. "You're an army man, aren't you, son?"

"Yes, sir!" I replied, picking up my fork to take a bite of food.

"I heard those army men like to drink a lot and beat their wives," the Reverend said. "You know anything about that?"

My fork froze halfway to my mouth. I glanced around desperately for help, but all I saw was chiseled Jamie staring at me expectantly while the Rev waited for me to say something smart so he could tell me to get up out of there.

"No, sir!" I replied definitively.

The Reverend proceeded to pepper me with rapid-fire questions and I did my best to keep up, until Jamie finally threw in a softball relief question for me.

"Do you plan on making the military a career?" Jamie asked.

"Yes," I said. "The military has given us an opportunity to see the world and earn an honest living."

I could feel the Rev looking me over, trying to find a weakness in me.

"Let me tell you one thing, young man!" the Reverend said suddenly, with intense ferocity. "God gave me only one daughter. And if God sees it fit, I will give her to you. Do you understand that, young man?"

"Yes," I replied, watching the seriousness in his eyes. I tried to maintain my cool as I wondered if maybe someone had told him I spent some time in prison or something, because the Reverend was as serious as a heart attack.

"If you ever put your hand on my daughter, I will get my shotgun and shoot you dead," he said gravely. "Do you understand that, son?"

I answered that I did understand, but I couldn't believe I was getting hammered like this after my graduation. I had a plate of food in my hand and had managed to take a bite by that point of the conversation, but even before this talk with the Reverend, I knew one thing for certain: I would never put my hands on my wife. I had experienced violence in so many ways and I couldn't even fathom touching a woman in that way. I had learned to respect the women who helped raise me; I deeply loved and protected my sister; and I had always looked up to my female cousins and teachers who had mentored me. However, I had never witnessed the love that a father has for his daughter until that moment, and it's something I don't think I fully understood until my own daughter was born. My father-in-law is missing a hand, something he was born without, and he understood the pressures and weight of a disability. He saw my disfigurement and wanted to know if I was mentally strong enough to hold up to the pressures of this world and support his daughter. The world can be cold and unforgiving, and sometimes we lash out at those we love because of the experiences we have to endure on a daily basis.

"When times get tough—and they will—go for a long drive or go to a closet and pray that anger away, but don't ever put your hands on my daughter," the Reverend said.

I understand now what he meant. As of this writing, my daughter is fourteen and my protectiveness over her echoes the kind of love Yolanda's father has for her. Although laws in Korea prevent me from having a shotgun, I believe I may have to purchase one when I return to the US and some young man comes calling for her. Perhaps the Reverend can come over and help put the fear of God into that young man the way Jamie helped him at my college graduation.

Following our graduation, my wife began teaching first grade at a local elementary school in St. Stephen, South Carolina as I finished my officer basic course and began my tour of duty in Korea. I really didn't want to risk losing her, so we set a date for Christmas Eve of 1994, right in the middle of my tour. After six months of active duty in Korea, I returned home with thirty days' leave. While I was overseas, I was lucky to avoid all the craziness of planning the wedding, and Yolanda put everything in place, including contacting all of my groomsmen so they were ready to go when I returned to South Carolina a few days prior to the ceremony. The wedding took place in St. Stephen, South Carolina, Yolanda's hometown, in her grandmother's church. Dezzaire was my wife's maid of honor and Junior was my best man. JB was also one of my groomsmen, along with Kem and one of the Stanley's. Instead of my military uniform, I wore a suit to blend in with my groomsmen. Had I been around for the wedding planning, this might have been different, but at the end of the day, I didn't really care. I had my woman and that's all that mattered to me. I never told Junior, "I told you so," but I didn't have to. He was there beside me when I said "I do" to the most beautiful woman in the world.

On the day of the wedding, the thundering clouds and torrential rain seemed to warn of a return of the Great Flood. It rained so hard that day, which the Irish believe to be a symbol of good luck. However, that seems like it might be something the Irish console themselves with, since it rains nearly every day there, but I have to say that maybe there's something to that superstition. As we ran from the church to the reception, Yolanda and I were so in love and it felt like the raindrops never touched us.

We celebrated our honeymoon in Charleston and about a week or so after the wedding, I had to leave my new bride and return for duty to finish my tour in Korea. I completed my tour at the end of June and returned home to the United States at Fort Jackson. My wife had already found an apartment for us near the installation in Columbia, South Carolina. It was the first time we had lived together, and as was to be expected, the transition took a little adjustment. We were adults now with real jobs, no longer dreaming of the possibilities of life, as we were living them instead. We had real bills and I worked long hours in my assignment at Fort Jackson, including some weekends. It was a major adjustment for Yolanda and me to share our lives with one another on a daily basis as husband and wife, and we really had to get to know each other on a new level that we'd never experienced before. But as of this writing, we've been married for over twenty years, so we must be doing something right. And yes, she is still the most beautiful woman I've ever seen.

Years ago, my mom and I had prayed for Yolanda when, as a little boy, I thought I would be too ugly to have a beautiful wife.

My mom still reminds me about that prayer to this day, and I realize how much we were actually given from this prayer. Not only is Yolanda beautiful, but she is kind, loving, a wonderful mother, and the best partner I could have ever hoped for. She later told me that the yes-or-no note was the corniest thing she had ever seen in her life and all I had had to do was ask her for her number. I told her that God had told me to write that note, and who was I to question God?

CHAPTER 15

Commissioning Ceremony

December 12, 1993: The day had finally arrived when I would become a second lieutenant in the United States Army. The occasion was made that much more special by the fact that I would be commissioned alongside my housemate and fraternity brother, Thomas. He was my line brother and we were tight as brothers could be, sharing our dreams with one another in the two-bedroom apartment we'd shared for quite some time. We were both raised by single moms, and wanted to provide for them and make their dreams come true. Thomas and I were also broke as privates and we couldn't wait for our real paychecks. We reflected a lot during the days leading up to our ceremony and planned for family members to come to town to see us. We were so excited and couldn't wait to take this next step forward.

The day before the commissioning ceremony, we filed into our supply room for the very last time, sharing stories of times past. We all had to purchase our official officer dress green uniform from clothing and sales at Fort Jackson. As a result, our ROTC uniforms filled with ribbons earned over the years were stripped. In a sense, we were starting over after all we had achieved over the past four years, or in some cases, four and a half or five years. Thomas had really excelled at advanced camp, receiving top scores across the board. Having achieved such honors, he had his choice of branches and would serve in the coveted medical service corps.

We had come a long way, both of us from humble beginnings, to being pinned second lieutenants in the army. *Wow!* we thought. We were going from scraping up enough money to pay our $300-a-month rent to making a decent income. *We had arrived,* we thought with matching grins. Thomas and I talked about our dreams, cars, and supporting our moms as if we had been drafted in the first round of the NFL. Actually, we saw one of our classmates get drafted into the NFL that same year. In my senior year of high school, I had played against Robert Porsche during a playoff game. Robert was the biggest human being I had seen in my life at that point—until I met Orlando Brown, also known as Zeus, who was also a SC State graduate signing as an undrafted free agent with an NFL team around the same time. We were a close-knit family at State and when someone hit pay dirt, we all rejoiced and celebrated. It was a big deal! The football teams were as legendary as the ROTC programs, producing many NFL players throughout the years, most coached by the legendary Willie Jeffries. Even our basketball team had made the NCAA tournament my freshman year, playing Duke in the first round. They were all great programs, and although Thomas and I were both part of this rich heritage now, we were not going to make Porsche or Zeus money, but it sure felt like it. When you go from having no money to a real job, it feels like you're incredibly rich.

The morning came and the time had come for us to report to the auditorium. My family had gone ahead as I waited on my brother to bring me my Corfam shoes he had purchased for me as a gift. He had convinced me to turn in the dull ones I had because he wanted me to look sharp, and the Corfams were the latest pre-shined low quarters worn with the dress uniform. The ceremony was due to start at 1000hrs sharp, with a 0930hrs dress rehearsal, and Kem arrived just in time at about 0930hrs. We raced to the auditorium, and I didn't say a single word to him. He had purchased my shoes, but was late, so I couldn't give him a piece of my mind because I just didn't have the time. And anyway, I was happy to see him, although I was frustrated by his tardiness, so I wasn't expressing that joy at that exact moment.

We made it to the auditorium and the senior non-commissioned officer (NCO) in charge of the rehearsal let me have it—my first chewing out as a lieutenant. Technically, the pinning hadn't commenced and I was still in between positions, so I wasn't quite a lieutenant yet. I couldn't blame Kem, so I took the NCO's words and fell in line. What was really funny was that Kem was in uniform as well, and he totally flipped on me when we entered the building. He went into big brother and NCO mode, telling me to hurry up and get in line as he straightened my collar as if it was my fault for being late. Thomas just grinned, and I knew he couldn't wait to hear the details of this one because he knew my brother and wanted to know what had happened. Anxiety over, I settled into the moment and relaxed into the ceremony. My turn came, and my mother and Kem came up to pin my bars. I was still a little upset with Kem, but he was still my big brother and my hero, just like he had always been. As I said, he was wearing his uniform as well and, as custom dictated, he gave me my first salute. I figured it was the least he could do for keeping my shoes hostage. I finally had more rank than Kem, but he still treated me like I was twelve years old. Then again, I suppose that's what big brothers do.

Even with my residual annoyance with Kem, I was still glad to have him there on stage with my mom and me. He had been such a huge part of getting me into the military and it felt right to have him there along with my mother, to whom I owed everything. My grandfather was watching from his seat and was positively beaming with pride. By that time, he wore a hearing aid and would often repeat himself. At the conclusion of the ceremony, he kept staring at me with a wide grin.

"Are you a second lieutenant in the army?" my grandfather kept asking me.

"Yes, I am," I answered each time, feeling a swell of pride.

Yolanda was there by my side, and I guess she looked as if she was in middle school with her baby face, because my grandfather kept commenting on how I was dating such a young girl. Either his hearing aid was down too low or he just didn't believe me, but no matter how many times I told him that Yolanda and I had met in college, he just didn't believe me. He kept looking at me admonishingly, like I should be ashamed of myself for snatching up someone so young. My grandfather was so proud of my commission, but I don't know if he ever believed Yolanda was only two years younger than me.

My grandfather was the last of the legacy and my mother adored him, even though he and my grandma had separated when my mother was younger. At the time of my grandfather's death, he was living with a woman whom we affectionately called "Mamma Bennie Mae." They never married, but she was his common-law wife. During the summers, Kem and I would either catch the Amtrak or hop a Delta flight to Philly to stay with them during the summer, just the two of us. Our mom would always send us off with an aluminum foil package full of fried chicken for the trip. Those were the days when security screenings were little more than a quick up and down before we were allowed to board; nothing like the modern airport screenings where we all shuffle through the line in our socks and have the contents of our suitcases dumped out on a dirty table.

When we arrived, our grandfather would greet us with the widest, most gregarious smile one could possibly fit on a face. I always felt so happy and welcomed when I saw him. He stood about six feet tall and was a fair-skinned man. He had a single gold tooth that appeared to be extra shiny when he smiled, as if he had some special type of equipment to shine just that one tooth. Due to my grandfather's hearing aid, he was loud, and we would have to repeat ourselves at least twice when we held a conversation with him. We called him "Boogie." Not "Grandpa" or "Granddaddy," just Boogie. In retrospect, that seems par for the course in our family because nobody in our house went by their God-given name. My sister, Lynnette, went by the nickname "Dimples" because as a baby, she'd had full cheeks with twin dimples. My brother was Kem, not "Kenneth" or "Ken." My mother's name was Rosa, but most people called her Rose. We, of course, called her "Ma," "Mommy," "Mom," or a combination of the above, depending on the situation. Typically, I called her "Ma" when I asked when dinner was ready. I guess it was a quicker delivery than the other monikers, but she'd ignore me anyway until she was ready to announce the meal.

Boogie had retired and was living off of his disability. He used his personal car as a taxi to earn extra money driving people around town, an Uber driver decades before Uber was even an idea in Garrett Camp and Travis Kalanick's heads. During those summers when we visited, Mamma Bennie Mae would leave me either a quarter or fifty cents on the dresser for spending money when she and Boogie left the house for the day. I could stretch those coins a little further if I won the weekly foot race we held on the block. The entry fee was a nickel per person, and we usually had about four or five kids in my age group to run fifty or sixty yards. I could run back then, but I was nothing compared to a guy my age who had the ultimate, well-deserved nickname of

"Flash Gordon." He didn't live on our block, but it seemed like Flash Gordon could still sniff out the racing time most weeks. If he didn't show up, I was a shoo-in to win. Those were fun times; we played stickball in the street and would race sticks along the sidewalk in the deluge of water when they opened the fire hydrants. I'd fill my belly with a Tastykake or two at the corner store, or we'd catch Boogie as he was coming home and he would treat us to a slice of pizza or a Philly cheesesteak.

The summer when I turned ten was one of my best summers with Boogie, except for the one time he caught me on top of the roof, preparing to jump over to the next rooftop to retrieve a halfie. A "halfie" was what we called one half of the rubber ball used for stickball. Kem was up there with me, but he ducked when he spotted Boogie coming down the street.

"Get down!" Kem hissed.

"What?" I asked. But it was too late. The next voice I heard was Boogie's.

"What are you doing on that roof?!" Boogie shouted.

"I was—" I started to explain, but Boogie cut me off.

"Get your butt down here. *Now*."

I glanced over at Kem lying prone on the roof before I began my slow descent down the ladder.

"You trying to kill yourself?" Boogie asked, still angry.

"No, sir!"

"Rose would kill me if you hurt yourself," he said.

I was more embarrassed than anything because that was the first time I'd heard my grandfather yell, at least at me. He kept rubbing my hands and arms as if I had stuck my hand in a hornet's nest or something and he was trying to rub the pain away. Kem was watching this as he eased himself off the house, putting his finger up to his lips in a silent plea to not tell on him. I looked back to Boogie who was looking through me instead of at me, rubbing and pleading with me to never venture up on the roof again. I promised I wouldn't and I eventually retreated to the stoop. Boogie went inside and Kem eased himself down on the stoop beside me as I sat with my head down.

"You know why he was rubbing you like that, Foots?" Kem asked.

"Why?"

"He blames himself for not being there for us when our father burned that house down. He was trying to protect you in his own way by rubbing you, man," he said. I didn't know if Kem was jiving me, but when he's caught up in his feelings, his eyes stretch wide. His eyes were wide, all right, so I believed Kem was giving it to me straight.

I looked at my grandfather a little differently after that day on the roof, for the better. I wanted to show him I was tough and durable, show him my scarred skin wasn't going to deter me. Despite my attempts at toughness, it was a fight against my skin. My burns were sensitive and a little nick would cause my flesh to tear and bleed. But I wanted to be strong like my grandfather, who had served in World War II. There was a little bit of mysticism in Boogie's service for me. Maybe it was because I loved GI Joe and those little green army soldiers they sold on the corner so much. Maybe it was because I used to watch John Wayne movies and viewed my grandfather as a hero just like the Duke. Whatever the reason, I loved my grandfather dearly. We didn't see him often enough over the years, but that story Kem told me on the stoop that day stuck with me and I wanted to make him proud. I remember so much about the summer we spent in Philly, not just because of that day with the roof, but because I remember Kem telling me that Elvis Presley had died. I didn't watch Elvis on TV, but Kem filled me in and the TV stations ran his movies all day and night in tribute. Kem was a storyteller and he had a way of making people come alive to me. He could paint a vivid picture with theatrics in a way that always left me captivated. Kem also loved Boogie and he'd spent a lot of time with him when we lived in Philly, back before the fire. I trusted Kem and tended to gravitate towards the people he cared about the most. If Kem told me they were good people, I let them in my space, too.

When my grandfather passed in 1996, Kem was stationed in Germany and I was stationed at Fort Jackson, having recently been promoted to first lieutenant.

"Foots," my mom began when she called, and then she stopped. In that pause, I knew immediately why she was calling, even without her saying it. Boogie had been sick for a while, and we'd traveled to Philly to visit him a few months earlier.

"Boogie passed away," my mom finally said. "I'm packed and on my way. I'll see you there."

I made arrangements and submitted my leave form to leadership as soon as I hung up the phone. I signed out on leave and Yolanda and I headed north to Philly. When we arrived, my mom was, of course, distraught. She was the only child, and his baby girl, so she began to look for anything and everything that belonged to her father that she could bring back with her. My mother was uneasy as she sorted through his home, and it was difficult for us to see her in that space. When Kem arrived with his wife and their two daughters, he, like our mom, was uneasy, his disposition swinging between quiet and moody. I found him difficult to deal with during this situation, but I understood. I didn't personally show much emotion; it was normal for me not to cry during times of grief. However, because I wasn't in the same space emotionally, I felt detached from the rest of my family.

We stayed with family until the day of the funeral. As we rode in the hearse, I remained quiet and stoic while my brother's and mom's eyes filled with tears. I was sad, but I didn't feel that same deep loss as my mom and Kem. When we arrived, we filed into the church and our extended family filled the first two pews. The preacher gave the eulogy and I found myself feeling kind of frustrated. Family members around me were pouring out tears, but I just sat there in my thoughts. Before long, it was time for us to view the body, so we queued up and I waited my turn. It was painful to see my mom and brother hurting so much, but I still wasn't feeling the same way they were.

Then it was my turn and I saw my grandfather's body lying before me. In that moment, it finally hit me. I saw him and I thought about his smile, the rooftop, his presence in my life and our family, and the time he had served in World War II. Instinctively, I reached up to my shoulder and unpinned my first lieutenant bar. I leaned over, and as the tears washed over my cheeks, I pinned my bar on his lapel. I was technically out of uniform because I only had one bar on my shoulder, but who cared? It was more important for me to be able to look down at my grandfather, Boogie, and see him wearing my first lieutenant rank. I hoped he was up there somewhere smiling at me, because in his own way, he was responsible for me wearing that uniform. He inspired Kem and Kem inspired me, and then there we were, Kem and me giving Boogie his final salute home. I had finally connected to my emotions and I was crying and grieving like my mother and brother. My wife had never seen me in this state, not ever, and she was a little taken aback. Yolanda gave me my moment, my space, and the time I needed to process it all, and then it was over for me.

I had cried so hard in a short period of time that I felt emotionally and physically drained afterwards. I felt as if I'd gone on a long road march with a full rucksack and I was exhausted. The man we'd called Boogie was gone, and now it was only Kem and me left with the responsibility of holding our family, our mom, together. Boogie had been our main connection to Philadelphia, and everything good about that city would be gone from us for a long time. The Tastykakes and authentic pizza slices, the hoagies and Philly cheesesteaks, the corner and the row houses. The noise, the beautiful noise of the city, and our history could only be told through the stories my mom still held in her mind.

We packed up the next morning and said our goodbyes to distant cousins and old friends before heading south down I-95. We drove until we connected to I-20 until we saw the Ridge Spring sign. We were home. This was the first time all of us had been together in a while: Kem and his family, Lynnette, Maurice, our mom, Yolanda, and me. We sat in the living room of my mom's house and reflected on the good times. My mom fried some chicken and made her cakes and casseroles, and we had collard greens and all the fixin's. We ate until our bellies ached and then we rested and ate some more. Kem began his round of jokes, usually on me about something to break the ice. But then later, when we were alone, Kem gave me his usual speech about family and how I needed to check on our mom and make sure she was all right after he left and returned to Germany. During that time at my mom's house after the funeral, we were together as a family, and I wanted to hold onto that feeling for a little while, especially since I knew our time was limited and soon we'd scatter back across the world to our own lives. The next day, we left my mom's house and returned to our own homes, continuing the march forward through our days as we dealt with the fact that our father was still alive and Boogie was gone.

CHAPTER 16

Officer Basic Course

I reported to my officer basic course on January 24, 1994, at Fort Leonard Wood, Missouri with only about fifty dollars to my name. I believe I had to be the brokest out of all the second lieutenants in the army inventory, but I had a job, a career, and I was a long way from Ridge Spring, as was evidenced by the snow stacked up on both sides of the road along the installation. It was freezing cold and I didn't own anything appropriate for that type of weather. I had come from the enlisted ranks and was used to everything being provided for me, including meals and clothing. I had no car, there wasn't a chow hall near the officers' quarters, and for the first time, it wouldn't be free if and when I could get to one. I guessed that this was what the adults called real life with real-life problems.

We received our modified training schedule and were told to report to the company in our physical training (PT) uniform for height measurements and a weigh-in. *Man!* I thought. *Don't they give you a few days to run off a couple of pounds, just in case?* But alas, this was not so. This would be the standard from this point on for all military schools, to show up in shape to meet army weight standards. No grace period; you were just expected to show up ready. Fortunately, I was lean during those days…well, maybe not lean, but I was conditioned enough to not worry about failing the height and weight. For me, this was reminiscent of a football combine, when we would all file in like cattle to get measured before being sent on our way. We also conducted some measuring of our own: surveying our new classmates and checking one another out as if we had a track meet the next morning.

It was natural to look for other minorities coming from an HBCU, and it didn't take long to pick out the handful that were present. It was at this juncture when I ran into my main man, Larry Sanders, a graduate from Alcorn State in Mississippi, the home of the great Steve McNair. Larry and I hit it off immediately because he was as country as me and just as broke. We were two raw second lieutenants with no idea what was ahead of us. We showed up for class the next morning in our uniforms and received a series of briefings on what was expected of us over the next few months. We also received a briefing from finance and learned we could get advance pay until the end of the month, and Larry and I jumped at this chance. We didn't even understand that most lieutenants didn't need this option, so we didn't know to be embarrassed.

I had served in an engineer unit during my enlisted years, so I thought I knew what to expect as a Corps of Engineer officer. However, no one had told me about the demolition part of the Corps, and the bridges and Mine Clearing Line Charge (MICLIC); all I knew were dump trucks and horizontal and vertical construction. Where was this part of the briefing during the displays at advanced camp? Blowing stuff up one was thing, but figuring out how to calculate the correct formula was something for which I was unprepared. As a matter of fact, I was flat-out embarrassed when I saw the calculators these guys pulled out of their bags and placed on the table. My calculator was missing a couple of buttons, to say the least. I had a feeling that this was going to be a steep learning curve for the kid.

Our class consisted of about 60 percent West Point graduates. As the classes began and we started to discuss previous wars, I realized I was at a deficit. I wasn't as well read as my peers, and for the first time, I felt academically inferior to some of my classmates. I had graduated cum laude from SC State, but I hadn't spent my time reading about the Civil War battles and World War II. It hadn't been my priority before, but I knew I had to make a paradigm shift if I was going to succeed. I immediately thought about my mom and the lesson she taught me that day in the car: *Ain't nobody going to feel sorry for you!* The wisdom of parents and our forefathers and the things they say hold true. My mother was right back then and she was right now.

This new environment and the responsibilities of being a second lieutenant meant that I had to keep up or get left behind. My classmates and I would be counted on to lead soldiers and make split decisions that in some cases meant life or death. As second lieutenants, we had to know our history and understand how to apply it to the current battlefield. I had some catching up to do, as did Larry and a few others. Those of us who needed some remedial work made the commitment to learn what we were lacking and we formed a study group to help us keep up. One of the most important lessons I learned—really, that *we* learned—was that our circle had to expand; we couldn't just lean on people who looked like us or came from a similar environment. We had to learn to reach across the aisle to other races and let our guards down. I couldn't be afraid to ask for help because my calculator didn't have a certain button, and until I finally purchased a calculator that did, I had to lean on someone else and humble myself enough to ask for assistance. After all, we were all on the same team serving in the US Army, and that made me proud.

Just when you think you have it made, you can't drop your oar. I was in the officer training course, but I was far from done and I couldn't slack off. There were exams every week that tested us academically, so I had to buckle down and play less basketball. Instead, I turned my focus on running faster, doing more push-ups and sit-ups, and studying harder than I ever had before. As the months passed, I began to gain more confidence, but, more importantly, I learned from some of my West Point brethren that I had to be well read and well informed on current events, as well as military history. Everything played a part and I finally felt like I got it. I had to realize that in some aspects, "the man" was imaginary, and I couldn't give anyone any excuse to deny me anything that I had prepared myself for and had rightfully earned, including promotions. I understood; We all had to not only look the part, but be the part. I received my commission on December 11, 1993, but I became an officer in the truest form during my time in the basic course as I stood amongst my peers, all of us training, studying, and growing together. The experience tested me, but I became an engineer officer over those five months of study.

When Larry and I received our first big checks, we thought we had hit the lottery. The four of us who hung out together all splurged, first by sending money home to our mothers, and then we went out to the local suit man and purchased three suits apiece. We just had to be the sharpest lieutenants on Fort Leonard Wood. Larry teased me relentlessly when he saw me with my suit and all the accoutrements on that first Sunday. He'd bought suits, but I had the suspenders and the handkerchiefs and everything in between. Larry told me that I needed to slow down and not come up to stardom too fast, and he finally stopped laughing once I decided to pull out the handkerchief to keep from looking too flash. Of course, Larry tucked the handkerchief back into my pocket with a smile, but he reminded me about my suits for years to come. We thought we had it made!

We were both making more money than we had ever seen, and in those days we didn't know a thing about investing or saving.

We had to open bank accounts when we arrived in Missouri because there was no online banking in those days, and who knew the routing number to the local bank back home? We sure didn't. It was just easier to open up something right there on Leonard Wood for convenience, and having an account there made it easier to check on our money as if we needed to guard it. We were complete rookies; raw, empty vessels starving for knowledge about life in general, but especially this new military life.

We learned how to calculate explosives and were introduced to the Bailey Bridge and pontoon boats. We learned about leading patrols and writing five-paragraph operations orders, the crutch of documents used in the army to lead formations and move troops across the battlefield. I had always enjoyed the outdoors and I loved the field exercises. It was exciting to paint my face with the camouflage sticks and sleep amongst the elements with my army-issue sleeping bag and shelter half. This was all fun for me and the basic officer course only magnified the patriotism that had grown in my heart during basic training.

I eventually began to soften my hard outer shell and I started to branch out and hang out with other races, and we shared our life experiences. I came from a small town where race was not an issue amongst my classmates, but these were people with whom I'd grown up. Jody, Billy, and Bobby were my brothers; they just happened to be white, same as Wendy and Lisa, who were like my sisters. A certain level of racial tension is inescapable in the South, like when my grandfather ensured Kem and I knew how to behave as kids to keep ourselves safe. However, amongst my peers, it hadn't really been an issue. As I began to open up to the other people in my officer basic course, I realized that it wasn't about race as much as it was about comfort and a level of trust. I, of all people, should've known better due to the misguided trust with my own father. The one person who should have protected me had tried to take my life, so my fears definitely transcended race into a much larger trust issue. But now, with the army, I was a part of a winning team with responsibilities, and it was great for me, because I felt good about my career. Even better, I felt like I'd made my mother proud, which had been my whole objective from the start.

In May, I returned to South Carolina to march across the stage in my college graduation and receive my diploma. That same weekend, I proposed to Yolanda and I was hoping for a stateside assignment to stay close to her. I only had a few weeks remaining before my officer basic course graduation, and I met privately with my assignment officers who dealt my fate: Korea. I would be going to the Second Infantry Division on an unaccompanied tour for one year. I'd wanted to see the world, but I hadn't been ready to go that far just yet, especially considering my recent engagement. However, I wouldn't be going alone because Larry had drawn the same short straw I had. I delivered the news to Yolanda and she took it in stride, staying positive about the whole situation, which gave me some relief.

Finally, assignments handed out, we finished our culminating exercise and prepared for graduation during the first week of June. My mother and Yolanda made the long drive to Fort Leonard Wood to watch the ceremony, which was nothing like graduating basic training. We were seated in an auditorium and a general officer gave a twenty-minute speech about the possibilities of what was in front of us, how we would make a difference, and so on. Then the officer basic course was done, and it was time to begin this military journey after taking a few weeks leave, which left time for reflection. In less than a year, I had received my officer commission, graduated from college, completed the engineer officer basic course, and proposed to the love of my life. I supposed I was officially an adult, although still without a car of my own.

I couldn't help comparing myself to my father, James J. Scott Sr. At this same age, my father's life had taken a drastically different turn. I understood that one mistake, one mishap in life, could take me on a similar path to his, so I had to focus on staying away from drama. Stay away from the weed smokers, don't drink and drive, just focus on my career, and walk that fine line. I did my best, and in the later part of June of 1994, I departed for Korea for my first tour of duty as a second lieutenant.

CHAPTER 17

Korea

I reported to Korea during the latter part of June, flying into Gimpo International Airport in the dead heat of summer. I was greeted by the pleasantries of kimchi as I boarded the bus to Seoul en route to Command Post Yongsan and the legendary Dragon Hill Lodge, a US Defense Department-owned hotel in Seoul open exclusively to active duty or retired military personnel and their families. It felt surreal to be in a foreign country. Arriving in Seoul was similar to entering the gates of Fort Polk, with the major difference being the sixteen-hour flight across the United States from the East Coast to the West, plus the long flight across the Pacific. I landed at Gimpo Airport with two duffel bags and an old suitcase in hand, my body filled with anticipation. I was a leader by rank, but I was still so green as I entered into the unknown.

There are Korean people everywhere I thought as I stared around the airport. Then I realized they were staring at me and it hit me: I was the foreigner! I was in their country. I had experienced being in a class full of mostly white people, but we'd all been Americans. By coming to Korea, I had entered a different world, where English was not the local language, and I was deeply intrigued. Back in the States, I'd grown up in the country around farm animals with nearby chicken farms. I'm sure that when Yankees came down south, the first thing that hit them was the smell. Korea was the same, in the sense that it smelled differently to me. Not bad or offensive, just different.

Once again, I had done it! I had begun an experience that many people I grew up with would never see for themselves. My tour of duty would last a year, and I couldn't just get in my car and drive for a few hours to get home. We were on a different time zone, fourteen hours ahead, and I was alone. Kem or my mom couldn't help me on this journey. I was twenty-four years old at the time, but I was sure this experience would advance me beyond my years.

The bus drive was at least an hour and a half from the airport. Evening had set in and I was just sitting there, taking it all in and thinking about how quickly things had seemed to happen for me, from college graduation to my officer basic course to now being in a foreign country. This was my life now, the life of an active duty army officer. We arrived at the hotel and the entrance of the Dragon Hill Lodge was something to marvel at, with its grandeur. It felt strange to have soldiers staying in a place as beautiful as that for the night. I would've been cool with barracks or something less grandiose, because I was new to this active duty experience and expected something humbler.

Instead, the hotel looked like something off of Fifth Avenue in New York City. There were restaurants, boutiques, nail salons, and even a high-end suit shop, of all things. *If only I was staying here for my tour,* I thought. In retrospect, maybe it would have been best to just stick me in one of the general purpose medium tents for the night instead of teasing me with such luxury. I had stayed in a hotel before, but it had been nothing like this, so I was extremely impressed. However, as of this writing, I've been living near the Dragon Hill Lodge for almost six years now and it's still just as cool as the first day I saw it.

It was late by the time we arrived on base at the hotel, and I was dog tired. We had been given a time to report in the morning, which I thought was a little too early after a fifteen-hour flight, but those moving up north closer to the demilitarized zone had to move out. We checked into our rooms to unwind for the rest of the evening. The room was standard with two full-sized beds, a mini fridge, and a small TV. However, when I opened the window to get a glimpse outside, there it was in all of its wonder: Seoul Tower. It was sitting right there in the distance, decorated with beautiful, glittering lights like the Eiffel Tower. It encapsulated all that Korea had to offer, the symbol of how far they had come since the Korean War. When I saw Seoul Tower, some of my nervousness eased. I thought about my duty, why I was there, and my responsibilities, and for a minute, everything was okay. There I was again, even further away than before—as far as physically possible—on the other side of the world from Ridge Spring, South Carolina. I was nervous, but excited.

Most of the people I knew from back home served in either the National Guard or the reserves. There were some of the older gentlemen who had experienced the tough war of Vietnam. All wars are tough, but it seemed that those who came home from Vietnam were reluctant to speak on it, my stepfather included. My military stories came from Kem, and boy, could he paint a picture! He would make stories of his time in Germany seem so real that I still dream of going there one day. Kem made me feel as if I was there with him at the parties or during the field exercises in the winter. He'd been stationed in Korea as well, but he hadn't talked it up the way he did Germany. However, I do remember the nylon zipper jumpsuits Kem had had made in Korea and the mink blankets he'd purchased there. I had lived vicariously through Kem, and now there I was, where my brother had once walked, but I would see it through my own eyes and I'd have my own experiences—and I was nervous.

It was sink or swim for the kid, because the guys in Ridge Spring had built me to be tough. Ridge Spring to Korea—man, if only Junior could've seen me. Junior was a former marine, or as he always says, just a marine, because once a marine, always a marine. Just like me, Junior drank the Kool-Aid, and to this day, he keeps all of his uniforms pressed and in a separate closet in pristine condition, despite the fact that he left the Marine Corps twenty years ago. We've had epic arguments over the years about our respective services and the only thing I will admit to him winning is the discussion about our dress uniforms. The army can't touch the Marine Corps when they put on those blue dress uniforms. We're making a comeback, but I will yield to my best friend on that one.

Junior had served in Okinawa, so he could relate to being on the other side of the world. However, it was my turn now, and although this was by no means a prison term, I initially felt that I had to do my time and return home to the Ridge. I already missed my mom and my fiancée so much, and I was nervous about missing the time hack of the 0700hrs reporting time, but I needn't have worried, because I was experiencing jet lag for the very first time. I slept for about four hours and then I was up for no apparent reason. *What is going on with my body?* I wondered. It was 0300hrs in the morning and I was awake without the slightest hope of going back to sleep, so I stared out the window at the Seoul Tower and imagined what was ahead. I thought about Yolanda and how much I missed her. I thought about my mom and my sister, Lynnette. I missed home already, but I thought about Kem and what he would say: "Suck it up, Foots! Be a man!"

Realistically, it wasn't like I could swim across the Pacific Ocean to the West Coast. I was stuck on the Korean Peninsula and had to make the most of this tour. I stared at the tower for a while and thought about the awesome opportunity I had to serve over there. I had arrived in the Land of the Morning Calm and it was all good.

In the morning, I, along with the rest of those Second Infantry Division Indian-patch-wearing warriors, loaded up in vans and headed north to Camp Casey and the turtle farm for in-processing. The turtle farm was the in-processing and out-processing facility. There was one building, a Quonset-type hut that was divided in two. Soldiers signed in to begin their tour on one end of the hut and signed out when they completed their tour, or permanent change of station. Therefore, the name "turtle" was invented because it took a year or so to go from one end of the building to the other—moving slowly, like a turtle.

We drove for what seemed like hours to Camp Casey and, upon arrival, I surveyed the scene. *Not so bad,* I thought. They had a Church's Chicken and a big post exchange, which is sort of a department store for a military base. I saw a few gyms and thought this setup was looking pretty okay. We were herded into a building and given instructions on height and weight tests, as well as times to report to the central issue facility to receive our combat gear. The army didn't play with height and weight standards back then, so we changed into PT uniforms and were weighed and measured as required.

The army height and weight standards apply to all soldiers serving in the military, whether they are in the army reserve, National Guard, or active duty. It applies to enlisted soldiers and officers of all ranks, both males and females. It is a standard that measures a person's height and weight based on guidelines listed on a chart. If you exceed the height and weight based on age or gender, you must then be measured using a body fat composition chart, now a database. If you exceed the body fat, you are considered over the required limit and must be enrolled in the overweight program. During the 1980s and '90s, being overweight meant you couldn't attend military schools, training courses, go on a pass, or many other things that would be considered beneficial in regards to a potential promotion. If you were overweight in the Second Infantry Division, you didn't ship to your unit, which could be an automatic career killer for officers, because you were expected to make weight and exceed the standards.

After having our heights and weights taken, we received enough gear to fight the Korean War all over again. *What is all of this crap?* I wondered as I surveyed everything, including the bear suit we were issued for the winter months. I shook my head but resigned myself to having enough stuff to qualify for my own episode of *Hoarders*. Then, just when I thought all was well, I was told I would be going to another camp.

"What?" I asked, surprised.

"You're an engineer assigned to the engineer brigade headquarters, so you're going to the Western Corridor, to Camp Howze."

Camp Howze was named after Medal of Honor recipient Major General Robert L. Howze, the first commander of the First Cavalry Division. This camp was one of six Western Corridor bases close to the demilitarized zone, which included Camps Greaves, Edwards, Garry Owens, Giant, and Stanton. I had no idea where I was headed, but I figured by the landscape rushing past the bus windows, it wouldn't be as nice as Camp Casey.

Camp Howze reminded me a little of Ridge Spring as we twisted and turned down two lane roads to Never-never Land. We drove for what seemed like hours, and then seemingly out of nowhere, a gate appeared.

"We're here!" the driver yelled.

What a desolate place, I thought as we entered the compound. We drove about twenty-five feet and started to drive up the road, which felt like climbing up a mountain as we went up and up and up. There was very little flat land there, with straight up or straight down as the only directions. Quonset huts that were built by the Twenty-Fourth Division, which had occupied the base from 1955 to 1957, peppered the grounds. This would be home for the next year of my life. Despite the rather vertical landscape, it felt very peaceful with all the trees.

"All right, sir! Here are your barracks," the driver said. "I'll help you grab your bags and take you to your room."

Because I was a lieutenant, I assumed I would have my own room. However, I got a taste of humble pie when I learned that I would be roommates with First Lieutenant Anthony Mitchell. It was a strange setup in the barracks, where the quarters only had one bedroom and the second guy had to sleep out in the open. Lieutenant Mitchell had seniority, which meant I slept in the living room area next to the kitchen. It was the humility I needed to show that I was not entitled to anything.

Lieutenant Mitchell was a serious officer, who didn't exchange a smile with a rookie second lieutenant at first greetings. He stood about six feet two inches and was very imposing. I tried to give him a grin to soften him up, but he wasn't having it.

"Who sent you here?" Lieutenant Mitchell asked, unsmiling.

"CPT Barbour told me to bed down here," I replied. Captain Barbour was a female company commander from the islands who didn't play around. She served as the Headquarters and Headquarters Detachment (HHD) Engineer CO, and I would be her executive officer for the next few months until a platoon opened up for me. Brigade headquarters are comprised of large staffs and have a need for a supporting element to take care of administrative functions. Therefore, the role of an HHD is to support the staff administratively.

I scanned the room as I waited for Lieutenant Mitchell's blow of a reply, when I noticed a familiar book on his table. It was a black and gold book that I recognized immediately, and before he could throw his verbal punch, I interjected.

"Are you an Alpha?" I asked.

"Yes, why?"

"I am, too!" I exclaimed. It was just the break I needed as he gave me a half smile.

"You can stay here for the night, but I'm senior around here and I get my own room," Lieutenant Mitchell said.

"Cool!" I replied.

"Put your things in the corner for now and relax," he said, and I did so. "Where did you attend school?"

"SC State," I replied proudly, my chest out. SC State Bulldogs always take pride in simply announcing our school, as if this instantly grants us a pass on all things.

"All right," he said. "I went to Prairie View, so I guess you're okay."

There's always a little tongue in cheek with the HBCU alums, so we had broken the ice, but I was still on my way out of Anthony's room in the morning to some poor second lieutenant's room instead. Anthony had served in Korea for almost a year already at that point, and he would be moving on to another camp in a few months to serve as the executive officer for his second tour of duty down the road at Camp Edwards. To this day, he is one of the sharpest officers I have ever met and he served as a mentor not only to minority officers, but to all of the officers he encountered. Every now and then you run into that type of person, especially military officers, who have the "it" factor. Anthony had it, and we all knew he would rise up through the ranks—and we were right. He became a great mentor to the younger lieutenants while he was there, and you could see his greatness from the beginning because of his demeanor and stature. As of this writing, he is currently a full colonel, still serving, with the possibility of being promoted to brigadier general.

After we connected over our fraternity and schools, Anthony immediately locked back into senior-lieutenant mode. He looked me over and gave me some advice as he sat with me in the living room for a little while.

"Learn your job and don't embarrass us around here," he said. "Look sharp and be on point all of the time, because someone is always watching you."

I understood his message and felt his tone as he held court and lectured a youngster for a minute. Finally, he stood.

"I'm stepping out for a few," Anthony said. "Relax! There are some beverages in the fridge and some food if you're hungry."

"Thanks, man!" I said. He looked at me as if to say, "Don't call me 'man,' but I'll give you a pass this one time because you're my fraternity brother."

Sure enough, I was out of there the next day and laced in a room with another second lieutenant who had arrived just a week or so before me, which meant he got the bedroom and I was still in the living room. Second Lieutenant Chong was a Chinese American and a Virginia Military Institute alumnus. We were both engineer officers who had just arrived from the same class at officer basic course. He had served as the class academic advisor and already knew a lot about me, at least in regards to my academic standings in the class. He had once lectured me about improving my scores and standings in class, to which I had taken offense. We exchanged some words that day because he seemed to look down on me a little because I wasn't a genius like him, and I resented the fact that he had come off as a snob with an elitist attitude.

Nevertheless, we were roomies, and for the first time in my life other than the open bays in basic training, I would be living on a regular basis with a person who didn't look like me. He was a neat freak and I was not, making me the Oscar to his Felix, which always caused a couple of pointed stares in our room. I knew this arrangement wouldn't last a year when I was frying some chicken tenders in the kitchen one evening and he came in the door and immediately covered his nose. Lieutenant Chong looked over at the mess I had made with flour and grease, and without thinking, launched into an interrogation.

"You're not going to eat that, are you?" he asked disdainfully, his voice slightly muffled by the hand over his nose.

"Eat what?" I asked.

"That has to be the unhealthiest meal I have ever seen in my life!" he exclaimed. He was probably right, but I dared him to go there, especially with the chicken, so that became our first official argument.

"I hope you're going to clean that crap up!" he yelled.

I couldn't wait to involve my friend, Larry, who had just arrived on pen. He lived upstairs and would be joining me in the feast I had prepared with a side of fries and the works.

"He doesn't understand a delicacy when he sees it," Larry said with a Mississippi chuckle.

"You're right, Larry," I said, my South Carolina grin stretched across my face. Lieutenant Chong glowered, but he served me one better a week later when he mixed up one of his home-cooked meals.

What is that smell? I wondered when I entered the door. There was Lieutenant Chong with his apron on, smiling and stirring his dish without saying a word. However, he didn't have to, because it clicked in my head: "Respect one's customs" was the phrase that came to mind as I sat on my bed out in the living room while he finished preparing his meal. This was a marriage of a different kind, and one of those off-the-record life lessons I got free of charge. We had to respect each other's cultures and ideals. I had to learn to pick up after myself and turn the music down, because we shared a room.

Lieutenant Chong served as the assistant maintenance officer for the Forty-Fourth Engineer Battalion and worked some long hours. Most nights, he arrived in the room after 2200hrs, which I thought was ridiculous. Was there really that much work to do every day? I hoped never to get that job. Lieutenant Chong was grumpy most of the time, and rightfully so, with that position. He had already made plans to exit the military once his commitment was complete. He eventually found a way to get his own room ad made his exit after rooming with me for about four months, leaving me with my own room and no roommate for the rest of my tour.

I served under Captain Barbour's leadership, learning the intricacies of leading soldiers and working as a staff officer. I was in charge of our personnel administrative section consisting of an energetic sergeant, a specialist, a private first class, and a couple of Korean Augmentations to the United States Army, also known as KATUSAs. They were typically young college students who had to serve their mandatory two-year military obligation as required by Korean law. They were great soldiers, and it was a unique experience to have the opportunity to learn Korean culture from them. They immediately introduced me to the Korean snack bar and some Korean dishes I enjoyed immensely: cheese ramen and Yaki mandu, the latter of which is a steamed or fried Korean dumpling that looks a lot like a Chinese pot sticker.

Captain Barbour was a straight shooter and got the question out of the way immediately. She had a Dezzaire-type of personality and just fired away: "What happened to you?"

I knew it was coming, so I gave her my standard line about a house fire.

"Well, if you're in the military and you're over here, I guess you're fit for duty, so get ready to work," she said.

"Yes, ma'am!"

She was a firecracker, but she was exactly what I needed as my introduction into my active duty army life. I learned how to task and delegate, supervise and train. I received an opportunity to see the big picture, first by working at the brigade level and interacting with senior officers while I processed paperwork for them. I saw a chief warrant officer four for the first time, and it was like talking to a general officer back in those days. Warrant officers are unique in that they are commissioned officers, but they specialize working in specific fields; you don't typically see many of them. They come from the enlisted ranks prior to their selection into the warrant officer field, making them, for the most part, already seasoned soldiers. There are warrant ones, twos, threes, fours, and fives, and they are all extremely smart and talented in their chosen fields, especially because it's not easy to advance through the ranks. We show them a lot of respect at every rank, but when you see a chief warrant officer four or five, you pay them their respect as if you are talking to a general. As I quickly learned in the army as a commissioned officer, although you outrank a sergeant major and a chief warrant officer, you better tread lightly and show them their respect. There are three people to whom I never talk back: my mother, a sergeant major, or a chief warrant officer.

I was responsible for the monthly unit status report, which required me to interact with Chief to obtain some important information. Chief would scold me when I didn't get the process right and he talked to me like I was one of his teenage sons or something. I listened to him and learned a lot. I was the lowest-ranking officer around the headquarters, and of course, the senior officers had the typical jokes ready for me.

"Are you old enough to drink, lieutenant?"

"Do you even have a driver's license?"

However, in between all the ribbing, they taught and mentored me. We had a first sergeant as well, and he was the man. First Sergeant was the uncle I'd always wished for, sharing stories with me about times in Europe when the army was, according to him, the "real army." I lived vicariously through his stories and hung onto his every word. He also played a little basketball from time to time, so we had that in common. We were located on Camp Howze, which was a small compound, but we made the most of it. We had barbecues every weekend and First Sergeant would always tell me to put the word out and pass the hat to purchase the food. I believe it is a requirement that all first sergeants know how to grill, and he was the best until he got tired and delegated the tongs to some up-and-coming sergeant to take over while he sipped his beer and chatted with the rest of us. First Sergeant began teasing me constantly once he found I had a fiancée waiting for me back home and would be getting married soon.

"What do you know about marriage, lieutenant?"

"You haven't even received your first paycheck yet, have you?"

"Can you even grow a mustache?" (I couldn't, but I didn't care).

"Let me see a picture, lieutenant," First Sergeant said. When I showed him, he raised his eyebrows appreciatively. "Man, you sure she's still waiting on you? She sure is pretty and you've been over here for all this time," he kidded good-naturedly, elbowing me a little. "Just joking, lieutenant," he said quickly with a smile when he saw the look on my face, as if I needed to call home immediately to check, just in case. First Sergeant was the best, and he made my time there fun.

I survived my time in the HHD and it was time to get my very own platoon, the most coveted position in the army for second lieutenants. I was so proud that I would have my own soldiers as a line platoon leader in Charlie Company, Forty-Fourth Engineer Battalion. I would be replaced as an executive officer by Second Lieutenant Calvin Hudson, the most charismatic and squared away officer I had ever encountered as a peer. Calvin had arrived in the Land of the Morning Calm by way of Albany State as an engineer officer as well, and he already had the voice and demeanor of a seasoned officer. He immediately knew what he wanted and told me he wanted to be the best lieutenant around and he expected the top evaluation. Initially, I thought he had to be the most arrogant lieutenant in the inventory, but he meant it and he backed it up. He was sharp in and out of uniform, one of those Kappa's with the cane and the talent to twirl it. Calvin's shoes were always spit shined and he would let us know he had the cleanest boots around, at least amongst the officers, because no one could touch First Sergeant's or Sergeant's Major boots.

So now there was Calvin the Kappa, Larry the Sigma, and me, the Alpha. We all hung out together and made the most of our time. Larry and I got our platoons around the same time and often compared notes. It was during these months that we truly learned our craft as we spent weeks in the field. We had our sapper engineers supporting the infantry and armor units, placing minefields, and blowing stuff up on order. It was fun! The winter in Korea was freezing cold, the kind of cold that makes you want to change your profession, but we survived. We wrote our operations orders pushing out to Army Training and Evaluation Programs (ARTEPs) and maneuvers, and we learned that in order to survive, you had to listen to your NCOs—especially your platoon sergeant. Lieutenants had to learn the balance of rank versus experience and respect versus loyalty. We ate and pounded some pickets together. We slept in the field together and shared stories about our families; we trained hard and partied harder when we left the field. They had my back and I had theirs, and this was the best time I ever had in the army.

I spent weekends in Yongsan or Osan when we received passes to go south. Knock-off Nikes cost about twenty dollars back then and typically only lasted about two or three games of basketball, unless you were really slicing and dicing, blowing out a tread on the spot. We purchased sweat suits with our names stitched on them, which were cool because you could easily convert them to summer wear by zipping off the sleeves and legs just above the knees. We also bought tailored suits, which ended up being a waste for me because I grew out of them within a year's time, but Korea was a blast.

Our camp was small, which made us a tight-knit group. We played a lot of basketball and would often travel to Camp Casey to enter the tournaments. We played softball and flag football, we grilled and barbecued often, and we talked about things we were going to do and buy once we got back to the world we called "The States." Some wanted motorcycles, but I wanted a Mustang, and we all dreamed about driving again since we were on unaccompanied tours and personal vehicles were not authorized in our area. There we were, only a stone's throw from the demilitarized zone, technically still at war with another country with the armistice in place, but at times it still felt so peaceful there. Additionally, I had learned about General Colin Powell's time served as a battalion commander in the infamous Second Infantry Division, and could now proudly mark my name down as an officer with time served in the division.

As my time started coming to a close, I began to work with my branch manager on my next assignment. Typically, young aspiring officers try to move on to other divisions like the Fourth Infantry Division, the First Cavalry Division, the Eighty-Second Airborne Division, or the 101st Airborne Division, but not me. I had no senior mentor at the time and I just figured I wanted to be close to home after a year away, so I asked for Fort Jackson, South Carolina. The branch manager told me that wouldn't be a problem, and a week or two later, I had my assignment locked in.

Major Walton, "The Hammer," who had served as our instructor during our college days, was assigned to the Twenty-Fifth Infantry Division in Hawaii and would be coming over to Korea for a training exercise. He contacted some of the old Bulldogs and arranged for us to eat lunch with him at the Dragon in Yongsan. I was excited to see the Hammer and happily took him up on that offer, and we were joined by Joe Bookard, another alum who was currently serving in Korea. At lunch, Major Walton asked us about our tour and he gave us career advice.

"Where are you going next, Bookard?" he asked in his hammer voice.

"I'm headed to the Eighty-Second, Major Walton," Joe said proudly.

"Hoo-ah!" Major Walton replied. "What about you, Scott?"

"Fort Jackson."

Silence fell over the table for several seconds.

"Did you ask for that?" he asked.

"No way!" I said, which was a lie, but I wasn't about to drop that on the Hammer in an open forum.

"You need to get that assignment changed immediately," he said gravely. Training and Doctrine Command (TRADOC) was considered a career killer in those days, but I didn't know any better. Tactical units that were part of divisions were more career-enhancing assignments. Most officers considered TRADOC as taking a break, or not working as hard as others in units that deployed and trained at the national training centers, spending weeks in the field. Senior officers wanted you to earn your pay and pay your dues to rise up through the ranks, just as they had.

"Do you want me to get involved?" Major Walton asked.

"No, sir," I said. "I will fix it next week."

"Okay," Major Walton said. "Because you are done if you go there."

I felt like a zero, especially next to Joe and his assignment. Joe and I had been close during our ROTC days, and he was another shining star; a walking, talking, all-in billboard soldier. He caught the bug after advanced camp and talked army in his sleep.

"You'd better listen to the Hammer," Joe encouraged me as we headed back to camp. "If you want to get promoted beyond the rank of captain, you'd better get out of that assignment."

I knew I wasn't changing anything, but I couldn't tell that to those hard-chargers at that particular juncture. I felt bad about the assignment, but it had been a long year away from home and I was a mama's boy, and a madly-in-love newlywed, to boot. Fort Jackson, here I come!

CHAPTER 18

Kids

Yolanda and I never had any kind of sit down discussion about trying to have a baby. We were just going through life and doing what newly married couples do, until she realized that she wasn't getting pregnant.

"Is there anything wrong with your sperm?" she finally asked me one day.

"I don't know," I replied, frowning. "I've never thought about it." I promised her I'd go get myself checked out, and although I didn't want to admit it, I was secretly panicking that there was something wrong. I had no idea how the process worked, but I made an appointment with the medical clinic and headed in. When I arrived, I felt like I was sixteen years old again and nervously trying to figure out how to tell the nurse at the desk why I was there.

"I need to get my sperm checked out," I whispered. I half expected her to start laughing at my boyish request, but as a professional, my request didn't even make her blink.

"Just fill out these forms," she said, handing over a clipboard. I felt relieved when this didn't seem like it was going to be a big deal—until I remembered that it wasn't enough just to tell the nurse; I still had to take the test. I won't go into the details, but suffice it to say, it was about as unpleasant as having a prostate exam. But I took the test, and then there was nothing to do but wait. Even though

Yolanda and I hadn't been actively trying to get pregnant before the test, the idea that we might not be able to have a baby because of a possible issue with my sperm was daunting. Fortunately, the results were clear and I passed. This pass was better than my bus license or driver's license, or even my commissioning. My wife and I even went to Red Lobster to celebrate, my ego sufficiently placated by positive results. Those positive results were all we needed, because we were off to the races towards actively starting our family together.

The following month, my wife took a pregnancy test and left the applicator on my nightstand for me to see. I overlooked the test at first because I'm a guy, and I missed the obvious clue. Tired of waiting, my wife finally pointed it out to me.

"Hey!" she exclaimed. "Look on the bed stand, stupid!"

As soon as I saw the pregnancy test, my heart started pounding. I knew if she'd laid out the test for me to see that it had to be positive, but I still had to see it for myself. I picked up the test and stared at the double lines. Yolanda was pregnant. We were going to have a baby. I couldn't believe it! I was shocked and thrilled and over the moon about our growing family. I later found out that weeks earlier, my battalion commander's wife had given Yolanda a book about how to conceive and supposedly how to choose the baby's sex. She'd had it all planned out! My wife wasn't usually big on the spouses' coffees the officer wives would have together on a monthly basis, but she attended once in a while, and I guess they began a discussion about kids and determining the sex of a child. The next thing I knew, Yolanda had a book from the battalion commander's wife on how to determine the sex of a child. There I was, a lieutenant, and my wife was borrowing books from the battalion commander's wife on *this*, of all topics. I wanted so badly to script the next staff meeting just to avoid a possible discussion with the battalion commander about it.

"You need to return that book as soon as possible," I insisted to Yolanda. "That's embarrassing!"

"Well, if they have it, then they must have used it as well," Yolanda said. I couldn't argue with her point, but I was still embarrassed. However, to my relief, the battalion commander never said a word about the book to me. Evidently, I was not the only one who didn't want certain topics to come up at work.

We decided to find out the sex of the baby instead of waiting for that delivery room announcement from the doctor. I said I didn't care if the baby was a boy or a girl, but secretly I was hoping for a son. When we went in to see the doctor for the ultrasound, we were both anxious and excited. Finding out the sex was one more step in solidifying the reality of having a child. No longer would we be talking about just a "baby," but a boy or a girl, a son or a daughter. As the ultrasound tech squirted jelly on my wife's stomach and began to examine the baby with the ultrasound camera, I felt the excitement welling in me, those final moments before the firework burst.

"Congratulations!" the tech announced. "It's a boy!"

I was elated! That same day, I went out and started buying stuff. I couldn't help it, just like so many other parents before me and so many that came after me. The urge to celebrate my son was overwhelming, and my baby boy was well stocked with basketballs and footballs months before his arrival. I couldn't wait to tell everyone at work, and I soon announced the news to my bosses and other leaders in a staff meeting. They gave me a round of applause as I beamed with pride. The military team rejoiced and rallied around its members during times like this, and it felt so good to bond over such a joyous time in my life. During a visit home, Yolanda and I announced the news to our family. I felt so swollen with pride and I couldn't help but be so over the top with my enthusiasm.

As the months passed, I still felt so proud, but nervousness had begun to creep into my thoughts. I had no idea how to raise a son. Kem and I hadn't had consistent male role models throughout our youth, so all I had to go off of was Charles Ingalls on *Little House on the Prairie* and Bill Cosby on *The Cosby Show*. While they were excellent TV role models, it wasn't like I could call them up for advice. Of course, there had been other men in my life: JB's dad, my cousin's husband, Luis, and my cousins, Vernon and Purvis. I wondered if I needed to pull what I could from these figures, or if I should just go with my instincts. My mother had raised us alone and had ruled with tough love. Was that the right blueprint to use as a parent? I had to figure out what sort of parent I was going to be, and suddenly it seemed like the months were speeding by all too quickly.

During the seventh month, my mother came up from Ridge Spring to visit us in Columbia. She wanted to spend some time with Yolanda and check on her to see how Yolanda was doing, so I decided to give them some space. By then, I was an avid tennis player and I decided to call up my good friend, Raheen, to play a couple of rounds. Our wives were both teachers and taught at the same school, and Raheen and I had hit if off immediately. We were best buddies, but we talked a lot of trash on the tennis courts and would play for hours at a time. While my mother visited Yolanda, Raheen and I lobbed the ball back and forth on the court. Although I didn't hear my cell phone ring, I checked it between sets and saw the missed call. A little tired from chasing the ball, I decided to use a call back as an excuse to get some rest. However, the call was anything but relaxing.

"Where are you?" my mother demanded.

"I'm down the street playing tennis," I started to say, but my mom cut me off and began to scold me for being away and playing tennis of all things, as if the tennis court couldn't have been where I really was because she didn't even know I played the sport.

"Your wife's water burst and the ambulance just arrived at the condo!" my mother exclaimed. "Yolanda is in labor and we're heading to the hospital now!"

"What?" I gasped in surprise. "But she's only seven and a half months!"

My wife stands at barely five feet, and at the time, she only tipped the scales at barely over a hundred pounds. Her small frame put her at risk during the pregnancy, and the doctors warned her of the possible difficulty in carrying our child to full term. Yolanda had continued to teach for a few months until December, approximately three months prior to our son's due date, before she was placed on bed rest. She was supposed to be on closer to six months of bed rest, but so far everything seemed to be going well. We knew that each week she edged closer to full term was so precious because it gave our son a better and better chance. We took every precaution and Yolanda held on for as long as possible. However, in spite of our precautions and the best-laid plans, my son had decided that he couldn't stay in any longer and it was time for him to enter the world.

In our hurry, Raheen and I broke some traffic laws getting to the hospital. We cut a thirty-minute drive almost in half, arriving at the hospital as the doctors were trying to do everything to keep our son inside for a little longer. Each day, each hour was precious. My mom reassured me that things would be okay and the doctor called me in. I started to listen to a litany of foreign terms, like "dilated" and "centimeters," "epidural" and "C-section." It was at that moment that I began to understand that women really are stronger than men in so many ways. I had jumped out of airplanes, played multiple sports at a high level, and wrestled with my older brother for many years, but I didn't feel ready for this, not even a little bit.

My wife received an epidural in her spine, was cut open, and propped up in what seemed like the most uncomfortable position in the entire world. All I had to offer at that point was a hand to hold and a few words of comfort. I was a role player sitting on the bench, but at least I was there. I watched the doctor's work, and suddenly, our son was on his way. My wife couldn't see what was going on, but I was right there watching the little fella make his entrance into the world.

James Scott III was born on March 31, 1997, in Columbia, South Carolina, weighing in at only two pounds—just like I had. He was so small! I was alarmed by his size, but my mom continued to reassure me that he would be fine. History was repeating itself, as my mom reminded me when she later told me the story of my own birth when I'd arrived two months prematurely and fought for my life, just as my son was doing.

"Have you decided on a name?" the doctors asked. I told them "James III"—"JJ" for short—and my wife agreed.

The doctors continued to work on him and Yolanda, and I was left alone in my thoughts with my namesake. I realized that the hospital was only a few miles from the prison that held my father, the first James Scott, and it all came full circle, the irony not lost on me. One life stalled with a life sentence because of what he had done to his own namesake, and me, with the opportunity to change the narrative and legacy of our name to become something honorable. I could've given my son a totally different name. After all, what was I trying to prove?

But I figured that instead of attempting to erase my past, I would take control of my narrative instead of letting it control me. It's like when I choose not to cover up my burns and instead opt to wear short sleeves and short pants, revealing that something happened to me. In doing this, I tell people that this is who I am and how I look; get over it and move on. My son is my future and we will not be defined by our tragic past. Did my son arrive early to show me how precious life is and not to take life for granted? Did he arrive early to allow me to reflect on my life and the responsibilities ahead? Maybe it was to show me that he was like me, a reflection of me, a reincarnation of me without the scars, to allow my mom and me to witness and show the power of God. Whatever the reason, James was here and fighting to be strong enough to go home.

James was born two months prematurely, only twenty-eight weeks to term. The doctors brought paperwork for my wife to sign, consenting for developmental therapy because our son was so early and tiny. I will never forget the tears in her eyes as she listened to the doctor. James was our first child and I felt her emotional weight. She was lying there, having just gone through a C-section, in an immense amount of pain, JJ was in the neonatal intensive care unit, and there were so many questions and concerns swirling around every moment. I wished desperately that I could make it right for her, but it wasn't up to me. It was in God's hands, but I felt the weight of the situation on my own shoulders all the same.

I wanted to walk down the hall and go to the elevator and exit the hospital doors alone; I wanted to walk around the corner and sink into my own emotions and just cry, but my wife needed me. She needed me to show strength and give her some sign of reassurance, and I knew I had to step up and give that to her. I summoned all the positive energy I had left in my body and focused on the birth and the fact that JJ was here, here on earth for a reason. That was reason enough to believe that everything would be all right, so I packaged that thought up and served it to my wife with a smile and jokes to ease the pain and stress she obviously felt at the time.

"JJ has a big head like his daddy, but he's a fighter like me, too," I joked.

As the days passed, I reassured my wife that JJ was getting stronger every day.

"The doctors say he's progressing very well," I updated her. I tried to be strong for her, and I really believed that he would be fine.

I traveled from the north side of Columbia to downtown every day to see my son at the hospital. He couldn't leave until he gained five pounds, and I never thought in my life that I would be praying for someone to gain weight. These days, my prayers are for me to drop five pounds, but I guess I used up all my weight prayers on my kids. Slowly but surely, JJ's scale began to tilt towards five.

"He's at three pounds, four ounces today!"

"He's progressing well and he's at three pounds, eight ounces!"

When he hit the milestone of four pounds and beyond, the anticipation of going home was almost overwhelming. The hospital was stressful, and even as we edged closer to our goal of five pounds, everything seemed endless. *Man, what is it about my family and this uphill journey? Why all the tests? What does it all mean? Haven't we been through enough, God? Please don't make this journey difficult for my son.* In my quiet time, my conversations with God became more frequent and pronounced. *Not to be disrespectful, God, but what is this about? I can deal with the scars and the stares and all of the struggles that come with them, but don't do this to my child. Allow us to bring him home and help him to be home. Please?*

JJ was getting better, stronger, and bigger, but he wasn't out of the woods yet. He still had mental tests and his heart was not as strong as it could have been.

After two months in the neonatal intensive care unit, JJ fought his way to five pounds. We were elated, but they held him for a few more days for observation, which only served to add to the anticipation. While we waited, I ensured we had the proper car seat so that when the doctors gave us the green light, we'd be ready. Then, finally, we got the call: It was time for JJ to come home. It felt like Christmas Day times ten for me. Finally, our son had reached the point where his health no longer posed a risk and we could take him home. However, he did need to come home with a portable heart monitor, which worried my wife to no end. But the important thing was that our son was finally going to leave the hospital. On that day he was discharged, I couldn't have been prouder. I had never driven so cautiously before in my life; it must have taken forty-five minutes to make the typically twenty-minute drive as if we were in a parade, but I had precious cargo on board and this was a momentous day. We were finally taking him home after two months in the hospital, and although he arrived at our condo with some instructions, we were overjoyed to have JJ with us.

The first couple of nights turned us into nervous wrecks because the heart monitor kept going off like a fire detector after burning some fries in the kitchen. The alarms constantly ripped us from what little rest we managed to catch, and we kept checking on JJ to ensure he was still breathing. I felt like I was on a long field exercise operating off three hours of sleep a night. I think I had that monitor checked for accuracy and battery life every time we went back to the hospital. JJ was my first son so I knew I had to just suck it up, but I promised myself that one day, when JJ reached the proper age, I would wake him up every hour, on the hour for payback—no explanation, just wake him up.

When he was born, JJ was so small. He fought for his life trying to gain those first five pounds, but now he stands six feet tall, at 190 pounds, and as of this writing, he's currently a college student at the University of South Carolina at Aiken. Just like his dad, he likes to eat, and maybe one day I will have to give him my box of prayers to reverse those pounds, because they aren't working for me!

A few months after James was born, we were due for a permanent change of station and headed to Fort Leonard Wood for the engineer advanced officer course. But that wasn't the only major change in our lives—Yolanda was pregnant again! If you do the math between James Jr. and our younger son, Joshua, they're the same age for five weeks of each year. We were excited, but also a little embarrassed to be expecting another baby so soon after our first.

"Don't you dare make some dramatic announcement in front of family!" my wife told me. I agreed, fully intending to do as she'd requested.

Prior to our departure to Fort Leonard Wood, James Jr. was scheduled to have his christening baptism. Yolanda's father, an ordained minister, would perform the ceremony, and all of the family, both mine and hers, would be in attendance. When the ceremony began, my wife and I stood up in front of the church with James Jr. I looked around at our family and I felt a swell of happiness and pride, and suddenly, I just couldn't keep the words in anymore. I leaned over towards my father-in-law's ear.

"We're pregnant again!" I whispered excitedly.

"What?" he asked, astonished.

My wife, however, was less excited about my announcement and wanted to choke me, but I just couldn't keep the news inside. Once the ceremony was over, my father-in-law checked with Yolanda, who confirmed that yes, we were expecting another baby. Then, when everyone had gathered together for the family meal after the baptism, my father-in-law dropped the bombshell.

"James and Yolanda are expecting another baby!" he announced.

Everyone stared at us in shock, while Yolanda gave me a look that, in no uncertain terms, told me that she thought I had a big mouth. However, she forgave me and we were able to let ourselves celebrate the fact that we were expecting another boy. I thought it was perfect that we were going to have another son, because now James would have a little brother to play with and the boys would have each other, just like Kem and me.

Joshua was born on February 23, 1998, at Fort Leonard Wood, Missouri Hospital, one month premature at thirty-two weeks, weighing four pounds. I was enrolled in the engineer advanced officer course at the time and was contacted by my instructor to report to the hospital immediately. I was a little surprised, because we still had a month to go before Josh was full term, but my wife wasn't exactly a full-term girl, so I gathered my things and headed to the delivery room. Fortunately for all of us, we lived on the installation and it only took a few minutes to get there.

Having been through this before with JJ, I considered myself a veteran by then, so I grabbed my gown as instructed and conducted my scrubs to sanitize my hands before entering the delivery room. I was ready…as if I really had a part to play in the birth at that point; my poor wife was the one who had to go through C-section number two. I thanked God that my father-in-law was on the other side of the country, because he surely would have lectured me about putting his daughter through this drama again. I like to think I would have pointed out that it took two to tango, but in reality, I know that's an argument that would have stayed firmly in my head. You have to know my father-in-law to know you have to get your shots in when you can, and even when something is my wife's fault, in his eyes, it's my fault, and he lets me know it.

Josh arrived with a full head of hair and he had to be the most handsome fella I had ever seen. Fort Leonard Wood, like most military hospitals, didn't have a neonatal intensive care unit, so Josh had to be flown to Columbia, Missouri. My wife was in no condition to travel due to the C-section, so I made the two-hour drive to Columbia to be with Josh. There were limits on the amount of time a student could miss in my advanced engineer course before being dropped from the role. I had a decision to make, and it was an easy one—family first, always—but the instructors were more than accommodating for me. We had another class beginning a couple of weeks behind our current class, so they allowed me to recycle to the following class to allow time for me to care for my son. The army's way of taking care of soldiers still rings true, and I couldn't have been more grateful to them for saving my career and allowing me to care for Josh when he needed me.

I took some leave and spent time with Josh as he built up strength, just like his older brother had. Josh only needed a pound before discharge, and he gained it pretty quickly. His independent spirit was apparent from the beginning, and although I know all parents are biased, I thought he had model-like features. He was as handsome as his mom is beautiful, and I just couldn't stop staring at him and smiling. It was amazing, seeing two different versions of myself in my sons with polar opposite personalities. The boys were my pride and joy and I saw so much of my brother and me in them every time I looked at them. I felt like I had an opportunity to raise them in ways that I had not experienced, like they had a chance for the do over I'd wanted for my own childhood. I could give them things I'd never had, play with them, and nurture them. I love being a dad.

My wife had already given birth to two boys, putting her body at risk in the process, so we thought we were done having children. Then, at the end of 2001, we found out Yolanda was pregnant again. After finding out early both times with James and Josh, we decided we wanted the gender to be a surprise. However, in all honesty, we were hoping for a girl. We had two sons who were close in age, not even a year apart. JJ and Josh had both been at-risk pregnancies, but my wife wanted a girl. We didn't plan to have another child, but neither did we plan to not have one, and four years after Josh was born, my wife surprised me with yet another positive pregnancy stick.

We had been used to preparing for doubles of everything because of James and Josh's ages: double stroller, double formula, and twice the amount of Pampers, two daycare bills, and bunk beds to boot. Boys were easy for me because I saw so much of Kem and me in them, and treated them as such: "Clean up your room!" "Pick up these toys!" "Stop hitting your brother!" "Let's go play basketball or go to the playground and swing high on the swing set and get dirty!" Easy!

Yolanda was ordered on bed rest for each of our kids, and her last pregnancy was no exception. My wife absolutely loves teaching, and the idea of having to stop working in her classroom was like punishment. She tried to be a stay-at-home mom early on in our marriage, but it only lasted about six months before she headed back to the classroom. Teachers are amazing, as I have learned through the years from witnessing my wife and her teacher friends. They work relentlessly in their classrooms for hours, including after school and on the weekends. It's something inside them that drives them beyond the little money they receive for the work they put in. As a matter of fact, at that point in my assignment, my wife would arrive home from work after me. There I was, a soldier on call twenty-four hours a day, seven days a week if required, and I was pulling up in the driveway before my wife. I felt funny about this for a while, but I learned over the years that at times, even soldiers can't outwork teachers.

However, the doctor put a stop to that and ordered Yolanda on bed rest for four months—but she only did it for two. Even so, she held onto Trinity the longest, carrying her close to full term, only a few weeks short. On August 29, 2002, our daughter Trinity Sanaa Scott was born in Fayetteville, North Carolina, while I was stationed at Fort Bragg. She was born only a little early at thirty-four weeks, and she was the only one of our children that did not require a cesarean. Her middle name comes from the actress Sanaa Lathan of *Love & Basketball.* Sanaa Lathan is one of my all-time favorite actresses, so my wife consented to give her name to our daughter.

I was there when Trinity was born and that day changed my life. Soldiers often miss the births of their children either due to deployments or training, but I was fortunate to be there for all three of my kids. We didn't know the sex at the time, but we both had a good feeling about this one. There was no C-section required, and Yolanda pushed her out without any issues. Well, really, I'm one to talk about childbirth because I had the easy job of just watching and not having to do any of the work. Trinity arrived after some cheerleading cries of "Push!" from the doctor, and out she came.

"It's a girl!" the doctor announced.

I saw my daughter and my wife and I knew for sure there was a God. For the second time in my life, I felt something close to the time I walked up to the front of that church so many years ago and gave my life to God. It was a serene feeling of complete joy and happiness. A baby girl! I saw the innocence in my daughter's eyes and I thought of my sister, Lynnette. I thought about my wife, my mom, my mother-in-law. I thought about Ms. Henman, Ms. Denny, Mama Gladys, and all of the other powerful women who had impacted my life. I saw them in my daughter, all bundled up in one little package, and I felt the magnitude of the responsibility that was now upon my shoulders to protect her with all of my being. I felt like I had just kind of been going through the motions, allowing my boys to be boys, not really knowing how to raise them, but just pulling from all of these different experiences with sports and TV. But here was this princess of mine, and I couldn't mess this up.

I needed to become a better man, a better father, and a better husband. I had to figure out how to prepare myself financially, emotionally, and spiritually to support Trinity, the boys, and my wife. I understood modeled behavior, and was cognizant of that in the way I treated my wife. I wanted to show the boys, especially as they got older, the importance of holding doors for women and taking off your hat indoors, but it became especially important because of Trinity. I knew that, by default, I would be her first experience of love towards a man. She would watch me and study me in the way I carried myself and the way I treated her mother. Trinity's birth brought that to the forefront and I resolved to do whatever I could to be the man I needed to be. I couldn't let her down.

I now had three different shades of me in two boys and one baby girl. They all had distinct personalities and were amazing kids. God had done this for me, for us. He had given my wife and me these gifts, these wonderful gifts, and now it was up to me to hold up my end of the bargain and try to right the wrongs of my past by raising two boys to be men and raising my baby girl to be strong and independent.

CHAPTER 19

Facing My Father, Part II

When I returned from Korea and was assigned to Fort Jackson in South Carolina, I was happy to be back in the States. I was closer to home, closer than I'd been in ages, although I was still an hour's drive away. Still, an hour is much better than an ocean. My new job required me to work most weekends, but it was still comforting to be closer to my mother. Yolanda and I had only been married for six months at the time and we were adjusting not only to marriage, but to life in a new environment.

About a year after I returned from Korea, a thought suddenly hit me: Growing up, my father had felt like he was a million miles away from me, locked up in a faraway land. But in reality, he was not only in the same city, but in Kirkland Correctional Center, only a stone's throw away from where I was posted. Physically, we were closer to each another than we'd been in years, but in other ways we were still so far apart. I was surprised it had taken me this long to realize this information about my father. Had I thought of it, I could've made that connection when I first got the orders about my transfer. I had spent so much time distancing myself from my father, and who he was and what he did, that to find myself so close once again was not only shocking to me, but a little unsettling as well.

I never shared these circumstances with anyone with whom I was stationed. Some would ask about my scars, but as I often did with people I didn't know, I would tell them I was in a house fire as a child and it was an accident. It allowed me to end the conversation quickly and still maintain my privacy. Even though I felt like I was somewhat past the incident, it still bothered me when people would ask what happened. Everyone involved in the conversation would feel uncomfortable, at least for a few moments, and I was forced to once again put up that invisible barrier to guard myself and my space. I wanted so badly for people to look past the scarred mask I was forced to wear and to just see me as one of them, a regular person. I understood their curiosity, but there's only so long that you can feel everyone staring at you like a zoo animal before you want to break free and blend in.

One day, I received a mission from my boss to find a location for a future exercise. While driving out to a location, I received a phone call from my mother.

"Your father called," she said. "He wants to get in touch with you."

"Okay…" I said hesitantly, my voice shallow, so unlike its normal cadence. "Give him my home number."

Although I did my best to focus on work, my mind was consumed with thoughts of my father. What did he want? Why did he want to talk to me after all these years? What was he going to say? What was *I* going to say? Years of pain and anger swirled around my mind until I was finally forced to push my feelings aside just to be able to pay attention to the task at hand. Wondering wouldn't give me the answers I wanted; I'd simply have to wait.

Later that day, after I returned home, the phone rang.

"Collect call from James Scott. Do you accept?"

It was so strange to hear my name on the other end of the phone. I hesitated for a moment, finding it difficult to speak.

"Yes," I finally said, my voice crackling. While I waited for the connection, my nerves began to overtake me. What would I say to this man who had put me through so much?

"Hello, son!" my father said, his voice both so foreign and so familiar.

"How are you, Daddy?" I asked reflexively, feeling like a child once more.

"Did you just call me 'daddy'?" he asked.

"How are you?" I asked again, omitting the moniker and ignoring his question.

"I'm fine," he said. "It's been a long time."

"Yes," I agreed. "It has."

He asked me several questions: Was I married? Did I have kids? How was Lynnette? And so on and so forth. I answered with short, one-line answers, until he caught me off guard with a question that shocked me.

"Will you come see me, son?"

I hesitated, unsure of what I wanted to say. Finally, I agreed, but my reasoning behind my answer was my own. I had questions, too—years of them—but I wanted to unload mine in a different way with a different tone than our terse, polite phone conversation.

After I hung up, I told my wife about the phone call. She was very eager to hear every detail, as if I was reading from a mystery novel. I told her that I'd agreed to visit my father and he'd be sending me the necessary forms. Yolanda stared at me, studying my facial expressions in an attempt to read fear or concern about the visit, looking for clues that I might not want to say aloud.

"Are you excited or nervous about the visit?" she asked.

I told her that I felt both. It was a mixture of emotions, and trying to pinpoint just one was nearly impossible. But I told her I saw this as an opportunity to unload my pain and show him that in spite of his actions and the pain he'd caused me, I had thrived in my life. By then, I was an officer in the military and I wanted my father to know that he had failed in his attempt to destroy us, to destroy me.

Before I could visit, I had to fill out a lot of paperwork. Because I had never visited a prison as an adult before, I had assumed I could just drive down and walk right in to see him. However, I realized how wrong I was when a bundle of paperwork arrived at my house about a week or so after my father called me. It reminded me of the first time I had to fill out an SF82 security form to obtain my security clearance in the military. *Do they really not want inmates to have visitors?* I wondered as I shuffled through the pile of papers that was very likely a deterrent for a lot of potential visitors.

It actually took me a few days to complete all the forms due to the sheer volume, but one thing irritated me about the packet: My father had had the nerve to include a canteen request form. The canteen request form consisted of a list of items you could purchase for inmates ranging from candy bars to toiletries. They struck me as weird items, but I'm sure that for my father, they were luxuries that were hard to get or afford in prison. It bothered me that he would include it, the nerve he had to ask for gifts after he had taken so much from me. All the same, I checked off most of the items he requested.

In the future, I struggled with filling out the request form because I was never sure if he was using me for items or not. During future phone conversations, I always waited to see if our talk would end with a request for something. It always did, which either frustrated me or left me feeling disappointed. I wanted a relationship with him, but I often wondered about the cost. Not the monetary value of his requests, but the cost of feeling used by him. Then again, maybe we were both using each other because my motives weren't always pure either. Our conversations were light, but I desperately wanted the truth from my father the way he wanted items from the canteen request. I needed answers. Instead, I kept filling out the canteen request forms when they arrived every six months or so. Each form came alongside a letter from my father telling me how much he loved me, followed up by requests for how much he needed.

When I finished filling out the rest of the paperwork, I mailed the packet back to the facility to wait for approval. It took a couple of weeks, but I finally received notification that I was cleared to visit.

Upon my arrival at Fort Jackson, I was assigned as a company executive officer. The position required long hours, but I really enjoyed working with the best NCOs in the army: the drill sergeants. To me, they were the epitome of what a soldier should be in all aspects of the army. I was a young officer, only one of two officers within the whole company. The other was the company commander. Although I had more rank than the drill sergeants, they carried more authority, and I definitely looked up to them and respected them tremendously. They showed me the ropes and the first sergeant treated me like his nephew. I clung to First Sergeant Collins like he wrote all of the army doctrine, and he schooled me daily. First Sergeant Collins was a throwback NCO, who kept his uniform and boots immaculate, and no matter how early I showed up to work, he always seemed to beat me to the office, a cup of coffee already in his hand. I'm fairly certain First Sergeants don't need to sleep, or perhaps they are issued a separate energy pack when they become an E8, the designation for a pay grade of an enlisted non-commissioned officer. Whatever it is, they're all amazing.

It was my job to ensure training flowed without a hitch. Bus and meal schedules, supplies, and training plans had to be laid out weekly. One flaw, one misstep, and the drills would let me have it with the lieutenant jokes.

"What's the difference between a private first class and a second lieutenant? A private first class has at least been promoted once."

"What's the difference between a private and a second lieutenant? The private *knows* he's stupid."

I never wanted to let anyone down, and I did my best to perfect the schedule, and I would go over the training plans with the first sergeant and commander during our nightly scrub. I was second in command as far as the rank structure, but dead last in terms of knowledge in the military, so I listened to my NCOs and learned from their experience. I served to the best of my ability as the executive officer in Company E for over a year before I was selected to move up the battalion to serve as the battalion operations officer. As a result, I was chosen to supervise and maintain the operations of five companies, including five of my previous executive-officer peers. It was a daunting and demanding task, but I felt that the experience I had gained from those amazing NCOs had prepared me for that moment.

I had been given a major mission by the battalion executive officer, Major Moten, to recon a suitable area for a battalion field exercise, which required me to go out to different training sites within Fort Jackson to find the proper location. He gave me a week to find a spot and report back to him. It was during this time that I was contacted by my father about the visit. No one at Fort Jackson knew about my father, and Major Moten had never asked me how I'd gotten my burns. I decided to schedule my meeting to see my dad during a scheduled recon day; however, I didn't tell my boss about the visit. I figured I could visit my father at the prison, only a few miles from Fort Jackson, and then return to my post and change back into my uniform and continue to work as if I had been out to the training site for most of the day, scouting locations. This was a decision I later regretted, but with the visit with my father looming in front of me, it was hard to think about much of anything else.

Finally, the night before I went to the prison, I called my mother and told her what I had planned. I could tell in her voice that she was concerned, although I couldn't quite understand why. Perhaps she was just being protective; I wasn't sure. Nevertheless, my mother hesitantly supported me in this endeavor. There was always a weird relationship between my mother and father. I'd never heard my mother utter a single negative word about my father. Instead, she'd always talked about the good times, the top of the wheel as we rode that continual cycle of relapse with him. My mother would, however, remind Kem, Lynnette, and me about our father's mental state and all the signs she'd missed over so many years. She in no way wanted my father to be released from prison at this point in our lives, but she didn't raise a fuss about my planned visit. Part of my mother wanted me to see him, but she didn't want me to probe into the past. More than anything, she wanted to ensure I was mentally ready for the visit. That, and she wanted to make sure I absolutely did not support his release from prison. She didn't want to focus on the bad times from our past, but she didn't want to repeat the mistakes of the past either, like when my mother had kept him out of jail in Philly. If you touch a stove and burn your hand, you don't have to spend the rest of your life focused on that time you burned your hand—but you also don't need to be foolish enough to touch the hot stove again either.

After we said goodbye and I went to bed, sleep eluded me. I tossed and turned all night, trying to decide how I wanted to express myself during this visitation. Should I unload my years of hurt by telling him how much pain he had caused my family and me? Should I tell him about the months I spent in the hospital, fighting to walk, fighting to live? Should I tell him about the emotional pain from classmates, from strangers, from the constant questions about my scars? What would I wear? I wanted to show him my success, to show him what I'd become in spite of him, but I couldn't decide whether I wanted to wear a business suit or my army uniform.

Ultimately, I opted to wear slacks with suspenders, a button-up shirt, and a tie. Because I hid my visit from leadership, I was worried someone might see me in uniform and report it back to my command. But it was important to me that I demonstrated a commanding physical presence during our visit. I wanted for my father to see me as tall and in shape, sharp in dress, and articulate. I wanted him to have to look up at me and feel my firm handshake, like a boxer before a fight. I wanted to intimidate him. I wanted him to exhibit some weakness in my presence as I represented my mother and my siblings. My nerves jangled throughout my body, but I didn't want to show them.

In the morning, I drove out to Kirkland Correctional Center, and the closer I got, the more nervous I became. When I arrived at the compound, I immediately noticed the triple concertina wire on the walls. I'd seen pictures on TV shows, but this was the real deal, a real-live maximum security facility. I parked my car and entered through the first checkpoint. I had to go through several checkpoints similar to an airport security screening, but with much more scrutiny. Belt and shoes off, emptied pockets, no pens, pencils, or sharp objects. Once security was satisfied with me, I moved through a series of iron doors and down corridors with buzzers and loud clanks, just like on TV. But as with the concertina wire, this was all very, very real. There's something surreal about experiencing an event after watching representations on film for so many years. But there was no pause button, no rewind, and no other channel. Just me, visiting my father in prison.

Finally, I entered a waiting room that looked similar to a school cafeteria with tables spaced throughout the room so visitors could sit and talk with the inmates. As I waited for my father to arrive, I looked around the room and observed an unusual scene. Seated at the tables was a mixture of young and old inmates, but I was surprised by how normal they looked. I'm not sure what exactly I'd expected, but the young guys were nicely groomed and appeared to be in great condition. They smiled as they conversed with their visiting loved ones. Many of them were of a similar age to me, and although outwardly you wouldn't necessarily know it, they'd committed heinous crimes. Their lives had taken a very different path from mine and they were now locked up for a stretch of time, some for life. Had I chosen to go another way, I could've been like them. I could've been on the other side of the table, waiting for someone to come visit me instead of the other way around. But I'd risen above my circumstances, I'd risen above my father's destruction, and I was that much stronger sitting in that room as a visitor instead of as a resident.

As I continued to wait for my father, I tried to decide what strategy I wanted to use. Should I stay seated or stand up when he walked in? I had a visual of him in my mind and thought I should stand to allow him to see how I had grown. I rehearsed in my mind how I would lay out my frustrations and anger, practicing over and over what I wanted to say. I thought about trying to thicken my voice to come off as stern and forceful; I didn't want to show even the slightest bit of weakness in front of my father.

Then, suddenly, there he was.

The guards opened a metal door, and then I saw my father standing about twenty yards away from me. I watched him scan the room for a moment before he found me and we locked eyes. As he walked towards me, I stared at him in disbelief. I'd held a picture of him in my head for all those years of how he used to be in photographs, but now he was only a shell of the imposing man he'd once been. The years had certainly not been kind to him. I wasn't ready to fold yet, although I suspect my eyes belied my tough exterior as he approached me.

"Hey, Foots," he said. "I am so glad you came out to see me."

I shook his hand and responded affirmatively, telling him that it was good to see him as well. I could feel myself shrinking, once again turning into that little boy yearning for his father. I fought that feeling with all of my might. I had questions and needed answers, but I felt my control slipping away as I stood before him.

In the visiting room, there were vending machines along one wall where you could purchase snacks and drinks. One of the vending machines was specifically for coffee, and you could pick your coffee type and the cup would drop down with your selected blend.

"Do you drink coffee?" my father asked. I nodded. "Would you mind buying me a cup of coffee and a Snickers bar?" he asked.

I obliged, walked over to the machines, and purchased two of each, then stuck the Snickers bars in my pocket so my hands were free to carry both cups of coffee. As I walked back to the table, I felt ashamed that I had weakened to his request. This wasn't how I'd planned for this meeting to go. Yet I felt pity for him. When I reached the table and delivered the snacks, he smiled and said it'd been a long time since he'd had a Snickers and a good cup of coffee. He thanked me effusively, as if I'd just purchased a color TV for his prison cell. I watched my father slurp his coffee and looked for signs of myself in his face. His hair was peppered with gray and he was much heavier than in the pictures I had seen of him in his younger days. He still spoke with a Philadelphia accent and asked me about my high school sports career. I later learned that Mr. Herrin had sent him newspaper clippings of my various high school sporting events through the years. My father knew all about me, and even remembered some of the details of the games as well.

"I'm proud of you," my father said. "And I love you."

I felt a strange mix of emotions in that moment. My father had pre-empted my angry strike and softened me, effectively destroying my plan. After that, I didn't know how to ask him about the fire and I didn't care at that point. I felt overwhelmed by the fact that he'd followed me through the years, and in telling me that he loved me, I felt like I had found part of what I'd been searching for all those years. We began to talk about sports like two school kids, and after a while, I realized that although I hadn't explicitly said the words yet, I had forgiven him—even though I don't remember him saying, "I am sorry." He didn't have to say the words out loud. His eyes said more than his lips ever could as I watched him study my burns. I could see the apology in his face and that would suffice for the time being.

As we talked, I realized that maybe this visit wasn't about determining a winner and a loser, or transferring my hate and pain to him. I realized instead that this meeting was about forgiveness, something I had accomplished without even having to say it directly. I ended up not mentioning the fire at all during that visit, but I had never felt freer. I realized that love is so much stronger than hate, and forgiveness had opened up my heart to release that hate and replace it with love and compassion. At that point, he'd spent twenty years in prison, and I was now the same age he was when he'd started the fire and entered prison. I took it all in, and even though I had additional questions when our visiting time was over, when I left the prison that day I told my father that I loved him, too.

As I drove back to Fort Jackson, everything seemed to be going according to my sneaky-day-out plan. I was still processing what had just transpired with my dad, but I still needed to close out the duty day to keep my secret in place. I walked into my office, thinking I'd successfully pulled off my absence without anyone being the wiser, when I was immediately greeted by Major Moten.

"Where in the hell have you been, lieutenant?" Major Moten demanded. "I've got a search party looking for you in all the training areas and we have been trying to contact you for hours!"

Busted.

He led me back to his office as I tried to process exactly how much trouble I was in.

"Okay," he said, closing the door behind me before taking a seat at his desk. "Where were you?"

A couple different scenarios ran through my head, but I knew the only real option was the truth.

"I was visiting my father in prison," I said.

"What?!" Major Moten exclaimed. He leaned back in his chair, shocked, as I unloaded this bombshell of a story on him about my visit.

I told him about my father being incarcerated and how he had started the fire that caused the burns on my face. Major Moten sat quietly as I talked, studying my burns. Truth is often stranger than fiction, and I knew he believed my story, because really, who could make up a thing like that? Major Moten was a West Pointer, as well as a history major, and he seemed to be almost intrigued by the details, although his inquiry was tinged with a deep sense of sorrow. He asked questions gently, asking how long my father had been incarcerated, and how my mother and I had overcome the fire. For the moment, Major Moten seemed to have forgotten that I had disappeared from my place of duty.

I could and should have been counseled for my absence, but Major Moten gave me a pass because of my unique circumstances. I admitted that I had been ashamed to tell him why I needed time off, and I had felt so conflicted with pressure to complete my assigned mission and to close a chapter of my life with my father. Major Moten was very kind and understanding, but I learned a very serious lesson that day about the importance of keeping my leaders informed, no matter what, because my actions could have a major impact on others. After that day, Major Moten and I became very close, and while I eventually found that suitable training area for the battalion, the chapter with my father remained open.

CHAPTER 20

9/11 and the Aftermath of the Twin Towers

I completed my company command at Fort Leonard Wood, Missouri, and chose Houston, Texas, of all places, to serve as an advisor to a reserve unit. I needed a break after command, and although these assignments could appear to be the kiss of death to one's military career, I figured I would roll the dice. There was a formula of sorts in assignments to advance one's career as an officer. To start, you would be a platoon leader before moving on to executive officer in a line company in your chosen field or branch. Then you went off to the officer advanced course and, upon completion, moved on to a staff job while awaiting company command. Post-company command, an officer would go back to a staff job or try to go to one of the training centers, such as the National Training Center in California or the Joint Regional Training Center at Fort Polk, Louisiana. Finally, one would attempt to make it back to the schoolhouse of their branch to instruct, or go off to advanced civil schooling (ACS) while awaiting the major's promotion board.

However, one would be considered "off-track" by choosing one of the three Rs, as they called them back in the day: recruiting, ROTC, or reserve training. These were the "kiss of death" assignments that could make the road ahead rough for future promotions. However, I'd always made my decisions, right or wrong, based on family wishes and location. I figured that I could just try to do my very best in whatever assignment I got and things would work out, one way or another. My career path was already about as untraditional as I could've had it. I kept grinding, choosing to be the big fish in a small pond. I was naive to proper counsel and was without a true military mentor to help me navigate through this journey, until I met Colonel Baker later in my career. However, I had been fortunate to survive many cuts along the way. I can't claim great military brilliance because I don't have that gift. Instead, I just believed that if I worked my butt off and treated soldiers the way I wanted to be treated, good things would happen—and they did.

My wife had a brother one year older than her, Julius, who was her father's namesake. He went by JB, just the same as my best friend growing up did, and he and Yolanda were extremely close despite living so far apart, with Julius in Houston. When choosing where to serve as an advisor to a reserve unit, my branch manager gave me a couple of location choices, one of which was Houston. When I mentioned this to my wife, she was more than excited at the prospect of living in the same city as her brother.

My wife and I arrived in the city of Houston and it was almost overwhelming from the start. I had been in traffic before in Columbia, South Carolina, and I had thought that was major at the time. I am not one for patience, and the idea of sitting in traffic for an extended period of time drove me crazy. As we attempted to push through the city down Interstate 10, I immediately thought that this move had been a mistake. There was no way I'd be able to regularly deal with this madness. A sea of cars filled the streets as we slugged towards our destination. *What did I get myself into with this assignment?* I wondered. We pushed and pushed until we finally made it to the heart of the city down an artery towards Old Spanish Trail, and were approaching the Headquarters building.

"Relax," my wife said, ever the patient one in our relationship. I just shook my head at the endless lines of cars.

We finally made it to the building and I pulled out my phone to have my sponsor meet me in the parking lot.

"What's up with this traffic, man?" I asked when he arrived. He laughed.

"It'll take some getting used to, but you'll love it here," he promised.

I couldn't see it at the time. There was no way I could get past that madness. I already had a pretty good idea of the area due to the advice I'd gotten from my brother-in-law, who had tried to forewarn me about the traffic: "You gotta be in it to understand it!"

After my quick introduction to my new unit, I immediately signed out to begin my search for a house to rent. I decided to move in the general area of Missouri City, Texas, and we began to house hunt with a realtor. As we started to canvass the area, the realtor also showed me some workarounds with the traffic to and from work. She very helpfully schooled me on the appropriate times to leave and the highways and interstates to avoid during certain times of the day. As that first week progressed, my tension about the city eased. I found Houston wasn't so bad after all as I rode along with my realtor, watching her cut through back roads and streets while I studied her driving skills. She also pointed out locations where famous people and athletes lived, such as Warren Moon, nine-time Pro Bowl quarterback who played for several teams, including, of course, the Houston Oilers. Being the sports junkie that I am, I was enthralled by the fact that the legendary quarterback could be so close to where I would be living. That alone put me in a different mental state about Houston, and I started to think this would work out after all.

We found a nice little house in a neat community within Missouri City. I also found the synchronicity interesting, and thought it a little amusing I'd just left Fort Leonard Wood, Missouri, and now we lived in Missouri City, Texas. I began to really feel the city as the weeks passed. I noticed affluent homes where people who looked like me lived were everywhere. I started to experiment with the cuisines, such as the Cajun boudin sausage, the crawfish, and the famous briskets. One night, we ventured out to Carrabba's Italian Grill in Sugar Land, Texas. After we sat down, I happened to look over at the table next to us and I couldn't believe my eyes. Seated right beside us was one of the Los Angeles Lakers greats: A. C. Green. It was my first time seeing a star of sorts up close and personal, and I recognized him immediately. I stared at him until he looked at me, and then I quickly turned away so as not to disturb him. I immediately turned twelve years old again, whispering to my wife as if we were involved in some kind of top secret mission.

"Do you know who that is?" I hissed.

"Who?" Yolanda asked.

"That's A. C. Green who used to play for the LA Lakers!" I excitedly whispered.

My wife didn't have a clue who he was, but she was still excited at the idea of someone famous being near us, especially after seeing my enthusiasm. I don't remember eating much of my meal that evening; I just kept staring and trying to avoid getting caught until A. C. Green and his dining companions finished their meals and departed. Unfortunately, this encounter predated cell phone cameras, so there was no proof I'd really seen him and I couldn't exactly call home to boast about my sighting, but that was fine.

Another time, I had to travel to California to check on a training site and I saw Kenny "The Jet" Smith walking out of the airport. I just stopped and watched him walk away! I'm such a chump when it comes to stars, especially pro athletes, but oh well. Aided by that encounter with A. C. Green, Houston became cool to me. The weather was perfectly hot and there was something magical about experiencing something new; the toll roads, the traffic, the tall buildings, and the stars. I enjoyed the variety of sporting options, entertainment, colleges, and young African American professionals doing well. It gave me a sense of pride and hope.

I attended a sporting event at least twice a month, either going to a Comets or Rockets game or heading to Enron Field to see the Astros. I was in heaven watching the pro teams. I often went with another captain who was a big fan of the Comets. She loved the whole team and insisted we escape the office and head downtown in the middle of the day. Once, we made up some excuse to leave the office, and off we went to the Comets' victory parade. We got as close as we could to the platform, and there they were, in spectacular form. I knew how we had escaped the office, but I wondered about the rest of the crowd. There seemed to be thousands of people there, and what kind of jobs did they all have to be able to just up and leave? Nevertheless, we were all there to witness one of the greatest pro teams ever assembled, led by Sheryl Swoops, Cynthia Cooper, and Tina Thompson. My fellow captain and I soaked it in, realizing that we were witnessing history. On the ride home, we talked about how awesome it was to be stationed in Houston, Texas—where else could you get to see all of this? And she was right—Houston was awesome! I came to really enjoy the city. There I was, a soldier just blending, unnoticed, into this metropolis…until 9/11 changed everything.

I was assigned to the 1/289th TS Battalion Fourth Brigade 75TS Division, headquartered off of Old Spanish Trail near the Astrodome. For the first time in my military career, I was off the reservation with no major military installation, within a three-hour drive of our brigade headquarters, which was technically located at Fort Sill, Oklahoma. It was a strange setup, but it was my new assignment and I had to make the most of it. Initially, the most challenging part of this assignment was navigating through traffic to get back and forth to work every day. I served as one of two active duty team members supporting a twenty-person reserve team responsible for the training and mobilization of units across the states of Texas and Louisiana. Sergeant First Class Jimmy Smart was my active duty non-commissioned officer (NCO), and wing man who taught me the ropes.

Jimmy had been on station for a year already and he knew the lay of the land. It was fun traveling with him and going temporary duty across the state with other team members. We had a superb team, including Staff Sergeant David Owen, who had served in the guard for many years by that point. He was the most experienced and talkative NCO I had ever encountered, including my good friend, Stanley Frazier. Staff Sergeant Owen had previously served in the Marine Corps and had never let go of that Corps spirit. He enjoyed the Guard and took it seriously, volunteering for every mission available. Staff Sergeant Owen knew the city and the state, and we needed his guidance just as much as he wanted to be a part of the team. It almost seemed like he was a full-time soldier for as much as we placed him on orders to support us. He was a good soldier, who eventually advanced to Sergeant Major, which was a proud day for us all. Even though I had served in the National Guard for many years, I really earned a new appreciation for what reservists brought to the table in working with my team. They have to balance regular jobs while supporting and serving in the military, and I learned that it could be challenging with each one pulling on you to include those who had families.

Things were moving along, and the assignment wasn't a big strain on me, so I began working on my master's degree in exercise science at Texas Southern University. I was fortunate to be so close to TSU, as well as many other schools, like the University of Houston and Rice University. They were all within about a ten-mile radius, and it was neat to see students of all nationalities walking around the campuses. The weather was always nice, so I often saw people outside when I frequently visited those schools to use their libraries for research. Additionally, my brother-in-law earned his PhD in electrical engineering from Rice University. I was enjoying Houston so much that I briefly considered leaving the military and staying in Texas permanently. That Cajun food, especially Pappadeaux Seafood Kitchen, almost ensnared me. Months passed and I was closing in on completing my degree. Life was good, and I was due to rotate out in January of 2002 to my next assignment if I didn't extend my stay in Texas. Then came the morning of September 11, 2001.

I was sitting in the family room at our house, watching *The Today Show*, when a report came in about a plane hitting the first tower of the World Trade Center. *Strange,* I thought, wondering what was going on. Then a few minutes later, I, along with the rest of the Nation, watched the plane hit the second tower. My heart started racing and I grabbed my boots and my shaking fingers attempted to tie the laces. *What the heck is going on?* I wasn't even thinking war at the time. I wasn't thinking much of anything outside of accountability, so I jumped in my Isuzu Rodeo and sped down the road. My mind was racing faster than my car. I didn't know what to expect when I arrived at work, but I had enough time to think about it with a thirty-five- to forty-minute drive ahead of me, depending on traffic. I practically flew down the road. I'm not sure why I thought I needed to hurry, but I did.

I pulled into the parking lot of headquarters and there were already guards there, which was not normal. The division headquarters didn't have many full-time soldiers, and I assumed we'd be joining in on the rotation pretty soon. Since this wasn't standing practice, the guards were only checking ID cards, but the threat level had been elevated. I ran up the steps to the major's office, but to my shock, he wasn't there. As fate would have it, he had a dental appointment that morning and had gone to it. He'd left early from home to beat traffic, which meant he'd missed the highlights, and I was left as the senior guy in charge until he showed up. We worked inside the division headquarters, but our brigade was out of state and I didn't know what the protocol was for something like this. I called the brigade headquarters in Oklahoma and the brigade executive officer answered the phone. He had to be the calmest lieutenant colonel I've ever met, and he put me at ease.

"Captain Scott, just ensure everyone is accounted for and have Major Wineglass call me when he arrives," he said.

"Yes, sir!"

I figured he would tell me to stand by for orders to report to war or something, but we were watching things unfold just like the rest of the country.

Major Wineglass finally showed up and instructed us to coordinate with the guards to begin a rotation with them. We all had to pull a shift, no matter our rank, from captain down to private, whoever was available. We didn't know if another plane was going to come down, or if a truck was going to plow through the barriers. We were all caught off guard for the first time in a very long time, both as a military and as a country. Anxiety turned to anger as we watched videos of the planes hitting the buildings again and again. Who would do this to us?

As the days passed, there was no doubt that we would ramp up to avenge the perpetrators. As Sergeant First Class Smart and I began to go back to our daily grind of training soldiers and getting out in the city, we felt a difference in the way we were treated. The surge of patriotism throughout the United States was palpable. When we were out there away from headquarters, we tended to stick out while walking down the street or getting lunch while in uniform. I don't remember paying for many lunches after 9/11, and the spirit of the flag and country was in full effect, something I began to feel very strongly myself. The more people gave us respect, the more I wanted to do, and the more I wanted to be a part of paying back the people who had caused our nation harm. There would be no extension for me in Texas; I needed to go back home to where soldiers lived and trained, so I headed back to Fort Bragg, North Carolina.

I was still on an unconventional career path, and headed to Fort Bragg to serve as an advisor to the local National Guard unit to train another training support brigade located on post. It was early in 2002, and I figured my family and I would make this area our permanent home, so we purchased a house in Raeford, North Carolina. It felt like being in a different world out in the middle of God's Country, a minimum of thirty minutes away from the nearest interstate. I believe this is where God made the first soldier, because you couldn't go anywhere in the region without seeing a soldier training for something. All of our streets were named for something related to the military, including our street, which was Bugle Call Drive. It was as common to see parachutes in the air as it was clouds, and the sound of cannons frequently rattled our windows. This became our norm for the next three years. I served as the engineer team chief of a five-man team consisting of a master sergeant, one sergeant first class, one other captain, and a warrant officer. We zigzagged across the state, training other units to ensure they were ready to go to war when called upon. It was a relaxed job…until it wasn't.

We got the word that National Guard units would get some action, and when 2003 rolled around, we began to ramp up heavily. I was personally dealing with some difficult feelings about not being deployed yet, as well as being responsible for training soldiers that would see action. I remember as the war kicked off with the shock and awe of everything, we were sent out to Fort Polk, of all places, as the testers to serve as observe controllers. I would watch General Vincent K. Brooks, then Brigadier General Brooks, give the daily press briefings as the spokesperson for the United States Central Command, also known as CENTCOM. He painted a picture of the situation for us all, and I looked on with curiosity as he laid out the war.

General Brooks stands at six five, and is one of the humblest leaders and people I have ever met. He made me proud to be a soldier as he briefed us with confidence, articulating each word. I saw General Brooks and I wanted to go overseas, too. He made me want to be a part of the mission, and over time, I became overwhelmed with guilt. The guilt stayed with me for a long time and I couldn't shake it. My mom was proud of my achievements, so why did I need to do more and go through a deployment to Iraq?

Most soldiers who didn't know my story about the fire assumed that I had been injured in the military, which was a story I could've just ridden like a wave. In fact, I once overheard someone "explaining" my circumstances to another soldier. The guy talking made a story up for me which, although heroic, was not my truth. Was that what I was looking for with a deployment to Iraq? Some John Wayne-type story to elevate my truth? Could I somehow change the narrative of a father intentionally harming his son to a heroic story of a soldier going into combat and receiving these burns? That would be more fitting and less shameful, but it was not my truth. Even with my inability to change my background, I still needed to be a part of this war. I needed to be over there. Was I running from something? If my wife knew what I felt, would she be angry with me for wanting to leave our kids behind and go to a war she didn't understand?

Our really low-key assignment of training National Guard and reserve units suddenly ramped up as the war escalated. My five-man team began to fan across the state, and we even pushed down to Fort Stewart for several months to train one of our brigades. During the middle of the madness, I received the best news of my career: The brigade commander's secretary called me early one morning and told me to stand by for the boss's call. All eligible senior captains had been waiting with bated breath for the announcement of the promotion list. It was customary for the senior officer to call you and say whether or not you made the list.

"Captain Scott?"

"Yes, sir?" I asked.

"Congratulations on your selection to major!"

"Roger, sir," I said, doing my best to stay stoic and professional—until I hung up the phone. I am not a dancer—I am missing that soul gene—but I busted a couple of moves as I whooped and hollered and celebrated, my voice booming through the house.

I was now a field grade officer, and this promotion gave me renewed confidence and energy. I was definitely a career officer at this point, and it was time to plan out my future with my branch manager. He gave me a school date for command and general staff college, the New Intermediate-Level Education program (ILE). My branch manager also broke the news to me that I would now transfer into a new functional area called information operations, a diversion from my basic branch of the Corps of Engineers. The year 2004 was drawing to a close and I was staring ahead at a promotion and a new career path.

CHAPTER 21

Third Army and the Middle East

I departed Fort Bragg as a newly promoted major with permanent change of duty orders in hand and two scheduled schools before heading to Third Army in Atlanta, Georgia. Location, location, location! Who didn't want to live in Atlanta? It was such a vibrant city and there would be so much to do and so many places to see. I was so excited and I liked that it was close to home, but not too close. However, my first order of business was to complete intermediate level education at Fort Gordon, as well as my information operations course at Fort Leavenworth in Kansas. I was ready for my next assignment and this next step in my career.

The Third Army was first activated during World War I at Chaumont, France, and consisted of three corps and seven divisions. However, it is most famous for its involvement in World War II under the command of General George S. Patton Jr. Upon taking command of the Third Army when they arrived in England in January of 1944, he gave the following speech:

> I've been given command of the Third Army for reasons which will become clear later on. I'm here because of the confidence of two men: the president of the United States and the theater

commander. They have confidence in me because they don't believe a lot of lies that have been printed about me, and also because they know I mean business when I fight. I don't fight for fun and I won't tolerate anyone on my staff who does.

You're here to fight. Ahead of you lies battle. That means one thing: You can't afford to be a fool, because in battle, fools mean dead men. It's inevitable for men to be killed and wounded in battle. But, there's no reason why such losses should be increased because of the incompetence and carelessness of some stupid S-O-B. I don't tolerate such men on my staff.

We're here because some crazy Germans decided they were supermen and that they had a right to rule the world. They've been pushing people around all over the world, looting, killing, and abusing millions of innocent men, women, and children. They were getting ready to do the same thing to us. We have to fight to protect ourselves.

Another reason we're here is to defeat and wipe out the Nazis who started all of this trouble. If you don't like to fight, I don't want you around. You had better get out before I kick you out. There's one thing you have to remember: In war, it takes more than the desire to fight to win. You've got to have more than guts to lick the enemy. You also must have brains. It takes brains and guts to win

> wars. A man with guts but no brains is only half a soldier. We whipped the Germans in Africa and Sicily because we had brains as well as guts. We're going to lick them in Europe for that same reason.
>
> That's all. Good luck.

This speech set the tone for the Third Army, who went on to display an impressive showing in World War II, most notably, including the Battle of the Bulge when General Patton made one of the great moves of the war by rotating the axis of advance by ninety degrees to counterattack the German flank. This move ultimately helped secure the Allied victory at this battle, which was the last major German offensive of World War II. British Prime Minister Winston Churchill later said of the Battle of the Bulge, "This is undoubtedly the greatest American battle of the war and will, I believe, be regarded as an ever-famous American victory." After World War II, the Third Army was the main striking force in Operation Desert Storm and beginning in 2003, it was deployed again in Operation Iraqi Freedom.

With this distinguished history of the Third Army behind it, I was proud to be part of its present and future. I already knew what to expect because of my army buddies and classmates who had served in the legendary Third Army, and because they issued desert uniforms to wear daily due to the frequency of deploying to the Middle East. I was ready to go because I was still struggling with the guilt of not having my combat patch. Therefore, when I showed up to Third Army, I was satisfied with the knowledge that I would possibly push out to Iraq in a matter of months. I had found a house prior to going to the information operations course, so the family was pretty much settled into our new town of Newnan, Georgia, on the outskirts of Atlanta, while I reported to the Headquarters, ready to work. As I settled into my cubicle space—the first time I'd had to deal with this type of setup—I began to hear the stories of the guys returning from the theater. In the military, a theater is an area in which important military events happen. This can include the entirety of an airspace, a land area, or a sea area that could become part of a military operation. I would say about 90 percent of the soldiers at Fort McPherson had seen combat, and the more stories I heard, the guiltier I felt. They talked about the mortar attacks and improvised explosive devices and the heat of the desert. This should have turned me off combat duty, but it didn't.

When my good buddy, John Boston, returned from Iraq, the guys at Fort McPherson immediately noticed how much weight he'd lost. I'd hear John over in the next cubicle, talking about how terrible it was over in Iraq and how he never wanted to go back to that place. Finally, one day I joined John in his cubicle and told him how much I wanted to deploy. John looked into my eyes, his face grave.

"Stay away from that place if you can," he said. "That place will mess you up mentally."

I went back to my own cubicle to continue working on my own project, but my mind was awash with questions. Should I just sit this thing out? Was this really the right choice for me? I wanted so badly to go, but I couldn't ignore my friend's words either. He'd been there, he would know…right?

We were working at a frantic pace at Third Army, with all of the working groups and planning meetings supporting the war. Third Army was a little unique in those days as well, because it appeared to send every black officer in the US Army through this unit at some point. I'd never seen so many black colonels in my life! They looked like a unit of modern-day buffalo soldiers. It made me proud and it gave us all a sense of pride, but we found out that the mission was colorblind. If you weren't at the top of your game and didn't know your craft, you would get flamed—regardless of your race. There was no favoritism or extra credit for being black. As the saying goes, it was what it was.

Third Army felt like home, and it reminded me of ROTC back at SC State in many ways. I also got an opportunity to see the strength of female NCOs and officers in the army. I had worked with females, particularly minority females, sporadically throughout my career, but the army sent the very best, as it appeared, to Third Army. I had never seen so many minority women in one place since college, and it really took me back to those days. There were female officers, from colonel to second lieutenant, all over Fort McPherson. In my section alone, I worked with Major Catina Barnes, a public affairs officer; Captain Angel Wade, an intelligence officer; Lieutenant Brittanie Martin, a signal officer; Captain Camala Coats, INTEL; and Major Renee Russo and Amanda Azubuike, who were both public affairs officers. They were all African American female officers with whom I worked every day, sharp and articulate women who came from various HBCUs and waved their colors proudly. They were some of the smartest officers I have ever worked with and they all rose up through the ranks and achieved at least the rank of lieutenant colonel. We all planned together, deployed together, and learned from one another. We were like family and these were my sisters.

Captain Wade and I were truly like brother and sister, as she was one grade my junior, sharp and witty. We deployed and worked side by side on many projects, laughing and sometimes arguing like siblings. These were truly the best of times, and we have all remained friends throughout the years. Although Angel became my sidekick, there was one who led the pack. Major Azubuike stood about five nine, was slender, and she had the prettiest shade of brown skin. She routinely ran ten milers as a warm-up, and was confident, but not arrogant. Amanda was a team player and had the ability to teach and guide, and I saw her as a mentor of sorts. She and I deployed to Egypt and Kuwait to work on operations together, and I got the chance to see a future colonel in her element. Watching her prepare for briefing and projects was like watching Michael Jordan practice. Amanda's ability to brief the public affairs slides during our daily update briefings was something to admire. I typically briefed after her, and it was like performing after Pattie Labelle or Whitney Houston back in the day. It came to a point that I begged her to brief before her, for the sake of my career. She was a rising star and she made it look effortless. As of this writing, she's currently a full bird colonel, as we call them, and everyone had known it would happen. If anyone doubts the abilities of minority leaders, I only wish they could have seen us perform back in those days.

There was an exceptional officer who reported in who had previously served in Third Army as a captain, by the name of Lieutenant Colonel Prentiss Baker. He was well known and respected in the halls of the unit by those who had served with and for him. I had heard stories of him and knew he was coming, but I really didn't understand the breadth of his stature until he arrived. He came through the door and on first sight, I knew I'd hit the lottery because he would become my new boss. He was all everyone had built him up to be and more. They called him the "Big Dog," and only the good ones in the army get a call sign.

I'd served all of these years in the military, and for the first time, I had a true mentor. We had been advised early in our careers to find a mentor, someone who could give us career advice. I never had. Maybe it had slowed me down career-wise, but I hadn't felt completely comfortable opening up to people, especially males, and I'd never reached out to anyone before Lieutenant Colonel Baker; he reminded me of Ray Lewis, but more polished. He even resembled Lewis in feature and build, but obviously without the facial hair. Lieutenant Colonel Baker had played running back in college and didn't appear to have lost too much of that muscle mass. He had the voice to match, speaking in a way that made you want to suit up and tackle somebody for him, not unlike General Patton taking command of Third Army. I listened when he spoke, and when he spoke there was so much substance to take in.

Once, Lieutenant Colonel Baker had one-on-one counseling sessions for all of his junior officers. He called me in and had a piece of paper in front of him with a timeline on it with career benchmarks.

"Scott!" he said, looking me square in the eyes like an old defensive line coach. "Where do you want to be in five years?"

I jumped a little when he said my name and hesitated for a moment.

"Where do I want to be?"

"Yup," Baker said. "What's your five-year plan?"

I had never been asked that question before and I wasn't entirely sure how to answer.

"Well, I guess I want to make lieutenant colonel and retire," I finally said, unsure.

"You guess?" he asked with a chuckle. "Scott, your goals ain't real if you don't write them down, and you can't achieve them if you don't have a plan."

Chills ran through my body as he spoke. He started walking me through his own personal timeline, showing me his career path and goals, and I became a sponge, trying to absorb everything I could.

"I'm going to put you in the right situations to make you a lieutenant colonel. I'm going to push you in ways that you think are unfair at times, but I'm going to get you there," he said to me in closing. I nodded, ready to move forward. I kept his words in mind as I saluted the flag and later deployed back and forth to the Middle East to Camp Arifjan and to Egypt on the Bright Star exercises.

Operation Bright Star is a series of joint training exercises between the US and Egypt, held every two years, dating back to the 1980 Camp David Accords. Following the liberation of Kuwait, the exercises have expanded to include eleven other countries, including the United Kingdom, Germany, Jordan, and Kuwait, among others. During one instance, we were conducting an exercise in the local area. I served as the night counterpart to Lieutenant Colonel Baker's days, and I had the responsibility of conducting a shift brief with him before leaving. He was pulled into another briefing prior to the shift change, so I assumed I could just leave a couple of notes for him before sliding out of the tenting and heading back to the hotel room thirty minutes away. I knew I was being lazy and I felt it inside me when I departed.

Sure enough, the Big Dog called my hotel room about thirty minutes after I arrived and dressed me down. He broke me down so badly that I knew there was no chance I would be able to fall asleep after that. The way Baker talked to me was reminiscent of the way my mother used to drop the hammer on me back in the day. As Baker talked, I felt ashamed and like less of an officer because I had let the Big Dog down. I had an impulse to hop on the shuttle back to the exercise site and pull a double shift to make up for my earlier laziness, but I knew I couldn't. Instead, I stayed in the room and stared at the walls, unable to sleep. I lay awake in bed and replayed Baker's words to me. The thought of facing him that evening was almost too much to bear, but I knew there was no avoiding Baker.

The next day, I showed up an hour early, feeling incredibly nervous at the idea of getting another thrashing. When Lieutenant Colonel Baker entered, he took one look at me and saw I'd gotten the message. Not only had I gotten it, but I carried that lesson with me for the remainder of my career. It was a lesson of tough love, not thinking only of myself and how tired I was, and of what it meant to be a professional officer. There are no shortcuts in life; if you want to succeed, you have to put in the work. The Big Dog was the best, and he eventually earned his eagle by being selected as a full colonel in the army. The insignia for a colonel is a silver eagle which is a stylized representation of the eagle. Colonels are sometimes referred to (but not addressed as) full colonels, bird colonels, or full bird colonels because lieutenant colonels are also referred to and addressed in correspondence as "colonel." To this day, he remains one of the finest officers and coolest full birds I've ever known and by far the best mentor I ever had in the military.

As the months rolled on, my number was called to deploy, but it wasn't to where I thought I'd go. The mission had changed a little for Third Army, and we were supporting the war more from Kuwait, which was still considered a combat zone. Although I'd wanted to go to Iraq, I figured this would be the next best thing. I told my wife and kids about my orders, and began to make my preparations for my six month rotation in the desert. However, the thing about family and kids is that time away from them is still time away, no matter where you're going. I could've been in California for all they knew, but regardless of my location, I would still be gone and they wouldn't get to see their daddy—and I wouldn't get to see my kids.

This deployment would end up being one of many rotations that I went on while at Third Army. I had more in my bag than the average soldier going back and forth to Kuwait. I had finally earned my combat patch, but it wasn't in one of the two major theaters of Iraq or Afghanistan, and so I was left feeling unfulfilled. I didn't have a death wish, but I didn't want to be that soldier who said I didn't go when twenty years down the road someone questioned me about serving in one of the wars. I continued my tours to Kuwait for the next two and a half years until the opportunity arose for me to jump and I heard about individual taskers for deployment time: one year tours as an individual augmentation to one of the staffs in theater. The idea intrigued me, and I figured that since I was going back and forth to the desert anyway, why not the major sandbox? I decided to discuss this with Lieutenant Colonel Baker, who encouraged me to go for it, so I called my branch manager.

"You want to volunteer for a Worldwide Individual Augmentation System tasker?" he asked incredulously.

"Yes!"

"Well, if you volunteer for this tasker, I'll get you wherever you want to go next," my branch manager said. There was a lot of pressure on branch managers to fill these positions. Soldiers would pull out all the stops—including throwing other people's names into the conversation—to avoid getting deployed on these taskers. I wasn't on my branch manager's radar yet because I still had time on the station, so he was understandably shocked. I asked him to return me to Atlanta to United States Army Forces Command, which was literally the building next to ours, only with a different mission. I wanted to keep my family stable and in place, and my branch manager happily obliged.

"No problem, Scott!" he said. "I'll cut your orders soon."

Now, all I had to do was tell my wife. As I headed home to tell her, I had time to make up one of the biggest lies of my life. I even had time to come up with "why me" theatrics and everything.

"I've got to go to Iraq!" I announced.

"What?!" my wife exclaimed.

"Yep," I said with a sigh. "I just found out today."

"They're deploying your unit?" she asked.

"Nope, just me," I said.

"That…doesn't make any sense," Yolanda said.

"I'm the only one who hasn't been yet, so I'm up," I explained. I could see the hurt in her face, and I was convinced that had she known I'd volunteered, she would have divorced me on the spot. I mean, who volunteers to leave their family for a year to go to Iraq, of all places?

Despite my deception and the fact I'd have to temporarily leave my family, I felt good about my decision. Perhaps I was going to Iraq for selfish reasons, but I needed to do this. At this point in my career, my body was a wreck; I had bad knees and my back ached. I was on my third knee surgery, and I probably should've been looking at retirement instead of deployment. I still had five years remaining for twenty good years, but that didn't matter; I was going to war. As June of 2008 approached, I received my orders and began to make my deployment preparations. Coincidentally, my twenty-year class reunion was approaching as well, and the planned dates for our reunion and my deployment were dangerously close to one another.

CHAPTER 22

Iraq

I was notified by my superiors of my report date to Fort Benning for pre-deployment training. I had waited so long for this, and yet my heart sank. My reporting date was the same night as my twenty-year high school reunion. I graduated high school in 1988 with sixty-three other classmates, a whopping sixty-four people in all. Our group of friends consisted of a band of thirteen brothers and sisters, and we attempted to round up everyone into attending. I immediately scrambled to make phone calls to my contacts, both in Iraq and at Fort Benning, to talk to them about the situation with my reunion. After all, the war would still be going on if I could get a one day extension. They discussed the seriousness of being present that day, but when I explained the situation, the officer on duty said it wouldn't be a problem, I could just report to Fort Benning the morning after my reunion. It would require a six-hour drive from my mother's house in Ridge Spring in the middle of the night after an evening of carousing with my friends, but it was totally worth it. In fact, when I arrived at Fort Benning, I was a little upset because there was a whole lot of standing around and there was no real sense of urgency or deadline; they only signed us in, went over the training schedule for the week, and then released us for the day. I couldn't help but think I could've spent more time with my classmates, but such is life.

I only had that one day and part of the night to spend with my classmates, and I wanted to maximize my time at the reunion. My wife didn't attend because of the crazy hours I'd decided to take on by driving to Fort Benning in the small hours of the morning. As I headed to Ridge Spring, I had so much going through my head. I didn't know what to expect during my deployment, or if I'd even come back, so I wanted to see my classmates. We had decided to have our reunion at our friend Tonya's parents' house. They had a nice home with a pool, back in the country off the beaten path, a great spot for a party. We had all agreed to BYOB, and I'd picked up a whole bunch of beverages from the Class VI at Fort McPherson prior to departing. My classmates and I had tried to reach out to as many members as possible at the last minute, but not many people showed up, maybe only about fifteen of us hanging around and reminiscing about times past. I was there, but I wasn't. I thought about the drive ahead to Fort Benning and my upcoming deployment. I told my friends about my departure and they couldn't believe I'd made the trip and would be leaving that night.

We took a group picture together to commemorate our reunion, we played music and talked sports and kids. As the night slipped away, I said my goodbyes and gave my hugs before I departed for Fort Benning. I left all of my beverages behind, as I hadn't been able to partake in all aspects of the celebration because of the drive, but it was fine because my mind was elsewhere. Adrenaline alone took me down the interstate as I thought about what was ahead of me. I called Yolanda and talked with her for a while down the road about the reunion, but mostly I listened to music as I drifted in and out of my own thoughts about the upcoming week. My wife and kids would be able to see me off prior to my deployment, but I still had a few days of training ahead.

I reported to Fort Benning for my training, and when I arrived, reality began to set in that my long-awaited tour in Iraq was really going to happen. The training consisted of first aid training, mine training, rollover drills, and qualifying with your assigned weapon which, for me, was a 9mm. Everyone also had to be cleared via medical exam screening, and I could have gone home due to a prior knee surgery that required a waiver that I had to get from Fort Bragg's Womack Army Medical Center in order to deploy. However, I got my waiver and was cleared for duty. It was hotter than hell at Fort Benning and I was soaking wet every day. The training was nothing extreme, more like familiarizing us with everything to be sure we were ready to be deployed to a combat zone. Fort Benning was only about an hour's drive from my house, and during that week of training, I made some late-night trips back home to be with my family. During those long drives back and forth to the base, I began to truly realize that I would be in a combat zone for a year, far away from my kids.

I left for Iraq on my birthday, July 4, 2008. My family came with me when I reported to the processing site and the kids watched in astonishment as I drew my 9mm. I will never forget the look on my children's faces for as long as I live. At the time, Junior, my oldest, was eleven, Josh was ten, and my baby girl was five. JJ saw my weapon and had this look of horror on his face as he surveyed the gun in my hand. The kids hated when I had to travel, but this time JJ realized that it was a dangerous trip, something that required a weapon.

"Why do you need a gun?" JJ asked.

"I'm going to war," I said simply.

"War?" he asked, looking even more concerned.

"Combat!" I said quickly, trying to make it sound less threatening. "I'm going into combat."

"I thought you said you would be in a safe place," JJ said, still eyeing the gun warily. "Why do you need that?"

"I'll be all right, son," I said reassuringly, placing a hand on his shoulder. Nevertheless, JJ's concerned face never changed all morning, and it bothered me to no end. As a parent, you want to protect your kids, keep them from worrying about anything, especially you. But JJ was getting older and I couldn't wave away his worries like a bad dream anymore.

"Daddy, that gun is cool!" Josh exclaimed. "Can you bring it home with you?"

"No," I said quickly.

"Are you going to get to shoot somebody?" Josh asked.

"I hope not!" I said. Unlike his brother, Josh was more preoccupied with the weapon itself instead of what the implications were for me being in a situation where I would need the gun.

"Is that your gun, Daddy?" Trinity asked. "Will I go to jail if I touch it?"

"No, sweetie!" I reassured her. "You shouldn't touch it, but you won't go to jail."

I could tell James was still bothered by my weapon, as could my wife.

"Don't worry," Yolanda reassured him, her signal to me to make up some story to calm him. But I couldn't come up with anything and instead tried to change the subject. The sendoff became uncomfortable and I needed my family to go. I could tell my wife wanted to cry, so I gently told them to leave. Not in a mean way, but in a "you-should-get-back-to-beat-the-traffic" kind of way, and my wife understood what I was really saying beneath my words. We hugged and said our goodbyes and I was filled with regret as I watched them drive away. *Stay focused,* I thought. *You volunteered for this, John Wayne.*

I have endured a lot in my life, more than many, but the most difficult thing I ever had to do was leave my children to go to Iraq in 2008. I didn't even care that I deployed on my birthday. As I left Fort Benning, I realized at that moment the significance of my role as a father. Fathers, you will never fully realize the depth of your role in your children's lives. It is not about you anymore, and it never will be again. Everything is about them. Leading up to my departure, my wife was a ball of emotions, but she remained very brave on the day I left. I was so proud of Yolanda that whole week, even though I know she cried when she was alone and the kids couldn't see her. She supported me to no end that week, preparing the kids for my deployment, helping me pack, and traveling to see me off, giving me just a little extra time with my kids that I wouldn't otherwise have had.

I arrived in the IZ (short for IRAQ) around 0200hrs, nervous and lost with two duffel bags, a backpack, and twenty extra pounds of fat that I wished I'd lost years earlier. I was tired, hungry, and sweating as if I had walked across the desert from Kuwait to Iraq. Looking back, I was probably a hilarious sight to see. However, during that time, if I could have faked a heart attack to go home, I probably would have. But there was no one to help me at that point in time anyway; I was there. I was in Iraq. Just like I'd wanted for nearly seven years. Part of me wondered how this had happened, seemingly so suddenly. Just a few weeks earlier, I had gone on vacation with my family in the mountains of Tennessee, riding my mountain bike against breathtaking scenery. Now, instead of feeling fast and free from atop my bike, I felt hot and heavily weighted down in a sweaty desert.

My third day in Iraq, I continually entered the dining facility, also known as the DFAC, calculatingly positioning myself in the space to avoid conversation with anyone. I have always been a private person, and strangely enough, the DFAC was the one place that I could find some solace; ironic solitude in a crowded place. It's like F. Scott Fitzgerald said in *The Great Gatsby*, "I like large parties. They're so intimate. At small parties there isn't any privacy." I hunkered down two seats away from where a female soldier and a civilian engaged in conversation, far too preoccupied with each other to draw me into their talk. I was all alone until suddenly, a man of African descent sat catty-corner to me. I did my best to avoid his eyes and keep from having my quiet time interrupted. Eventually though, we both looked up at one another.

"How are you?" he asked, his words encased in an accent I couldn't quite place.

"Fine," I said with a smile, giving into this interruption of my solitude. "What country are you from?"

"Kenya," he answered.

"How long have you been in Iraq?" I asked.

"Four months," he said.

"Do you like it?"

At my question, his voice turned dark and gloomy.

"I miss my family so much, but I have to make money for them," he said.

I nodded, understanding. It struck me in that moment that all of us there were making sacrifices of some kind in Iraq to make a better life for someone else. I was sharing my lunch and space with a Kenyan, a new friend, who just wanted to make his family's lives better. But he, like me, was far away from his loved ones, sitting instead in a war-torn land.

I had been in Iraq for about two weeks and I had a serious case of the blues. I had gotten over the shock of being in a combat zone, and we were fairly safe in the green zone. I had heard the stories of mortar strikes and rounds hitting the CHUs, or living huts, on the base, but I hadn't seen anything so far. We had barriers and bunkers everywhere and where we lived looked pretty fortified. One night at around 2200hrs, I was getting ready for bed after a long shift. I had showered and pulled out my Bible to read a couple scriptures like I usually do to end my day. Since being in Iraq, I had started at the beginning with Genesis and had already worked my way up through Exodus. I opened to where I had left off and was reading with my flashlight when suddenly—*BAM!* It was the loudest sound I'd ever heard in my life, including when the C4, a plastic explosive that is used by the military went off during demo training in the officer basic course. The sound was up close and personal and it shook our hut like something had landed next door. Huts were connected in twos with a community bath and shower. When the round hit, I popped up and got the door open, all in one motion. I don't remember my feet hitting the floor, but I was there, flinging open the door and stepping outside towards the bathroom. The guy next door was on the same battle rhythm, because he met me in the middle and we just stared at each other for about five seconds.

"What the hell was that?!" he exclaimed.

I don't curse that much; I never have. Not because I was super spiritual or overly religious, but we just didn't do it in our house when we were growing up. My mother didn't use profanity, so we didn't either, simple as that. Every now and then, my mom would say "what the hell," but she had to be really pissed at either Kem or me for doing something stupid. According to my recollection, it was usually directed at Kem, but either way, profanity was not something used in our home.

"What the hell was that?!" the soldier exclaimed.

"Yeah, man, what the hell *was* that?" I replied. I had to be scared because I let one loose without even thinking about it. We stared at each other for a moment before we turned and went back to our rooms without saying another word to each other that night. I got my flashlight and Bible and decided to start from the beginning, and without any additional thought, I flipped my book back to Genesis 1:1 and began to read, which I did until I fell asleep. That night was definitely a wakeup call for me that I was in a combat zone, but the next five months were relatively calm after that until we moved from the green zone to Camp Victory for the remainder of my tour.

I worked on the COIC floor, which stood for Combined Operational Intelligence Center. It was set up with stadium-style seats, about ten seats across and about fifteen or so rows deep. There were colonels and lieutenant colonels and majors from every service and all different countries. It looked like one of those scenes in a movie when they show the NASA scientists getting ready for a space shuttle launch, but everyone had their uniforms on. Well, most of them did, anyway, since we had a bunch of interagency folks there as well. *What did I get myself into?* I wondered. I was a long way from Ridge Spring, and this certainly wasn't a training exercise. This was the real deal and I figured I better know what I was talking about when someone asked me a question. I felt like a fish out of water around all of these super brains.

One day, after about a week or so of being there, I had just gotten to work from the chow hall when a lieutenant colonel told me the commander was going to be there that morning. I wasn't exactly sure who the commander was; it could have been any one of the generals walking around the palace. Then, the Multi-National Forces-Iraq commander entered and someone ordered everyone to rise to their feet, as was standard protocol. We did so and waited. In walked General Petraeus with a trail of brass and powerful-looking civilians in tow. I had seen him on TV and in photos, of course, but there he was in front of me, in the flesh. My eyes were glued to him. I couldn't believe it. He was already legendary by then, and there I was, up close and personal. Well, I was about ten rows up, but I could see him.

I was in complete and total awe of him when the lieutenant colonel told me to pay attention just in case he asked me a question. I outwardly kept my cool, but on the inside, I was vigorously shaking my head no. We all had microphones on our tables in front of us, but I was not about to jump to answer a question from the man himself and risk being eaten alive. I had heard too many stories about people getting chewed up for saying something stupid during the update brief and I definitely wasn't about to be that guy. I was a major at the time and trying to make lieutenant colonel, and I had no plans to lose rank during my deployment. My boss, who was sitting behind me and monitoring our conversation, caught my eye and gave me the cut throat sign and pointed to the mic as if to say, "Don't you *dare* key that mic." I grinned, relieved, and sat back to watch General Petraeus work that room with the most intellectual thoughts and questions. This was a PhD-level briefing with the general that I had the privilege of witnessing on a weekly basis, and I thought it was amazing.

I worked for an army colonel who is still the smartest, most humble person I have ever met in my life. His name is William King; he's a chemical officer, and in my opinion, a genius. Serving under him was the one time in my life when I wished I had the mental capacity to serve another officer better. I thought of myself as a pretty good officer, able to tackle complex tasks, but Colonel King was on a different level. He was on track to become a general officer, and as such, I was one of his team members. The environment was a lot like basic training in the way that no one asked what had happened to my face. They probably just figured

I had been wounded in combat and I was on my second tour of duty or something. It was street credit I hadn't earned or deserved, because there were soldiers out there in the thick of things, losing limbs and suffering disfigurement and burns in that horrific war. Nevertheless, I was there doing my part and assuaging my guilt over not having deployed in combat before then.

I was assigned to the assessment section within the Cell composed of a cross-section of subject matter experts from various fields with unique skill sets. It was my responsibility to listen to several update briefs, along with collecting reports about casualties and weapons or cache sites found during the course of the week. My report was then staffed up the chain to the Multi-National Forces-Iraq commander to read. It was cumbersome and the reports generally ran about ten pages or so. My boss would chop on it, red ink it, and send it back to me for any additions or corrections that were needed. Additionally, I was responsible for setting up a weekly video conference between the Multi-National Forces-Iraq Joint staff operations and the Central Command commander. Our staffs were numbered based on support areas: J1 was personnel; J2, intelligence; J3, operations; J4, support; J5, plans; J6, signal/communications, and so on.

Setting up the video conferences was always a pucker factor moment for me because it was a zero defect operation. It was either ready to go, or you were fired and they got someone else to do it. The general liked his chair positioned in a certain manner with no chairs to his rear. He had to have a full-sized slide deck and the mic pushed back. I always had to fight for video time, no matter how many times I dropped the general's name; I forgot that there were hundreds of generals running around that place. We always did a sound check and the door was held open prior to the general's arrival. That one event stressed me out more than hearing that mortar round going off…well, not quite, but you get my drift. It typically went off without a hitch and the general would leave without saying a single word. However, Colonel King would always hit me with a good job which made it all worthwhile.

As an additional duty, Colonel King wanted me to take over the responsibilities of the money transfer from another officer who would be leaving Iraq soon for redeployment, so I linked up with the officer to see the process. We made arrangements during the appropriate time and headed to the Iraqi Ministry of Defense headquarters to conduct the transaction. I had only been in the country for a short time, but there I was, organizing money moves for Iraq. I'd showed up to the meeting with a Navy lieutenant at one of Sadaam's palaces when it hit me: What were the chances of a country boy like me ending up in a palace in Iraq meeting with Iraqi leaders to coordinate a move of this magnitude? I laughed inside when I thought about what my best friend, Junior, might say if he were there to see it. *What in the world are we doing here?* He would have asked.

This was my first time going to a headquarters occupied by mostly Iraqi military, and it was spooky, to say the least, when we arrived there in our armored vehicle. We were all suited up in our Interceptor Body Armor (IBA) equipment with ballistic helmets and weapons in tow. We entered the building and it looked like one of those old abandoned warehouses or buildings that should have been condemned years ago, but people were still working there. We had bombed the country pretty well by then, and the electrical grid across Iraq was a problem, but you couldn't tell how bad it was until you traveled off the compound to the local areas where the Iraqis worked. In this building, there was still a ceiling, but it was riddled with holes from the bombings. Having grown up in the United States, seeing the state of this building was a bit of a surreal feeling as well as the pinch I needed as a reminder that I was truly in a warzone. Well, that and the occasional shelling.

As we sat at the table with our translator and the Iraqi leadership, I drifted into my thoughts about the fact that I was really there with a different army doing business. While overseas, it always hit me that I was a long way from Ridge Spring, and if Stanley and Junior could have seen me, they would have been shocked. My friends would have found a way to make a joke of it as well, seeing as how we had barely had enough quarters to play Ms. Pacman growing up, and then there I was, making a money exchange.

As I watched the officer discuss the payment to the Iraqis, the lights went out in the building like the incident during the Super Bowl between the Ravens and the 49ers. No one reacted but me. I scanned the faces of both the Americans and the Iraqis, but there was nothing, not a hint of surprise or shock at the power surge. Instead, they kept their poker faces and steely eyes like we were at war or something. I tried to do the same, but I'm sure it showed on my face as I stretched my eyes like car lights switching from low beams to high beams at night.

What in the world is going on? I wondered. *That's not normal.* It finally clicked for me that this was real. This wasn't a movie and things shouldn't look or feel normal. I felt uneasy, like a kid at a stranger's house who was more than ready to go home. *Let's just exchange this money and get out of here,* I thought. I tried to play it cool, but I didn't know what was happening or what had caused the outage. A few minutes later, the power resumed.

"What's that about?" I asked my buddy.

"This happens all the time," he assured me.

I found out later on the drive back that Iraq had an energy crisis with the failing electricity sector and crumbling infrastructure. We had power generators on our compound, so we didn't feel the effects the way the locals did in town. Instead of really focusing on the money transfer process, I found myself thinking about how I had gotten to this point in my life. I thought about us being shot at or bombed out in the city, and I was suddenly eager to get out of there as well. As I stared at the Iraqis with a strange look on my face, they stared back at me with the same expression as if to ask, "What happened to you?" and "What are you doing here?" We were guests, if you will, in their country, which we had to keep in mind. I ended up not taking over that particular responsibility due to the arrival of another officer shortly afterwards, which was just fine with me. However, that visit stuck with me and painted a true picture of what the Iraqis had to deal with in a war-torn country that had to be rebuilt.

We worked a grueling schedule in Iraq, starting our day around 7:45 a.m. and working into the night until 2000 to 2100hrs, on a good day. We were located in the green zone, co-located with the American embassy. To break up the monotony of working on the floor, we scheduled some gym time as well as time at the makeshift coffee shop inside the embassy. They had created a pretty impressive library within the embassy and books were donated to us from all over the country, all over the world, and we could check them out for a predetermined amount of time before returning them. It was always kind of mystical to walk through the palaces, like walking back in time through a movie like *Raiders of the Lost Ark*. These palaces must have been a thing of beauty before the war when they were first constructed, but we pimped those palaces out when the US Forces arrived, adding office space and cubicles. After years of war, we had a makeshift movie theater with popcorn and everything in the basement, as well as a cafeteria inside the palace. It was still a combat zone, but they made it livable because a year was a long time to be away from home, and many soldiers were on their second or third deployments, some even more than that. Due to some previous suicides in theater, we were encouraged to break up our days and get away for a few minutes whenever we could to get our minds off of the war.

Everyone had some sort of countdown calendar to leave Iraq. You could tell by the looks on people's faces where they were in regards to the duration of their tour. The new arrivals had a "why me?" expression on their faces, but they still kept up the appearance of freshness and sharp eyes. Those in the middle of their tours looked as if they had been in prison for ten years and had aged at least that much since the start of their deployment. We were all sleep deprived, but it really showed in the mid-tours' faces. However, those who only had sixty days or less looked as if they had caught their second wind as they climbed the mountain, looking back at us newbies as if they hoped we could make it up the hill with them.

It was a grind. My own emotions ranged from patriotic to "What was I thinking?" to "This sucks, and if I survive this tour, I pray I never see this place again." There were state department people in Iraq, along with soldiers and military support from so many other countries. We had a strong coalition, and it was fascinating for me to see and meet people from different countries. If you were lucky enough to temporarily forget the war, escape mentally for just a minute, you could really gain an appreciation for the culture and beauty of Iraq. However, the many barricades and concrete walls quickly brought you crashing back to reality. There was no doubt that we were in a war zone; the mortar rounds never let us forget.

When days were tough, I'd see a squad or team come in from one of the forward operating bases, or FOBs. You could tell they were in the thick of things because of the dust on their uniforms, the grit of the war all over them. They came to our location for a little rest and relaxation, which always reminded the rest of us of a little perspective—you couldn't feel sorry for yourself for too long after seeing those soldiers. After all, some of those soldiers, mostly young ones, never returned home. Those were the guys and girls I prayed for each night. Those were the true heroes who protected all of us, even me. There were also units who had their deployments extended involuntarily for three or four months during the surge. When I heard about this, it made me feel ashamed for complaining about my twelve-month tour. Who was I to complain when these soldiers had home in their sights, only to have it yanked away from them, pushed further away from their families.

Nevertheless, it was hard for all of us. "One day at a time" was the name of the game over there. My mood ran the spectrum as I thought about my classmates, family, and friends back home. *They don't even understand how fortunate they are to be safe and at home,* I thought. *We are over here protecting them while they're just going through their carefree lives.* Then I remembered that I had volunteered, and I was upset at my thoughts envying those back home. I thought about the end state and what it would mean to my kids and my future grandkids, and it made me proud. I thought about the fallen military members about whom I would read and write during my weekly assessment reports to the general, and I felt an ache in my chest I couldn't shake.

It always seemed like the young ones who had not even begun to experience their lives were the ones who lost them, and that made me emotional. It didn't seem fair, but war isn't fair. I questioned the war, but I spoke to Iraqis and heard the stories of how Saddam Hussein had tortured them for many years, and I realized we had to be there. Kem defended me that day when we were kids from those bullies, the Morris clan, because I needed him. He taught me to fight my battles and to learn to defend myself, but he also said he had my back no matter what, and I guess that's why we were there. At least that was my mantra, and it was enough to sustain me after I realized that it had probably been stupid to feel guilty about not serving in the war. However, I was in the thick of it now, and just like my first tour in Korea, there was a large ocean separating me from home and I wasn't going to give in.

After about four months of my tour, our command received orders that we had to move from the green zone to Camp Victory. We had to pack up the shop and make the move down route Tigris to the sprawling base. Camp Victory was a beautiful place—well, maybe "beautiful" isn't the right word, considering we had bombed the heck out of it prior to occupation, but it was still something to marvel at. This fortress looked like something out of *Game of Thrones*, with a huge castle as the main attraction where we worked. The place was immense and surrounded by a moat stocked with fish and a drawbridge to cross it. Military members and civilians alike could feed the fish prior to entering the grand doors that opened up to a sweeping ballroom with glittering chandeliers hanging above.

By the time I arrived in 2008, we had built office spaces and installed cables in all of the rooms. We'd also built miles and miles of living space consisting of Connex-style rooms, called CHUs, where palm trees had once peppered the landscape. "CHU" stands for "containerized housing unit," and was the standard housing for many soldiers deployed to Iraq. CHUs are aluminum boxes measuring twenty-two by eight feet, a little bigger than a commercial shipping container. They have linoleum floors and cots or beds inside, with a door, window, top vent, power cabling, and an air conditioner for the summer. Depending on how the CHUs are configured, each one may house four people or be split into a two person unit. Some have a toilet and shower between the rooms, but each living space has a bed, an end table, and a wall locker, and some soldiers get refrigerators and TVs. Many of the

FOBs, or Forward Operating Bases, consist of many units, thus earning the nickname of "CHUville."

Throughout the camp that was large enough to have its own zip code by US standards were smaller scale castles, including baby castles in the middle of a lake that reportedly belonged to Saddam's torturous sons. We once took a PT test using the road around the lake for our two-mile run and someone uploaded tons of pictures onto a shared folder on our computers that showed Camp Victory prior to the invasion. The photos were amazing and I couldn't believe I called this place home for eight months. However, as time went on, the breathtaking landscape became just another route I walked through to get to work.

When we moved over to Camp Victory, I no longer worked on the Combined Operational Intelligence Center floor as Colonel King formed his own assessment team. Our team consisted of people of all services and inter-agency personnel, additionally augmented with Army National Guard personnel. Staff Sergeant Alvarez was our super NCO, and was the first person I had ever heard of extending in theater for a second tour. It seemed like something out of the Vietnam playbook, which instantly made him seem like a hardcore soldier, a reputation Alvarez lived up to because he was a special, one-of-a-kind soldier. The colonel could give him any mission, any task, and Alvarez could knock it out without complaint. Our team also had a sharp Air Force technical sergeant named Nichelle Nichols. The name sounded familiar, but I couldn't place it right away until later, when I watched one of the many movies that was loaded up on the shared drive.

"How'd you get your name?" I asked her one day.

"My mother loved *Star Trek* and Ms. Nichols became the first black actress to star on the series, hence the name," she explained. She was as pretty as her namesake and just as sharp as Alvarez. We all worked in cubicles within a large room, and on some Fridays, we'd reel up the days with office parties and some cigar smoking on the balcony. It seemed kind of crazy; people around the world supported us with everything from golf balls to hit off the back terrace into one of the many lakes across the camp to cigars and magazines and books. They were small things, but they made life overseas a little more comfortable as we served our country and dreamed of home.

Towards the end of my tour, I received notification from Colonel King that I would serve as the investigating officer for some missing vehicles. Some poor sergeant first class had signed for hundreds of civilian vehicles shipped in country for use to drive around the bases. As dictated by proper protocol, I had to call legal for assistance. I called the JAG office, and sure enough, Captain Biden picked up the phone.

"Bo Biden speaking," he said. I had heard that the vice president's son had deployed to Iraq, and I made the connection immediately.

"Are you…"

"Yes, I am," he confirmed. "He's my dad."

I'd almost forgotten what I called him for, but I arranged to meet with him to go over my preliminary investigation. I made the appointment and soon found myself in his office. This goes without saying, but Bo Biden looked just like his dad. It doesn't take much to get me star struck, but up to this point it had consisted mainly of athletes. As I showed him my paperwork, I just kind of stared at him for a minute as if to say, "Why are you here in Iraq?" He had to be the nicest gentleman I had ever met in my life. He was a captain, and I outranked him by one, but still, Bo Biden was so cool. After that meeting, I saw him from time to time in the chow hall line or heading down the road somewhere, and I just couldn't believe he was in Iraq. I waved to him whenever I saw him and he would just give me one of those gentle smiles. I told my wife maybe a hundred times during my tour and over the years since that I served in Iraq with Bo Biden, and when she saw him or his dad on TV or knew there was a possibility of me mentioning his name, she'd interject and finish my sentence.

"I know, I know! You served with his son!"

"Yep, he was there with me!" I'd say proudly. I was heartbroken when he passed, because I had personally met him and he was a comrade who had served in the long war with me. He was so young, and it seems like we always lose the good ones far too soon.

We were allotted two weeks R&R, and I had decided early in my tour that I wanted to get most of my tour behind me before taking my break to go home. I made it through eight months before I finally took my break. In hindsight, I should have taken it earlier because it took a psychological toll on me, giving me time, too much time in a war zone, time to read and write reports. I was mentally fried and felt really disengaged when I returned home. My kids looked at me as if I was a stranger, not unlike the first time I saw my father in prison: The person didn't match the picture. When my daughter saw me, she stared at me like the first time Lynnette saw me after the fire, but without the tears. Trinity just stared at me as if I was some intruder in her home. My wife had grown accustomed to making things happen while I was gone, and at times I felt as if I was in the way. The war had changed me, changed us. It made me sad and almost frustrated at the fact that I had chosen this path, and now I was a stranger in my own home. I didn't want to visit anybody or see any of my friends, but I knew I had to make a trip home to see my mom.

The days went by too fast, which made me even more anxious. In a strange way, I wanted to go back to Iraq where things were routine, and then I stopped. What was I thinking? I missed my family something awful, but I realized I was a different person now. Everything was different. The casualty toll had really beat me down, and without me realizing it, had caused me to withdraw from my family and friends. I had it in my mind that I wanted to just go home and see my wife and kids and be alone. I didn't want to hear "Welcome back!" or "Thanks for your service," especially at that point. I still had three months to go in Iraq and I just figured I would go home and hide out until it was time to return to the Iraqi theater to complete my tour of duty. I knew I had to call my siblings and I was dreading calling Kem. I love my brother, but Kem would always beat me up about seeing our mom and spending time with her throughout the years, even though he had spent many years away himself. Whoever was closer to Ridge Spring had to keep track of our mother. After I'd been home for a few days on R&R, I finally talked to Kem. He asked how I was doing, he asked about the family, and then the next thing out of his mouth was asking when I was going to Ridge Spring to see our mother.

"Well…" I said hesitantly.

"Well, nothing!" Kem exclaimed. "If you don't get down there to see your mother, we are going to have some problems." Then he hung up the phone on me.

I put down my phone, but the guilt treatment had already begun to take effect: I knew I had to go. It wasn't that I didn't want to see my mother, but I knew she would notice the change in me like only mothers can. No matter how tough I tried to be or how much I might try to put her at ease about my deployment, my mother would be able to read my pain. I hadn't seen combat close up and I didn't maneuver through IED-riddled roads on a daily basis like some of my peers and the young troops who really wore the gravity of that war. However, the war zone had beaten me down in my own way. I was enraged by the fact that those young soldiers and service members were dying and I could see their faces. They had left behind children, spouses, and parents before they had really been given a chance to live, and that weighed heavily on me. When I wrote out those reports, there would be a number alongside the word "casualties," and over time I grew numb to it until the commander would highlight a soldier who had died during an update brief. It would hit me then that all of those casualty numbers were real people and it bothered me. I didn't want my mom to see that in my face, because she would cry, and I couldn't deal with that.

Nevertheless, I made the trip to see my mom. She embraced me like she had when I graduated from high school. She stared at me like the day I had returned from basic training. She also cried like the day we came home after her time in the hospital, when all of us were finally together again for good. My mother knew me and she saw everything in my eyes, but she just left it there.

"You're almost done. I can't wait until it's over," she said. "It's time for you to get out of that military." My mother always mentioned that during my deployments, but she knew I loved being a soldier and wanted to provide for my family.

"Let's eat!" she added, changing the subject. She didn't pry, which is what I needed. Mothers know when their kids are uneasy and my mom knew me well. We ate so much food that day, which is what I really needed—a good meal with my mother. I didn't get to see Kem during my break, but Lynnette drove down to join us and we laughed and reminisced until late in the evening before I returned to Newnan.

While overseas, the other troops and I got frequent visits from coaches to athletes to senators and everyone in between. During my tour, I saw Senator Obama (and again later, as President Obama), President Bush, Stephen Colbert, David Robinson, and Senator Clinton. Both presidents seemed like these perfectly made human beings with auras around them, not unlike the way Charlie Murphy described Rick James. They literally glowed. Once, Technical Sergeant Nichols was selected to stand behind President Obama, along with a host of other military members, as he spoke to the mass of people in the castle. She made the cover of a magazine and everything, becoming an instant star amongst the team members. In hindsight, my tour wasn't that bad. Just as Bob Hope visited Vietnam, we had our entertainment as well, and the visitors were welcome distractions. Laughter helped, but at the end of the day we were still in a war zone, far from home.

I left Iraq a few days prior to my birthday, mission complete, and I had already made arrangements for the family and me to go to Disney World together to celebrate my homecoming after a short stopover at home. I still didn't want to hang around non-army people, including my extended family, but my wife had already planned a joint welcome home/birthday party in our backyard. So, I sucked it up and enjoyed my day.

The party was supposed to be a surprise, but because Yolanda knew my desire to be left alone, she'd warned me ahead of time to act surprised and try to keep my spirits up. I had a friend from church named Bob, who had introduced me to car shows and helped me purchase my gold '53 super beetle. Bob picked me up to keep me away from the house for a little while so Yolanda could set up for the party. As we drove to Bob's house to check out his newly repainted candy-apple-red bug, I drifted into the story of the first time I brought my own 1953 super beetle bug home to show the kids. I had been so excited to show them my new wheels and had pulled into the driveway and told them to gather around as I gave them a onceover of my new pride and joy. However, my sons' reactions were similar to the first time I introduced them to SPAM and they were already frowning as I opened the car door.

"What is this?" Josh asked.

"What do you mean?" I asked.

"This car is old!" he exclaimed.

"That's the point, Josh," I explained. "It's an antique!"

I made my kids get in and I instructed Josh to roll the window down. He stared at me as if I had told him to start speaking Chinese.

"Roll the window down?" he asked. "What does that mean?"

I burst into laughter, realizing that my kids had never seen a window handle that you had to crank down.

"Why would you buy this car?" my kids asked. "How much did you pay for this?"

I finally realized that their taste for old bugs was the same as their taste for SPAM, which is to say, it wasn't good. You never know what your kids are going to like.

I smiled as I remembered that day while I rode along with Bob, playing along with the pretense of him keeping me away from the house to buy some set up time. Finally, after spending a few hours together, Bob and I returned to my house where everyone was gathered, including my sister and her husband, Cedric, who had made the three-hour trip for the occasion. When I walked into the backyard, I saw the space filled with people from the church as well as a few other friends in the neighborhood. They'd strung a "welcome home" banner in the backyard, and on the picnic table was a birthday cake. Standing there in the backyard, I realized I felt free. I didn't have to carry my weapon everywhere and it was comforting to see green grass instead of the brown desert dust. However, I still wasn't sure I felt like I was 100 percent home. The party was special and I really appreciated everyone coming out for me, but mentally, I wasn't there. I had physically come home, but emotionally, I was still in the sandbox.

A week earlier, I had been really bothered by the death of Michael Jackson. In a strange way, I had somehow convinced myself that I should have been home before he died. I'm not sure why. It was just one of those weird things that made me think something was wrong with me. It was similar to when I went off to Korea in 1994 right after the OJ Simpson slow chase in the Bronco, and then I returned home before the verdict, but the whole feeling was amplified. I felt like I'd lost so much time and missed so much, especially when it came to my kids' lives. Guilt was creeping in because I had chosen this deployment. But I tried to push that aside and enjoy my party. We had so much food and we sang and danced in the backyard. Well, I just *watched* the dancing part, because I have two left feet. Even as fun as it was, I couldn't wait until everyone left. I'd always been sort of a loner, but now it was worse. I needed to be around army people, but I had taken thirty days' leave, so that had to wait.

It took a few months before I started to snap out of it and started to blend back into my natural environment, but I knew I wasn't the same. I found I was more irritable and standoffish than I had been before. I'd made it back alive, but I would never be whole again. I'd never really been whole since the fire, and now I had a new heightened awareness of my environment. After months of writing those reports highlighting the number of casualties each week, I'd become a little desensitized to the fact that those numbers represented real people who had been robbed of their innocence and their lives. And yet those numbers and those lives were inescapable. They're still inescapable.

CHAPTER 23

Facing My Father, Part III

In 1996, my father requested I attend his parole hearing, a request that deeply concerned my mother. When I told her what my father had asked, she became very upset and drilled me on his health care and where he would live if he was released. When she asked me that, I realized I hadn't thought about that when I'd agreed to be present. My mother also brought up the safety of Yolanda and our newborn son, James Jr. As she talked, I grew more and more horrified at the idea of my family's safety being compromised. But my word was my bond, and I felt that I couldn't back out of the agreement I'd given my father.

This time, I arrived in my service dress uniform. I had spoken to my father's counselor prior to the hearing and he had told me that the chances of my father being released were very slim, largely due to the nature of the crime and the fact that my mother had a vote in the matter as well. I felt relieved, knowing I could safely fulfill my promise to show my father support at his hearing with the knowledge that his parole would be denied. Once inside the hearing, I made a short statement about how I thought my father felt remorse for his actions. I shared with the board how he had found God and his faith had strengthened him, but their decision was quick and my father's plea for parole was denied; he would have to wait another two years for his next parole hearing. This was the first and last time I showed up for a hearing.

Through the years, my father wanted me to pay for an attorney to support his efforts. I always told him I would look into it, but I never really had any intention of supporting his petitions for release, due to my mother's concerns, as well as my own for my family's safety. But when we spoke on the phone, I often allowed him to dream by helping him to paint a picture of where he could live if he was ever released. I would take him on a mental trip with me wherever I was stationed and tell him about the town. My father would fantasize about going fishing with his grandchildren, or going out to a nice restaurant.

"Tell me about Atlanta again," he would say.

I would set the scene for him, describing the house and the area, adding in rich, full details to complete the picture.

"That sounds real good," he'd say. "That sounds real good."

After a time, he began writing letters to my kids. To this day, I still have one in my dresser drawer beside my bed. It was a letter he wrote to James Jr. in which he warned my son about the danger of drugs and he talked about the importance of studying hard and going to college. Even now, when I reread that letter, I feel tears prickle at the corners of my eyes and emotion closes my throat. In spite of everything, my father and I developed a relationship. It wasn't the relationship I'd longed for as a kid, but things rarely work out exactly the way we want or expect them to. For the first time, I had something good from my father, and I held onto that. I still do.

One day in 2010, my father's counselor called me and told me that my father was in desperate need to speak with one of his kids. The holiday season was upon us and I knew it was time for the yearly Christmas package, so I assumed it was something pertaining to that. I had just finished a five-day rotation at work and was off for the next few days and had been looking forward to spending some times with my family, so I initially said no. However, my heart softened a little when I heard the deep concern in the counselor's voice, and I told the counselor I'd make the four hour trip to South Carolina to visit my father.

On Friday morning, after seeing Yolanda and the kids off to school, I packed for the overnight trip. As I did so, the counselor advised me to call prior to the visit to ensure I was on the visitor's list. Lucky for me that I remembered this, because when I called, I was told that my visit had to be scheduled two weeks in advance and I would not be on the list. Usually, I would have accepted this answer and given in, despite my suspicion that this wasn't completely accurate information, but something pulled at me and called for me to be persistent.

"Hold on, let me transfer you," said the voice on the other end of the phone.

This turned into the Greek chorus of my phone call. I was transferred over and over and over until I felt like I'd spoken with nearly every staff member of the prison. However, my endurance paid off and my visit was eventually confirmed, so I set off on the long car ride towards my father. As I drove, I called my mother, Lynnette, and Kem to help pass the time on the drive. Part of me felt guilty that I would end up spending more time with my imprisoned father than with my mother on this particular trip, but the urgency in the counselor's voice still pulled at me and I felt like this trip might be different.

Finally, I arrived at Kirkland Correctional Facility. I checked in, and then I was left with nothing to do but wait. I felt restless as I waited for the metal doors to open and for my father to appear. Too anxious to sit, I stood and paced back and forth like a tiger in a zoo, trying whatever I could do to distract myself. My father wasn't expecting me until the following day, so I knew he'd likely be surprised to see me. As I paced across the room, it occurred to me that during my last visit, I'd been a first lieutenant. Now, I was only a month away from becoming a lieutenant colonel. I'd grown and changed so much, no longer the young newlywed who had visited my father or the little boy who had unknowingly wandered into my father's sinister ambush. In thinking of myself, I wondered who my father had become. Had I ever really known who he was?

While I waited, the guard engaged me in some small talk. She spent several minutes complaining about her job, her distaste already very evident to me. It wasn't the work itself that bothered her, she told me, but rather her peers and leadership that made her sick. I found it rather ironic that the murderers, molesters, and drug dealers were more tolerable for this guard than her coworkers.

Suddenly, the doors opened and my father appeared, and just as I had fifteen years ago, the macho army officer in me turned into that little kid who yearned for his father's attention. We embraced as if reuniting at the airport after a weekend trip and we quickly fell into our hurried game of catching up on one another's lives. Due to delays on both of our parts, we had lost forty-five minutes of our visitation time, and my agenda was set: I didn't want to waste a moment of our two remaining hours. Before our visit, I had purchased a key card to use at the vending machines. I knew his vices and had prepared accordingly by loading twenty dollars onto the key card. I knew my father liked his coffee and his sweets, so I wasted no time in offering him some treats, which he happily accepted.

As we walked over to the vending machine, I began to study my father's physicality. The years in prison had not been kind to him, as evidenced by his stooped walk, his left hand clutched close to his body not unlike a stroke victim. The diabetes, high blood pressure, and mental illness had taken a huge toll on my father's frame. Standing beside him, I noticed his shortened height, the drag and limp of his steps, and I found myself thinking, *I'm taller than you.* The revelation felt a little surprising to me, and on a subconscious level, I think it made me feel superior during our visit, like I had the upper hand over my father. On that day, I planned to ask my questions, my ego would be stroked; I would be in charge.

"What do you want?" I asked my father.

"Coffee, cream, extra sugar," he said.

You'll get what I give you, I thought darkly, but I said nothing and instead I obliged and prepared his coffee.

"Anything else?" I offered.

"M&Ms and a Snickers bar," he added politely.

I collected the candy and we made our way over to a table. An attractive young lady passed us. She couldn't have been older than twenty-eight, and looked to be visiting her boyfriend, or at least that's what I guessed based on the absence of a wedding ring. She was beautiful by all standards, a fact that my father did not miss when he whispered to me about the package on her. I was shocked at first, because I had expected my father to keep the saved and sanctified persona he'd had before in an attempt to win me over, but he didn't. I smiled a wide, teenager's grin, not because of his comment about the young lady, but because I knew this visit with my father would be true and authentic. No putting on airs, no smoke screens, just two humans talking.

We sat across from one another at the table. I've always found it difficult to focus during a conversation; my brain is constantly racing, drifting in and out, locking on the individual one moment and then inadvertently ignoring them the next.

"How are you?" he asked.

"I have more good days than bad," I responded.

"How's Kem? And Lynnette?" he asked.

As we talked, he reeled off question after question as I began to study him like a psychiatrist. I studied his face, his mannerisms, his eyes, and his hair, looking for myself in him, looking for the resemblance. Then, he caught me off guard by bringing up his mental illness. Suddenly, he had my full attention. My father told me about the diagnosis that labeled him a manic schizophrenic. He told me about the cocktails of wine combined with acid-laced weed he consumed on a regular basis starting in his high school days until the day he was arrested for the fire. I had heard these stories from my mom, but hearing it straight from the horse's mouth was an entirely different experience altogether. It wasn't that I hadn't believed my mother, because of course I had, but hearing this confirmation from my father gave the stories new weight and validity.

"I hear voices and have bouts of rage," he admitted. None of this was new, but to hear my father admit to this felt monumental. We talked some more, and then he started to ask me questions again.

"Do you like going to clubs?" my father asked.

"Clubs?" I asked.

"Yes, clubs, or bars, as we called them in Philly," my father clarified, a tone creeping into his voice.

"Oh. No, I don't do clubs," I replied.

"I thought you were like me," my father said with a smirk.

I am nothing like you, I thought.

"No. I never liked the club scene," I told him instead. Uncomfortable with this shift, I redirected the conversation in a way that I wanted it to go. "Do you think it was your sickness that made you start the fire?"

My father sighed, thinking.

"I know I was drinking a lot that night," he said. "I remember being mad at your mother and turning over the gas dryer."

I was careful not to interrupt. Instead, I watched, looking for a kink in my father's armor to see if he was lying. Blinking his eyes, shifting, voice inflection, or one of the other signs I'd been trained to find.

"The police said I lit a match that caused the fire, but I don't remember," my father said. "We all smoked! Your mother, grandmother, and me. Any one of us could have lit the match." He paused for a moment. I think he was trying to place the blame, push it away onto someone else. "I don't remember who lit the match, so I took the blame. But the fire wasn't intentional," he added.

Regardless of whether it was true or not, my father was telling me what I wanted to hear. I probed deeper and he opened, his life and secrets unfurling like flowers. Through this conversation with my father, I realized that we were more alike than we were different. The high blood pressure, the back pains, many of the mental issues as I battled some of my hidden demons. The trauma of the fire and the devout secrecy with which I had held it close were hard to bear, and I often felt that the good in me struggled to suppress the bad. Was I only a mistake away from sharing the fate of my father? People have always told me that I'm very kind and generous, well-mannered and polite, but they don't know my struggles and flaws. I haven't let them know my struggles and flaws. Without God, I'm not sure where or who I would be.

My father and I talked about the fire, but at that point he was not in good shape, mentally or physically. Diabetes had reduced him to a shell of his former self and I am sure that forty-plus years of serving in the penitentiary weathered him tremendously. In my mind, this meeting was going to be beneficial for both of us. I needed answers about the fire that I'd never gotten in the past, I wanted to know about his childhood, and he needed to see me. However, at that point in his life, he was there, but he wasn't.

I asked him questions about the fire and he claimed he'd been framed, insisting that Uncle Willie James, my maternal grandmother's brother, wanted my father locked up because he hated him. Of course, I knew this was false because I'd been there that day. I'd seen my father sitting on that porch, waiting for us to walk right into his trap. However, despite having every right to get angry over his declarations, I didn't. My father, on the other hand, started to get angry, thinking about the injustice of his supposed framing, but then he immediately calmed down and asked me about getting a lawyer for him so he could get out of jail. I tried to redirect him and pull for details about his childhood and his mother, but my father couldn't stay on topic. Then, he shared a story with me of how he was sent to a mental ward because a youngster stole his newspaper. My father was in another space as he described his story, his eyes far away and his mind elsewhere, and I knew the man I called "Dad" was lost.

I spent the rest of the time trying to put him at ease, helping him escape his mental shackles. I told him I would bring the grandkids to see him and that I would do my best to get him out of prison. I shared with him the stories of Atlanta and the beauty of the city and how wonderful it would be to have him there with us. I watched my father's face and saw him take that leap with me as I continued to mentally pull him out of prison and into this fantasyland I'd designed. He needed it desperately. The diabetes had caused his left hand to clench and shiver, and he fought against his own body to pull the cup of coffee to his lips with both hands. One slurp, then two, and then his trembling hands worked hard to steady the cup and set it back down onto the table.

Why does he shake like that? I wondered as I watched him. I studied my father's salt-and-pepper hair, his receding hairline, to see what could become of my own hair. Was it the drugs? His mental state? Or was it hereditary?

"Tell me about your house in Atlanta again," my father said.

"It's huge," I said, stretching out the details a little for effect. "I have a room on the first floor for you when you get out."

My father's face broke into a grin, but I got a chill when I said that. Not because it was a lie—I did have a room—but because I knew he was never leaving that place.

"I have a pond in the neighborhood and we can go fishing with the kids on the weekends if you want to," I continued.

"I would like that, Foots," he said, still smiling.

We kept talking, fading in and out of conversational topics like sports or requests to send him money for a new TV or about him mailing me one of those holiday wish lists.

"I'll see what I can do, Dad," I said.

"Do you think you can get me another one of the candy bars and another cup of coffee?" he asked.

"Sure."

As I walked over to the vending machine, it really sank in that my dad was mentally imbalanced and this might be my last visit to the prison. I watched my father slurp his coffee down and eat that Snickers bar as if it was the very first in his life while he talked about prison restrictions and their cut-down on sweets as he battled diabetes. I found myself thinking about my own health as I continued to study him. After a little while, I noticed that I began to focus on other things in the room. My fact-finding mission was over and it was time to get home to my family.

I looked around the visiting room at the blend of young and old faces of men who looked like me, save for the prison uniforms and the slight expressions of shame and fear on their faces. The men didn't look like killers or bank robbers. They had nice haircuts, some had the latest shoes. It was also interesting to see the spouses and girlfriends visiting these convicts in prison, some of them very attractive. I thought about all of those college students who would love to be with some of these young women, but I guess they were loyal to their men. What path did those guys take to end up there? Some were so young, just like my dad was when he'd entered prison. The place was so depressing and I started to get a little irritated. I resolved I would never put myself in a situation to be locked up in a place like this.

"Dad, I've got to go," I said.

"Okay, son!" my father said. "Do you think that lawyer in Atlanta will be expensive?"

I knew there wouldn't be a lawyer, but I played along anyway.

"I can afford it, Dad," I assured him.

"Are you going to be there for my parole hearing?" he asked hopefully.

"Of course, Dad. You're coming home this time."

We embraced for what would be the last time while I fought back tears. As I watched him walk back towards the big metal door, I gave my father a final onceover and I waited until the guards opened the door. My father didn't look back at me, which I suppose was ultimately a good thing. Maybe it was easier that way. Once he was gone, I turned towards my own exit. I walked back through the corridor to retrieve my items, which had a series of doors that had to be buzzed each time they opened while officers monitored my departure.

"Here's your belt, sir," one of the officers said as he handed it to me. It made me think of boarding a flight after 9/11, and with half a laugh, I thought about how I'd made it out alive.

When I got back in my car and began the drive home, I called my mom to give her an update on the visit because I knew she was anxious about what had transpired. She never had an issue with any of us wanting to visit our father, but there was always something that seemed to be on her mind when we did; a concern for him, but also the hope that he wouldn't lie to us or convince me to help him get out.

"How was your visit, son?" my mom asked.

"He's gone mentally, Mom."

"What do you mean?"

"His body has deteriorated and his mental capacity just isn't there anymore. He's a shell of the man I once knew, and you don't ever want to see him like this."

My mother began to cry as I shared some of the details. She knew, but she hadn't wanted me to see that side of him, in spite of everything he'd put us through. My mother is not a vengeful woman by any means. Before we hung up, I told her I was on my way to her house and that I would see her in an hour.

My mom and I visited for a while and I departed for home around six thirty or seven that evening. There was no cell phone coverage for the next twenty or twenty-five minutes on the back roads leading to the interstate, so I just cruised along, checking out the scenery and reminiscing about years past in Ridge Spring. As I approached I-20, my cell phone began pinging with messages from my wife. She doesn't usually call unless she needs something, so this was odd. Yolanda has never been one to spend much time on the phone, and she typically leaves me alone when I'm visiting home. But now, seeing my phone, I had a whole bunch of missed calls from my wife, and since I hadn't told her I was stopping by my mom's house, she hadn't thought to call there to find me. I knew something was up, so I called Yolanda right away.

"Where were you?" Yolanda demanded by way of greeting.

"I stopped by my mom's house," I explained. "What's wrong?" I asked, panic mounting in my voice as I heard my wife's desperation and fear on the other end of the line.

"The house caught on fire!" she exclaimed.

My heart was racing and I felt awful for leaving them in the first place to go visit my father.

"Is everyone all right?" I asked, painful memories flooding back into my mind.

"Everybody's fine," Yolanda said. I could tell she was trying to keep her voice level, but the nerves crept in around her words. "We're next door with the neighbors and there's a fireman here."

"Can I speak with him?" I asked.

"Hold on," Yolanda said. I waited anxiously as the phone was handed over.

"Hello, sir," a male voice said.

"Hi, are you one of the firemen?" I asked.

"Yes, sir, I am," he said. "Your family was very fortunate tonight. We contained the fire to your attic area and everything is okay."

I exhaled a breath I hadn't realized I'd been holding. I could finally breathe. My family was okay and my house was mostly intact. I thanked the fireman many times over and felt deeply relieved, but I was still anxious to get home. An interminable two-and-a-half-hour drive still stretched out in front of me, and I called back every thirty minutes to check on the family. However, the time in between the phone calls allowed me to drift into my thoughts. I thought about the irony of visiting my father and talking about the fire on the same day that my own home caught fire. What did it all mean? I didn't want to call my mom because she would have just lost it, and I didn't need those added emotions at the moment, so I drove and thought and continued to call home to check on my family.

"We're okay, but I don't trust this house," Yolanda said. "How close are you?"

"I'm an hour away," I told her. We said goodbye and hung up, leaving me alone with my thoughts again. I could have lost my family, but I hadn't—so what was the message God was trying to send me? I became frustrated at the fact that I had spent time with the man that had done so much harm to my family, and as a result, I hadn't been there for Yolanda and the kids in their time of need. *I shouldn't have gone,* I thought. *I should have known better and I shouldn't have gone.*

Finally, I was only thirty minutes from home. I was in the city of Atlanta, pushing through traffic, which kept my mind off things a little. Still, the closer I got, the faster I drove. I needed to slow down, but I couldn't stop thinking about my family and our house. I thought about the damage to our home and the repairs that might be needed and how to get rid of the house after the repairs were done. I knew I couldn't just get rid of the house like throwing away a shirt with an ink stain, but my emotions had shifted from panic to anger because now my wife didn't feel safe. As I hit the last stretch towards home on I-85, I thought about my mom and what we went through. That tragedy didn't compare to what I was now facing, and the thought was actually somewhat comforting. Of course, that was not the time to drop that particular sentiment on my wife.

I made the turn off I-85 up the ramp, off exit fifty-one, Newnan exit, and the light was green. I made the left through the next light, past the Hardee's on the left. Almost there, I made the next left past the submarine sandwich store and headed down the road for the last mile. I turned into the entrance of our subdivision and saw our house, the third one on the left. I slowed down and looked up at my home, trying to find the destruction. I couldn't see any obvious signs, but by that time it was dark outside. The fire trucks were gone and the neighbors were asleep, so I pulled into the driveway, still searching for signs. I got out and headed to the side gate, opening it and walking around towards the back of the house. Nothing.

I could smell some smoke, but nothing heavy. Surely, the smoke would be all throughout the house, but could it be if my family was still home? I opened the front door and disarmed the alarm. Suddenly, my kids poured into the room, all trying to tell their versions of the story at once. I couldn't believe it. My house was still intact and everyone was fine. The fire really had been contained to the attic. The smoke was only strong when I opened the attic door to peek in, and I immediately closed it. Then I went to my wife and wrapped my arms around her, so thankful she was safe.

"Do you think it could start again?" she asked. "Should we stay here tonight?"

"I think we'll be okay," I said, squeezing her a little tighter. "I'll check it out in the morning, but the fireman assured me it's all okay on the phone. He actually told me it was a miracle that the fire didn't spread quickly and that only the electrical box mounted to one of the beams in the attic caught fire."

Yolanda nodded. The situation really wasn't bad at all, and I was careful to avoid coming off with some over-the-top response to the fire. That would've been open season for her to bring up my experience with house fires, and I'd already spent too much time thinking about that during my drive home. I kept my mouth shut and reassured her that all was well and that she'd done well taking care of the kids. She'd done all the right things, and once cooler heads prevailed, we reconsidered selling the house.

In the days following the fire at my house in Atlanta, I found myself thinking about it a lot, sure that it was some kind of sign. I searched for a deeper meaning, wondering if it was a sign from heaven. The incident took me back to the original fire and the way it had impacted Kem, Lynnette, and me. I thought about how we'd all survived and lived to have our own families. I thought about the sacrifices our mother had made to ensure that we at least had the opportunity to make a good life for ourselves. As I drove, I felt the tears stand in my eyes as I thought about all the blessings we'd had, as well as the irony of my house catching fire while I was visiting my father, finally discussing *the* fire. Maybe this fire in my house would be the spark we needed in our home to finally have a conversation about my childhood. I had never discussed the details with my kids because they weren't really old enough, but now they probed into my past. They looked at me as if I was reading from a mystery novel, hanging onto my every word, asking about my dad and why he would do such a thing. They studied my face as they continued to pepper me with questions.

"Why did you name me James III?" my eldest son asked. I thought about it for a moment. *Well, why did I do that?* I wondered. *Maybe third time's a charm?* I figured I could straighten out this Scott legacy and break this generational curse. I had to right this wrong once and for all to erase this image of a monster. The fire in my house brought it all back to me, and no matter how hard I tried to protect my family and shelter my kids, this became a full-circle moment for me. I had moved away from Ridge Spring as if I was trying to escape my past and start anew, not wanting my kids to know about the hardships and pains of my early life.

I thought they didn't need to know that part of me. I was an army officer and they didn't know any real struggles, and that's exactly the way I wanted it. I wanted them to experience all of the good things in life, the YMCA, the Boy and Girl Scouts, nice subdivisions, good schools. I wanted my children's lives to be drama-free so they could avoid the sleepless nights I'd had to endure. However, because of the fire at our house and my last visit with my father, I had to share with them my childhood experiences and let them into the challenges I'd overcome in my life. My kids weren't completely oblivious; they'd always thought of Yolanda and me coming from two different worlds because of the differences in her family structure and mine. The kids could see the calmness when we visited my wife's side of the family versus when we visited mine, but they wouldn't dare complain. Now, they knew the history.

I think I understand the point of the spark that led to the fire in the attic. It wasn't about the minor structural damage at all, but about the conversation I had needed to have with my kids about why I am who I am. The fire burned down the wall I'd built around my past, and I was finally able to let my children see me—*really* see me.

CHAPTER 24

US Army Forces Command Assignment: July 2009-January 2011

I began to settle into my new assignment at Forces Command as a battle captain. It was my first time serving in a position that consisted of full-time, twelve-hours-a-day shift work. We worked a five-day-on/four-day-off schedule and I hated it. The people were great, but the assignment was awful for me. Up to that point, my shift work had only lasted for a week or two before resetting to our normal duty hours—at least, normal by military standards. However, I was now serving in a position that required me to work these twelve-hour shifts for a couple of months at night before switching to days for a couple months. It was very taxing on my body. I thought of some of my friends and others back in Ridge Spring who worked in factories with this kind of schedule for their entire adult lives, and I gained so much respect for them. I don't think we're designed to work at night on a regular basis; God made day and night for a reason.

Fred Dorsey, who was a reserve major at the time, served as my supervisor. He was a really cool guy and a talented officer who taught me the ropes. He called me "Scotty" and would school me on the details of the job. Most of our staff consisted of reservist and government employees, and I had returned from Iraq and literally conducted a permanent change of station next door from Third

Army. However, the two units were like night and day. Civilians seemed to outnumber military personnel, and for the first time, I was to have a government civil service employee in the grade of GS14 as my intermediate supervisor.

Before arriving there, I didn't understand the civilian government system. I didn't know a soldier could have a civilian boss, but I learned quickly. Mr. Paul Douglas had served in the army for a few years and had worked his way up to a senior civilian employee. He'd worked in Forces Command for many years and knew the inner workings of every section like the back of his hand. Paul was as calm of a boss as I'd ever had, and his management skills were as smooth as they come. However, if an officer screwed up a report or something, Paul had a very effective death stare. I quickly realized that the military depended on the civilian workforce in a big way to include the contractors who supported the mission as well. I already had a tremendous amount of respect for the National Guard and the reserve forces, but I got a renewed respect for them just by working with them every day. I had now touched almost every level of the military structure, from tactical and operational units to ground components and multinational forces. It was a unique unit and assignment, and I should have been in heaven because I didn't have to deploy anymore and was able to maintain stability for my family—but the shift work just killed me. I wanted out, so I called on the Big Dog once again to get me out of there.

"Scott, what do you want to do?" he asked.

"I want to get back into the IO business and go overseas somewhere, maybe Hawaii," I said. "IO" stood for information operations which, during military operations, pertained to information-related capabilities being used to influence, disrupt, corrupt, or usurp the decision-making of adversaries while protecting ourselves. It's an essential factor in a joint force commander's capability to achieve and sustain the level of information superiority necessary for decisive joint operations.

"Okay, draft an email and send it to Motley and I'll endorse it for you."

Vincent Motley was a great friend of mine who served as my branch manager. We'd all served in Third Army together and we were pretty tight. However, he couldn't just hand out assignments to all of his buddies, myself included, but if Colonel Baker cosigned, then Major Motley would get me out of there.

"Where do you want to go, James?" Motley asked. I told him that Germany, Hawaii, and Korea were my top three. "Okay, let me work it for you."

A week or so passed, and Vince came back with a quick no for my top two.

"Come on, man, you can't get me Germany at least?" I asked, feeling disappointed.

"Nope."

"Okay, what about Korea?" I asked.

"I can get you to Korea," he said.

"Cool, let me discuss it with my wife," I told him. Yolanda had never been overseas before and she was actually terrified to leave the country. I'd served all of these years in the military, but we'd never gone overseas together as a family. In order to sell my wife on the idea, I had to really sell it and pull out all of the tricks. I'd enjoyed my tour in Korea, but I was the soldier, and my enjoyment might not translate to my family's enjoyment. When I talked to Yolanda, I painted the picture of a fantasy land while I talked about the Dragon Hill Lodge and the close army community.

"Let's step out on faith!" I told her, invoking our faith into the equation. That sort of tactic usually worked with my wife being a PK ("preacher's kid"), so I pulled out everything I could and figured I would just ask God for forgiveness later for including Him in my sales pitch. However, God knew my heart. As a result, my wife's "definitely not" turned into "give me some time to think," before eventually changing into a "let's go for it!"

"What?" I asked, shocked. "Are you for real?"

"Yep, let's do it!" she said with a grin.

I called Vince Motley and told him to pull the trigger on my Korea assignment and get me some orders before Yolanda had a chance to change her mind. In the meantime, we had a lot of preparations to take care of, like getting our house ready for the rental market. We also had to hurry to get passports and medical screenings for everyone, and all the while I kept telling my wife and kids that they were going to love Korea. My family and I had to complete all of the requirements prior to getting my request for orders, the document I needed to submit for permanent change of station orders, and we scrambled to get everything done. All three of my kids had to get medical screenings, and we didn't live on an installation, making the process just that much more stressful and hectic.

Finally, I received my request for orders in mid-October of 2010, with a report date of January 20, 2011. In the meantime, my wife continued her teaching job at Welch Elementary while I ran around Newnan and headed back and forth to Fort McPherson, which was thirty-five to forty minutes away from our house, to check items off of our to do list. The longest step was the passports; my family hadn't needed them in the past and we had to apply for them. We were warned that it might take three to four weeks to receive them, but by that point we were entering into the holiday season, which didn't bode well for expediting the process.

Effective October 1, 2010, I was promoted to lieutenant colonel. I found out while I was on vacation with my family from a good friend, Keith Hayes, who had also served in Third Army with

Vince and me. Keith was a fellow SC State alum and someone I'd leaned on for guidance and mentorship during my days in Third Army. In addition to being two years my senior and having already pinned lieutenant colonel, he was also one of Colonel Baker's protégés, and Keith really knew his stuff. The promotion list was due to be released around mid-July and I was a nervous wreck with anticipation. Some people were obvious shoo-ins for promotions, but I wasn't sure I had done enough, achieved enough, or performed well enough to make that list. Then, while driving back from vacation, I received a call from Lieutenant Colonel Hayes.

"James!"

"Yes, sir?" I asked. Although we were good friends, I always gave him his due respect, especially when I thought our conversation was work-related.

"Congratulations!" he exclaimed.

"For what?" I asked, confused. The list had not yet been released, but Keith had called Motley to check for me so he could give me the good news. It was like getting a phone call from the commissioner of the NBA or the NFL telling you that you were nominated to the hall of fame, although my military career was far from over.

"Are you kidding me, man?" I asked, my shock sending my military courtesy completely out the door. "Seriously, are you sure?"

My wife kept asking me what was going on, but she knew it had to be good news, considering the cheesy grin I had plastered across my face. I took the next exit so I could pull over at a gas station to catch my breath.

"Trust me, James, you're on the list," Keith assured me. I gathered my emotions and thanked Keith as if he'd been the one to place my name on the list himself. I do give him partial credit, along with the Big Dog and many others. This promotion elevated me to join several SC State grads, including my good friends Jimmy Mills and Tyrone McGay, Thomas Hundley's first cousin. We also happened to all be fraternity brothers and members of the great Beta Delta chapter of SC State, as well as assigned to Forces Command together. I hung up the phone with Keith and yelled out a big, "YES!" as if I'd just purchased a scratch off lottery ticket and hit it big.

"What in the world is going on with you?" Yolanda asked.

"I made the lieutenant colonel list!" I exclaimed. "We did it!"

"What?!" she exclaimed, her own joy matching my own. It was truly an awesome moment because promotions in the military are a family affair. No one makes more sacrifices than family, and my wife had sacrificed so much for me, giving up so many teaching jobs to move across the country with me, and my kids had changed schools so frequently to accommodate my career.

Even in my excitement, I still felt a little shadow of a doubt in my heart because the phone call was unofficial. I needed to see the list in the same way I'd needed to see my name when Coach Stowe had posted the basketball team cut list on that door so many years earlier. The list was released the following week, and I printed the entire document. I scrolled through the whole thing, flipping page after page of alphabetized names until I finally got to the *S*'s, and then there it was: James J. Scott, the last four digits of my social security number, and FA30. I'd done it! The congratulations from my peers, superiors, and subordinates began to pour in while I checked the list over and over, highlighting my name just to make sure it was really real. This moment was monumental and the culmination of a long journey.

As the months rolled on and my sequence number came up, I began to make preparations for a promotion ceremony. We had a great team at Forces Command, and I reached out to one of the most squared away soldiers I knew to assist me: Sergeant First Class Jones. She was sharp, and a great planner, especially for events like this. She'd kept all of the officers out of trouble over the last year or so, and she agreed to assist me. My number came up for October 1, and I knew this might very well be my last promotion. A soldier knows when they've peaked in their career and I knew. It's the same way you know your kids when a teacher wants a conference with you about one of them. When the teacher explains the situation to you about a grade or behavior, you know as a parent if they did it or underperformed in an area. You might say, "Not my child!" but you know they did it, because you know your kids like you know yourself. I knew this would be my last promotion and I wanted to invite as many of the people responsible for this achievement as possible.

On October 1, 2010, I was promoted to lieutenant colonel in a grand auditorium that required special passes to enter. JB was there, along with Raheen and all of my SC State alumni in the area, as was the Big Dog and some of his staff from Third Army. My in-laws were present, as were Kem and Lynnette. I couldn't help but allow myself a huge grin when I saw my siblings. I had prepared a speech, which I adjusted a little as the higher officials and guests arrived. In my speech, I thanked Lieutenant Colonel Dorsey and the Big Dog and all of my heroes. I thanked my baby sister, Lynnette, and my big brother, Kem, for being instrumental in my life, and I boasted about my younger brother, Maurice, and his accomplishments. Maurice had recently graduated from Clemson with a degree in civil engineering and he was truly a representation of everything that was right with our family.

When I came to my mom, who was sitting front and center with her royal-blue dress and hat to match, I could feel my emotions spilling over like a pot of soup heating up on the stove with a lid that had been left on for too long. Everything was bubbling up at the mere mention of the name "Mom." I tried to start my speech again after saying "my mother," but it was like pulling the string on a lawn mower to start it and the engine just keeps fluttering. I could hear people in the back calling encouraging things like, "We understand! It's okay!" as I gathered my emotions to complete my speech. I looked at my mom and saw that she'd begun to cry as well, because without having to discuss our journey, she knew. We knew. She had given so much to make this day possible for me, and as fate had it, I had the opportunity to express what my mother meant to me, to all of my siblings who were gathered there that day to witness my promotion ceremony.

In that moment, I knew that none of this had anything to do with rank, a title or promotion; it was about the journey. It was about the sacrifices our mother had made for all of us, and I stood there as a witness to everyone that if you had a mom with the strength of a thousand lions, whose faith was firm, you could achieve anything. Titles can be so ego-driven, and I understood that, but my mother, who didn't have a clue about rank structure, could tell someone in the neighborhood or at the grocery store that her son was an officer in the army, and that made her feel good inside, so I was fine with the title.

I cried for the rest of my speech as I moved on to my wife and kids. I was a complete mess by that point as I discussed what Yolanda meant to me and how proud I was to be James Jr., Josh, and Trinity's dad. I had lost my military bearings by that point and was just dripping with tears. I made it through the rest of my speech with applause from the audience, but all I could think about was my mother. When I see different award shows where actors, athletes, and musicians make their acceptance speeches and mention their mothers, I grin inside, because just like me, I know that the tears are coming because I've been there. I know the importance of mothers, and as a result, my dream has always been to have my kids mention their mother as I did that day. But I hope our kids at least think about me, too. I want to hopefully have made a difference in their lives as a result of changing the narrative of my life from negative thoughts of my dad to someone of whom they can be proud.

CHAPTER 25

Returning to Korea: The Final Military Journey

January 2011-Present

That day of rejoicing came and went, and the preparation of another permanent change of station (PCS) commenced. A permanent change of station (PCS) is the official relocation of an active duty military service member along with any family members living with him or her to a different duty location, such as a military base. The Army waits for no one, and it was time to get ready and move. We frantically prepared for the move to Korea, and as we checked off items from our to-do list, I reported to the processing point to get my orders. There, I found out that my family would have to join me at a later date due to a lack of housing space in Camp Yongsan, Korea, my new duty station leaving me to report unaccompanied for a few months. In hindsight, this worked out well because my wife and kids got an opportunity to finish out the school year in Georgia, while I went ahead to get things set up in Korea to await their arrival.

I made my flight reservations and flew into Korea, traveling sixteen hours on Korean Air with a direct flight from Atlanta. I arrived back in Korea at Incheon Airport for my second tour of duty in seventeen years, and boy, was it different! Since my last tour, they had built a whole new airport. Looking around, I decided that this had to be the cleanest and most elaborate-looking airport I had ever seen. *What happened to Gimpo Airport?* I wondered. Korea had modernized so quickly in my absence.

I reported to the military desk inside the airport, which served two purposes: accountability for personnel reporting to Korea to support the military, and to provide transportation to the assigned base. After I checked in, I boarded a bus similar to the one I'd driven in high school and headed to Yongsan. As we drove from the airport toward the base, I couldn't believe the landscape. Approaching Seoul, building and apartment complexes seemed like they'd sprung up out of nowhere. Traffic thickened around us as night fell and we entered the heart of Seoul while I stared out the window in amazement. *Holy smokes!* I thought. *Is this New York City or Seoul, Korea?* The buildings and lights were an incredible sight to see as they glittered across the landscape. *I'm going to enjoy this tour,* I thought as we pushed towards the Banpo Bridge and headed towards the camp. As I admired the view out my window, I saw the one landmark I had missed seeing the most for all those years: Seoul Tower. It still had that mystic aura about it, just as it had so many years earlier. By then it was dark outside, and although I was drained from the flight, I couldn't help but stare out the window like a little boy who had just arrived at Disney World, eager to see the rides.

We arrived at Camp Yongsan's main gate and the gate guard hopped on the bus to check our IDs and passports for entry. Once we were all cleared, the bus rounded the corner and headed up the road, and there it was: the Dragon Hill Lodge. I grinned, immediately flooded with good memories. The in-processing building was next door and the bus pulled up close to the building before stopping so we could disembark and unload our bags. As we walked up, I smiled again when I remembered that there was no turtle farm waiting for me this time. After signing in, the young soldier at the desk gave me my training schedule for the following week. We had arrived on a Thursday and wouldn't start our in-processing until that Tuesday due to a four-day weekend, so I asked him about receiving a pass to go off post. The young soldier looked at me strangely.

"Sir, you don't need a pass to go off post," he said. "You can just go!"

I felt like an old soldier stuck in a time-warp device and sent twenty years into the future, with nothing but questions. Back in the day in the Second Infantry Division, everyone needed a pass before coming to Yongsan and hanging out off-post. Now, I had the freedom to roam alone based on my rank. I pulled my bags down the walkway to the Dragon and signed for my room. *I'm back, baby!* I thought to myself as I entered my hotel room. I hurried to the window to catch another view of Seoul Tower, but this time my room was shielded from the view. Oh well. I figured I'd check it out later.

As fate would have it, my sponsor for my new unit was a fellow SC State graduate by the name of Benjamin Barlow. I had been in contact with Ben for a few weeks, getting details about the job and what to bring to the country, and Ben was the best sponsor, showing up on my second day back in Korea to check on me. Unfortunately, he couldn't spend too much time with me because of the situation in Korea at the time, when tensions were running high between North and South Korea.

Over the past few months, the North had sunk the Cronin, a South Korean submarine. The Cheonan sinking occurred on March 26, 2010, when Cheonan, a Pohang-class corvette of the Republic of Korea Navy carrying 104 personnel, sank off the country's west coast near Baengyeong Island in the Yellow Sea, killing forty-six seamen. The cause of the sinking remains in dispute, although overwhelming evidence points towards North Korea. They had also shelled YP Do, an island that belonged to South Korea, where civilians lived along with a Republic of Korea (ROK) Marine unit. The bombardment of Yeonpyeong was an artillery engagement between the North Korean military and South Korean forces stationed on Yeonpyeong Island on November 23, 2010. Following a South Korean artillery exercise in waters in the south, North Korean forces fired around 170 artillery shells and rockets at Yeonpyeong Island, hitting both military and civilian targets.

You couldn't tell the seriousness of the situation by looking at the locals or the average soldier walking around the base; everything seemed normal, but it wasn't. Nevertheless, I ventured off post during that weekend to check out the sights. This wasn't Iraq and I felt safe, although I was still in total disbelief at how times had changed in Korea. It really was like living in the States without the crime; Korea's strict gun laws had made it extremely safe in the country. The possession of firearms is generally forbidden in South Korea. The law specifically lists people who are allowed possession, which is generally limited to soldiers, law enforcement officers, secret service agents, and so forth.

Korea was still freezing cold, but I was prepared and had purchased a thick coat prior to my arrival. That was one thing that hadn't changed, the brutal winters. As I walked through Itaewon, I immediately noticed the Korean locals, both men and women—especially the women—dressed as if they had just walked off a fashion runway. All the incredible clothes you see in the magazines and in fashion shows on TV were being worn around me in real life. It was fascinating to see and watch.

When the time was right, I called home to tell my wife about the culture, the environment, and how much she was going to love Korea when she and the kids arrived. I Face Timed her on my laptop, which was a major change from my first tour. My first go-around consisted of calling cards, and we laughed at how much money we spent back then on phone calls alone. The next day, I ventured out to the tourist area of the Myeong-dong shopping area, and it was almost too much for me take in. It seemed like there were about a million people concentrated into one shopping district. If there was major tension on the peninsula, you wouldn't have noticed it from this area, because the crowds compared to a Black Friday sale at Walmart times a hundred. It was a crazy scene, and I attempted to take pictures to send back to Yolanda, but pictures can't really do the experience justice. She would just have to experience it for herself when she arrived.

As I completed my in-processing over the next week and signed for my bachelor officer quarters, I began to lock in on my main purpose for being in Korea: my assignment and job. I reported into the headquarters of the United States Forces Korea (USFK), a sub-unified command of the United States Pacific Command. USFK was established on July 1, 1957, and is the joint headquarters through which US combat forces are sent to South Korea, including ground, air, naval, marine, and special forces commands. I would be working in a joint environment assigned to the J3 operations serving as the J39 deputy. This would turn out to be one of my most challenging jobs in the army, but I felt that the Big Dog and my experience in Iraq and Third Army had prepared me for this assignment. My tour would consist of two years serving on the joint staff and I reported in, ready for the ride.

Ben had already been there for a year and a half at that point, and he brought me up to speed as quickly as possible, going over the war plans prior to a major exercise that was quickly approaching. He served as my information officer planner and he was very squared away, a term used by all branches of the United States military services to describe one whose performance is even with or above satisfactory level, and who has continued such performance consistently for an extended period of time. Key resolve was one of two major training exercises we conducted at the joint level in Korea, and I would have to drink from a firehose in preparation for my duties (metaphorically speaking, of course).

It was back to shift work for me serving on the night shift for my boss, who worked days. I'd been promoted, but my full Colonel boss still trumped me and worked days. It really didn't matter for him because he worked seventeen- or eighteen-hour days anyway. Most colonels, and especially generals, have another gear when it comes to working. They have this ability to work insane hours for days upon days, but I suppose that's why they're colonels and generals. They work their regular hours, and as the rest of us faint with fatigue, they shift into overdrive and continue to press on.

I thought I knew all of the acronyms in the military, but in Korea I had to learn a whole different set. It takes about six months to learn half of the terms! We were a combined staff as well, working alongside our ROK counterparts, which required translations for most meetings and discussions. It was amazing to experience this environment. I'd gone from an army-level headquarters to a multinational headquarters, and from an all-ground-forces headquarters in Forces Command to a joint staff in just a couple of years. *What a journey,* I thought as I survived my first exercise without getting fired.

The weeks turned to months as I anxiously prepared for my family's arrival. A spot on post had become available and I immediately put my name on the list to sign for my new quarters. My family was set to arrive on June 1, and I was excited. However, I really had to keep talking up the location because some of my wife's colleagues had caused her to start stressing over the reports of tension on peninsula. The news back home always appeared to make the southern end of Korea seem dire, but I convinced Yolanda that things were calm. She'd never flown overseas before, and I was so proud of her for taking charge of everything back home, from getting the house prepared for renters to dis-enrolling the kids from school and getting them ready for travel. I couldn't wait to see them.

I arrived at the airport and waited anxiously to collect them. As soon as I saw them come out of the baggage claim area, my face broke into a huge grin; I was elated! Yolanda and the kids had arrived safely and all was well now that I had them back. We arrived back on post and I began to point out the schools and Seoul Tower and everything else, as if I was a tour guide. The jet lag and the flight had obviously beaten them down, so I'm not sure if they heard a single word that came out of my mouth on the drive. However, we were all together again and that was all that mattered. We lived in a housing area behind the commissary called Blackhawk Village, and our quarters were located by a large baseball field. The village also had three playgrounds that were color coded as red park, white park, and blue park. Of course, I didn't know about the park color coding until later when my daughter began to make friends and would tell me she was going to the red park if I needed to find her.

"What?" I asked. "Where in the world is this red park?"

"That's the color of the swing sets at the park, Daddy," my daughter said.

It occurred to me that my wife and daughter finally knew something about the military life that I didn't and they wanted to rub it in my face. However, I kept that to myself and just smiled as I thought about the quick adjustment they were making to Korea. We were settling in and we were happy.

We traveled to Osan Air Base to hit the village that had the best shopping. There, they had the best mink blankets, purses, and suits, among other things, and my family appeared to be in Candy Land the first time they visited. The prices were not the 1994 prices I remembered, and I realized I was still stuck in the '90s in so many ways. I bargained for everything as if the prices were still the same, although Korea had closed the gap with the United States in many areas to include technology and pricing. But it was a new experience for Yolanda and the kids, and they loved every minute of it. All of the horror stories they'd heard from people back home who had never set foot in Korea were quickly erased. Camp Yongsan and the rest of the country were safe and my kids could roam around the base freely and safely. My kids had access to places I had only dreamed of as a child: youth centers, two gyms with basketball courts, playgrounds, and youth sports year round. They were in heaven. The boys and Trinity quickly settled into a group of friends, and it was great to see kids of every race and ethnicity knocking on our door to play with my kids. It was a true melting pot on the base and it was a joy to witness.

Military bases, especially overseas, level the playing field for kids in certain ways, because they all attend the same schools, visit the same hospital, and for the most part, live in the same kind of house. It's truly one of the greatest experiences I've witnessed after growing up in a black and white town divided by the train tracks. Everyone adjusted quickly as school began, and as fortune would have it, Yolanda's substitute teaching job at the beginning of the school year turned into a permanent position. As someone once told me, "Happy wife, happy life," and Yolanda was certainly happy and in her element. Time went by, and as the year progressed, my family fell in love with Korea, enjoying it even more than I did.

"Can we stay here until we graduate, Dad?" my sons asked.

"Wait, what?" I exclaimed. This was only supposed to be a two-year tour and Josh and JJ were in eighth and ninth grade respectively. But I saw how much my family loved Korea and I knew what I had to do. The following week after the boys made their request, I put in my own request for an extension turning my two-year tour into a three-year tour. Yongsan became home, and everyone on post knew each other, creating an environment reminiscent of Ridge Spring. Everyone checked on each other's kids, and I felt like I couldn't have planned it any better with the decision to come over to Korea. We adapted to the culture and began to eat an extensive amount of the Korean cuisine. The Greek fraternity and sorority life was great in Korea, and we fanned out all across Korea to participate in organized community projects together, such as feeding the homeless and visiting orphanages to entertain the kids. We raised money for the senior high school kids who attended the American schools on the different posts, settling into a network of wonderful people to include our churches that supported one another and mentored our kids. As my two sons entered high school, they both began to travel across the peninsula and abroad to Japan to participate in sporting events. I'd never seen anything like it, where kids got to travel to different countries to play football and basketball games, but I was so glad my kids had this unique opportunity.

My family was in paradise, but I had been working hard, especially in light of all the craziness going on with North Korea and the training exercises. Provocations from the north continued sporadically over my first two years, requiring long hours at work during certain periods, and yet I enjoyed it; we all enjoyed our time in Korea. We really grew to respect the culture and we liked traveling around to different countries, like Thailand, Japan, Guam, Australia, New Zealand, and the Philippines. It was fascinating, realizing what a gift I had been given of this second chance at life. I should have perished in that fire when I was a kid, and yet here I was, living the good life with my family.

The only downside was that I'd begun to notice that my body was breaking down physically and I had started to think about retirement. I could tell my mood had begun to shift and I would get more irritable about things than I normally would. The old soldiers had always told me that I'd know when it was time to retire, and I realized that they were right—my time had come. However, before I could move forward, I needed concurrence from a few people. My wife had always been supportive of my career and my decisions to continue or retire, so when I posed the question, she said that she would support whatever decision I made. Next, I called on someone upon whom I'd always leaned for advice about life: Kem. I called him up and told him I was tired and ready to hang up my boots.

"Did you check with Mommy?" Kem asked.

"You know she wanted me to shut it down years ago because of the wars!" I said.

As Kem and I talked, he just wanted to ensure that our mother would be okay financially and emotionally. My mother, in turn, wanted to ensure Yolanda and the kids would be okay. I assured Kem that everyone was okay with the decision, although I had not physically called our mother about my choice to retire within the year.

"Okay, then," Kem said. "Let's hang it up!"

I was pleased, because I needed Kem's blessing, and I truly would have kept going if my brother would have told me to hang in there for a few more years. However, I think he could hear it in my voice that I was ready to stop.

I submitted my retirement paperwork, and on September 1, 2014, after twenty-seven years of combined service, to include the years I served in the National Guard, I officially retired from the military. It was finished! I felt as if I'd been wearing twenty-pound ankle and arm weights, along with a fifty-pound rucksack, for almost thirty years, and on that day, someone told me I could drop all of it after crossing the finish line. It was incredible. I'd begun serving as a volunteer basketball coach at the high school, and both of my sons had made the varsity team. They still wanted to finish high school in Korea, and fortunately for us, I landed a government job in the same unit on the base.

It was during this period of my life when I received one of my greatest gifts as a father, aside from the birth of my daughter. Both of my boys were on the varsity team and I was sitting on the bench, keeping the stats as one of their coaches. Typically Josh and JJ didn't spend much time on the court together during a regular game, but on one night during a home game, Coach Jim Davis called their numbers and there they were together. I was just sitting there on the bench, and suddenly they both popped up to check in the game. I saw them and the Scott name on the back of their jerseys and my throat tightened with emotions. I saw Kem and me in my sons, but I also thought about my father and me. Even though Kem and I had never played on the same team due to our age gap, I still saw him and me in that moment. I allowed myself to ever-so-briefly imagine my brother and me walking onto that court together, my father in the stands watching us, the way it should have been.

The juxtaposition of my brother and me and my two sons gave me a moment of sadness, thinking of what could have been, followed by an overwhelming joy that flooded every inch of my body. My chest was bursting with pride. My father didn't give us that gift, and there was a void in our lives as a result—and that stung—but there I was, witnessing a gift from heaven, a better gift. The ghost of my father and the bad memories were fading, and there seemed to be a changing of the universal order, a breaking of the cycle of the absentee father. I was there for my sons, unlike my father had been, and although I might seem like a gloating parent looking for some type of praise or extra credit from other people, I needed that moment for the healing of my soul.

Josh and JJ checked into the game and my fellow coach and friend, Keith Fointno, made eye contact with me and grinned. Keith knew what it meant to me and could probably read my face, no matter how hard I tried to be stoic. I was beaming with pride as I watched my boys, and I didn't care if they scored a single point. It really wasn't about winning or losing the game for me. I thought about the many days I'd spent participating in sports and how I'd wished to have my father at just one game, and I felt God smile on me once again. I watched my sons run up and down the court together and reflected on what a full circle moment this truly was. The other parents knew those were my boys out there, and they cheered when they saw them together, but they didn't know what it truly meant for me as their dad.

It was the crowning moment for me and my tour in Korea, the ultimate affirmation for me that this was the right place for us. There they were, my two sons, and they didn't shy away from the attention they were getting. They had no idea that, although I wasn't the one on the court, I needed it more than them, and I relished the moment. That night came and went, but the memory still lingers. If I could go back to that night of the fire in 1974 and erase or alter some of those events, the only thing I would wish is to have my grandmother back. However, if God told me He would erase my burns and all of my scars, but it might alter my life to take me away from the life I have now, I wouldn't change a thing.

EPILOGUE

In the end, I am left with the truth of the matter: I miss my father, no matter how strange that may sound. I miss seeing his face and hearing his voice, because in so many ways, he is me and I am him. The little boy that still lives in me needed that relationship, no matter how dysfunctional it was. My father left this earth, and when he did, he left me with a yearning for so many more answers to questions that'll never be answered. Half of my lineage is from him, and when he died, so did a part of my history. Our history. Maybe that's why I miss him; selfish reasons, stories untold. All the same, I still have this void.

I'm glad my father is free, because no matter how devastating those events were on that night in Ridge Spring, I believe that he paid his debt to society. I dreamed of seeing him in the stands during so many of my games, but maybe his absence drove me to be a better version of him, a better version of what I could have become than if he had been in my life. There's a lot that I don't know, but I do know that there is a hole in my heart because my father isn't here anymore. Perhaps that's part of the PTSD. I do know that this journey has made me a better father. I know that every time I look at my two sons, I see myself, and each time, I think about my father. Every single time. There's something in the universe that instinctively connects our lineage, and they are better versions of me—and maybe that's the point. My sons' hearts are bigger and they're both good people inside, with manners and a caring spirit just like their mother, and that gives me peace.

The truth is that I have come to terms with my life, although there are times when I drift back into that dark place. These scars have given me humility that I may not have otherwise had, and I can now see the value in that. When I think I have achieved something in life, I still have a mirror to serve as a reminder that I am not all that, and it's only through God's grace that I'm alive. My good days far outweigh my bad ones; I don't bump my head on the pillow these days thinking about my father, and the sweating has ceased, although my wife would probably prefer the pillow pounding over my snoring.

Growing up, I wanted to know why this happened to me, and that search for answers allowed my father and me to meet and reconnect, although it was initially on admittedly less than gracious terms. I'm glad to have reached out to him, even though I may never know why he intentionally started those flames that altered all of our lives. I'll also never know why my father decided he no longer wanted a family and launched a plan to kill us instead of just leaving. The truth may never be told, but I'm here and that's all that matters. I'm here to tell this story of my journey, my trials and tribulations, and my will to fight for a better life. Maybe that's the point, and if my story heals one person or even inspire a group of people, then this journey has been worth it.

My siblings are well, considering the circumstances. My mother succeeded in raising us, and my siblings and I are all professional, productive citizens with our own families now. If there is a winner and a loser in this scenario, my mother definitely won. Ken retired from the army after twenty good years and Lynnette work in the corporate world, while Maurice serves as a civil engineer for a great company. We survived. My momma did it! She asked God to save her life so many years ago so she could raise her kids, and because of her strength, we are here. Our mother is the hero, and we owe our lives to this incredible woman. She has the strength of a thousand lions, and although I yearned for a father, she stood in the gap and saved our lives, and as a result, my siblings and I hold her in the highest regard. She is our queen, our matriarch, and she should be celebrated for her courage. I hope these pages tell the story of a woman who never gave up, despite her early struggles in life, her injuries, and the domestic violence she survived. She fought to keep us together as a family and showed the lengths to which a mother was willing to go for her children. I have made mistakes in my life, but I always think about my mother and her faith as I try to correct my missteps. Any ounce of good in me is because of my mom, and I can tell my story because of the sacrifices she has made. She is our Rosa Parks, our Harriet Tubman, and this book is written in her honor. My achievements in life have been possible because of her, and I salute her for it.

Alongside my mother, I have been very fortunate to have met and been influenced by Ms. Henman, Mrs. Denny, Ms. Gladys Gibson, and Dorothy Gibson, who in addition to my mother, instilled in me the tremendous respect I have for women. My mother-in-law, Ms. Burnie Barnes, to me, walks on water. I've had role models like Angel Wade, Catina Barnes, and Dezzaire Gadsden, who achieved the rank of lieutenant colonel. Women like Shannon Wilder and Patricia White are throwbacks to the strong women in my early life and serve as trailblazers in the government; Mabel Holston and Dianne and Janice and Sandra inspired me. Then there is my sister, Lynnette, for whom I would go to the ends of the earth to protect. All of these women have changed my life and given me this utmost regard for women, and when I think about these women and see my daughter, I smile. It has been my lot in life to be surrounded by strong, incredible women and I couldn't be more thankful.

My father still remains in my daily thoughts. These pages have been churning in my head for many years, and maybe this has become my therapy as I emptied my thoughts into this book. Perhaps I may continue down this path while I wait for that one thing, that one answer to my question why, but it doesn't matter as much as it used to. I sought out that much-needed counseling prior to leaving the army, but it has always been my faith in God that has held me steady and strong. I had an opportunity to discuss what happened and create methods to cope with the scars, the mental and emotional ones more so than the physical ones. My counselor and I discussed the fire and my father, rehashing old wounds, and it helped me to deal with the pain—and I mean really deal with the emotional wounds. As a result, I'm moving in the right direction. I also reached out to my brother, in whom I confided about my counseling, only to find out that he was seeking help as well. Ken never told me because he was ashamed to reach out, just like me. We talked about our struggles and we discussed the fire with one another; we talked about the pain and the strength of our mother. There is still a wall that exists, and we've decided to tear it down one brick at a time, and in our own way.

I'm fortunate to have a minister in my father-in-law. I'm also blessed to have a Japanese American in Andrew Hirata, who serves as my current pastor in Korea and provides my spiritual food, as well as my fraternity brother, Michael Almond, who ministers to me. I believe in a higher being, and that is my truth. I still struggle with sleep at times, but I don't slam my head against the pillow anymore to empty my thoughts. It has taken years of ministry, counseling, and support from my wife and kids to finally release this pain. Growing up, I wished I could change faces, but in hindsight I realize that my true scars existed internally. I'm fine with my appearance, because I can't go back, and I'd rather look at the three shades of my face in my kids while smiling at the irony and blessings of life. My children give me peace and joy.

Sometimes, those of us who wear these scars are selfish in our thoughts. We think we carry the burden alone, but we don't. During one of my low points, my wife once asked me if I'd ever thought about how she felt, having to answer questions about how I got burned.

"What do you mean by that?" I asked.

"I'm just saying, I carry this burden just like you do," Yolanda said.

The statement hit me like a sack of bricks. I didn't probe, because as I stared off into my own thoughts, I understood and felt the blow in its entirety. Man, how selfish had I been for all of these years? I had lived with these scars, these burns for most of my life, and I'd grown accustomed to the stares, the questions, and all of their gravity—but what about my wife and kids? They were left with the questions, and I'd never thought of it from their side.

"What happened to your husband?"

"What happened to your dad?"

They're left to answer, to defend me at times, and deflect the harsh words. I felt ashamed the next day after my wife, in a sense, shattered my world with this bombshell. I thought about the millions of people who suffer with some type of scar, the victims of assault, alcohol abuse, PTSD, and so many other wounds, both seen and unseen. They carry a heavy burden, but they are not alone. Through my wife's words, I also gained a deeper appreciation for my family, especially Kem and Lynnette for all of their love and support.

I have come to realize that life is not a hundred-yard dash, where we all are given the same shoes and our starting blocks are set at the same distance. In life, you may not know how far you need to run in order to reach the finish line. When I reflect on my life, I think of the first time I ran the four-hundred-yard dash in competition. There were eight lanes, and each runner was staggered at a distance greater than the others. I was placed in lane three and I thought it was odd to see the person in lane eight so far ahead of me. We didn't have track and field at my high school so we had to travel to a neighboring school to run and train on an official track as if we were back in the 1940s. However, we were fast, and speed trumps any fancy facility.

There were so many variables to running your best race in the four-hundred-yard dash, from pace to short spikes to long spikes to confidence and so forth. I saw the eighth lane and felt doubtful that I could ever catch up to that runner before the race had even started. We're born into different lanes in life, and along the way we have to figure out how to overcome our fears, no matter what circumstances we're dealt.

Once, my family and I visited Cebu, Philippines for a vacation. I picked out a beautiful resort close to the water called JPARK Island and it had everything, including a water park and many restaurants, which created a self-sustaining environment for guests; there was no need to leave the resort. I've always been an early riser, and while my wife and daughter slept through the morning, I ventured out. As I walked the streets of Cebu, I wandered onto a full outdoor basketball court. I couldn't believe it. It looked out of place, but there it was, and people were already playing. They were just as shocked to see me, this black guy who had sprung up out of the streets onto their game. They stared and smiled, and the ones waiting on the side, either to jump into the next game or just spectating, began to chat with me.

"Where are you from?"

"America," I said proudly. They reached out their hands to greet me and I felt like a celebrity.

"Do you want to play?" they asked. I pointed to my feet at the sandals I'd worn out and told them I'd be right back. I was about a half mile from the resort, and I power-walked back to our room. I love basketball, and couldn't believe these strangers had welcomed me and invited me to join them. At that point in my life, my knees were worn out, but I couldn't pass up the opportunity. I opened the door to our room, and by then, my wife had awakened.

"Where were you?" she asked.

"I found a basketball court and people are playing!" I exclaimed.

"You are so crazy," she said with a smile, shaking her head. "Be safe and don't get kidnapped."

"I will or I won't?" I said with a laugh.

Shoes on and camera in hand, I made a mad dash back down the streets of Cebu to the basketball court. They seemed shocked to see me return, and some who were waiting started clapping. I didn't have my Bengay with me, or my super-duper knee brace, and there was no time to go into my thirty-minute stretching ritual, or even a prayer session, to help keep me injury-free. I asked to play next game and my time came quickly. I couldn't believe how talented they were at basketball! I guess I had stereotyped Filipino people's basketball skills and had assumed the game hadn't reached as far as Cebu.

It had been close to a year since I had worn a military uniform, and my physical fitness was a little lacking, to say the least, and I guess it showed, because my new friends began to call me Charles Barkley. Since they hadn't seen my game yet, I assumed it was due to my gut at that juncture of my life. I did have an advantage of height as one of the tallest people out there, since most Filipino men are not that tall. Nevertheless, I made a last-ditch effort at stretching before the ball was tipped. I knew as soon as we started going up and down the court a couple times that I would be the passer from the post, but then I realized I couldn't shuffle fast enough to the other end to get involved in the play.

I had the time of my life for the next thirty or forty-five minutes of either playing or just watching the other guys. I snapped picture after picture until I'd taken enough photos to last a lifetime. Before I decided to leave and head back to the resort, they had unofficially adopted me, and I had a newfound respect for my Filipino brethren. I smiled the whole way back, and on my way, I decided to stop by a local store to grab a bottle of water. Sure enough, one of the guys from the basketball game caught up with me, and instead of heading back to the resort right away, I decided to chat with him while I drank my water on the old patio outside the store. I asked him about his family and whether or not he had kids.

"Do you want to meet them?" he asked suddenly.

I was feeling a little apprehensive and my Spidey senses were starting to kick in a little. I was off the reservation away from the resort, and my wife didn't have a clue as to where I'd ventured off to play basketball. Nevertheless, I was touched that he thought enough of me to invite me to his home. I searched his eyes to see if I could detect any signs of hustle, but I saw none. Although it wasn't all good in my mind, I went with my gut instead.

"Let's go!" I said.

We hopped on a couple mopeds and headed up the street. I started to feel very nervous when we suddenly turned off onto a dirt road. We dismounted our separate mopeds and my new friend motioned for me to pay both drivers. I obliged, even though I felt like it was a little bit of a hustle move on his part. We started to walk down a path that looked like a landfill as we began to pass a block building and trash strewn across the ground. Suddenly, I began to see people little children and old women. One lady was washing clothes in the same area that I saw some pots used for eating. I saw what appeared to be a clubhouse, but it wasn't in a tree. It was poorly constructed and sitting on the ground, and as we passed it, I noticed a family inside. There were several more houses peppered across the landscape that were built the same as the first. The concrete structures served as stores, mini-stores with all types of items in them, like a scaled-down Dollar Store in the woods. I took in the whole town of people along the path, with laundry hung out on lines by the little wooden houses. The area was muddy in places, and I snapped both physical and mental pictures of the landscape, my first real view of poverty in its entirety, up close and personal.

There was a larger, open wood shack with laminated numbers on a table—a makeshift school for the kids. It was almost like a preschool or an after-school center for the village. The surprising thing of it all was that everyone I encountered had the biggest smiles on their faces. They were happy! This was the deepest poverty I had ever witnessed and I didn't see defeat on anyone's faces.

We arrived at my new friend's home, plywood and blocks, with a combination of tin and wood for a roof. Black smoke lined the front room from the coals used for cooking. There was a bench in the front room where my new friend directed me to sit as he introduced me to his family, starting with his wife. She smiled deeply as she greeted me, dropping her head in shyness. Then there were his kids, one after another, until I had met all six of them. Finally, I met his mother-in-law. They all lived in what appeared to be little more than a two-room shack of sorts. He offered me a cola, and I obliged as he pulled out a whole two-liter bottle of Coke from behind the door. I didn't see any cups and suddenly I didn't feel the need to quench my thirst. I began to do the math as he excused himself to go get a cup.

I couldn't resist, because I knew my wife wouldn't believe me, nor would anyone else, so I began to snap some pictures. I wanted to capture the moment I was in, as well as show people how fortunate they were in life. I pretended to position myself in a different area of the home to take their picture so I could peek at the other room. Then I saw it: the piece of foam laid out across the floor that acted as a bed. I felt tears prickling at my eyes as I realized what I was really looking at. There were no beds, and the foam was weathered and stained. This was home for them. Six kids, his wife, and his mother-in-law all lived here. Nine people in one shack with no running water, smiling at me and inviting me in with open arms. I emptied my pockets of all the cash I had and gave it to his wife, which she accepted with tears of her own. I knew to give it to her because of what I felt in my spirit, urging me to do something for this family.

I told my new friend I had to return to my family, and we left the village. We didn't leave the same way we came, and I didn't return to the resort as the same person I had been earlier that day. The experience had rocked me to my core, and I felt ashamed when I said goodbye to him as he left to return to his home, while I left to enter the gates into another world. I told him I'd see him later, but I had no plans of seeing him again. I told my wife about my journey and what I'd seen that day. She initially chastised me for being out for so long and then told me I was stupid for being so reckless.

Yolanda was looking out for me because she loved me, and knew she was right, it could have been dangerous, but I believe God took me on that tour. I ate really good food at the resort for the rest of our trip, but I couldn't help but think of the village every time. I thought I'd grown up poor, but I remember there was a family who lived a couple of miles down the road from us in the

Ridge who didn't have any running water at their house—which was still an actual house. I thought they lived in poverty until that day I took that tour in a village in Cebu, Philippines, and then I met poverty, real poverty.

Just like the four-hundred-yard dash, we begin this race at a staggered start. Some of us either stumble or acquire some scars as a result. Some are born blind, missing legs or an arm, deaf or mute—we don't get to choose. We are dealt this hand, either from the start or along the way. What are you going to do? Just fold up, pack it in, and quit? Rosa Scott Johnson taught me to just suck it up. So what, you've got some burns on your face? So what, your daddy isn't here and you've got to go back and forth to the hospital? Are you going to just drown yourself in a big old tub of self-pity? I couldn't let my mom punk me. I was going to figure out how to run this lane.

We didn't have a track to practice on, but I knew I could catch the guy in lane eight in the four-hundred-yard dash because I believed I could. I needed to pace myself around on the straightaway, but I felt myself gaining ground. I couldn't hear anything except the sound of my footsteps. The guy in lane eight was taller than me, but I still caught him. I was a little winded, but I still had some kick in me as we leaned into the last curve. Speed is colorblind. Sometimes the smartest person doesn't get the job, but speed doesn't discriminate. Nobody was thinking about my burns on that track because we were all running against the clock.

I am a man. I stand by my faith and believe in a higher being who watches over me. James Scott Sr. and Rosa Scott Johnson created me, and because of them, I exist. God gave me this path to walk, this fiery path with bends and hills and valleys. I have no regrets and believe I have been chosen to make this journey to share my experiences with the world. I am Philadelphia made; the small town of Ridge Spring shaped me; SC State University gave me purpose through family bonds and higher education; and the military saved me and gave me a life I would never have dreamed of having.

I have seen with my own eyes things and places previously unimagined because of the military. I visited Egypt and stood on the stones of the pyramids. I've traveled to countries all over Asia and the Middle East. I have been fortunate to see the beauty of Mount Rainier and the majestic mist emanating from Niagara Falls. I even crossed over the Golden Gate Bridge during a visit to Oakland, all compliments of the US Army. My life is not perfect—no one can make that claim—but I am fortunate. Cebu taught me that. When you think you have it bad, look around for some perspective. When you feel like giving up, keep living.

Army Strong!

ABOUT THE AUTHOR

After twenty-seven years of military service, James Scott is now a retired US Army lieutenant colonel, currently working abroad as a government employee. A first-time novelist, he was born in Philadelphia, Pennsylvania, and raised in the small town of Ridge Spring, South Carolina. He and his wife Yolanda Barnes are the parents of two sons and a daughter. He credits the military and sports for saving his life. He can be contacted via Facebook (@james.j.scott), and on Twitter (@jamesscott1906).

Made in the USA
San Bernardino, CA
31 March 2019